To Mark —

There: out of

SOFT LANDING

Shift the Culture!

How to Resume Our Roles as Responsible Members of the Community of Life

Everything is Connected!

We can Save the World!

By

Don Shepherd

Abolish Corporate Personhood!

MW00789637

For John Paul
and also
for every other Member of the
Community of Life

Published by Save the World, Inc.
www.savetheworldinc.com
Contact: Don@savetheworldinc.com

Copyright © 2020 by Don Shepherd

All rights reserved. May cite text with proper attribution.

ISBN for Paperback version: 978-0-578-77400-8
ISBN for Ebook: 978-163649787-7

Book cover and website design by Will Alkin
Editing by Catherine Rose Lee

SOFT LANDING

How to Resume Our Roles as Responsible Members of the Community of Life

Preface

If you have not already done so, there is another book I want you to read... It is *Ishmael, An Adventure of the Mind and Spirit*, by Daniel Quinn. *Ishmael* is a very important book. And it has been very important to me, personally.

I know that is an odd way to begin my own book. The reason is... I derive a lot of important, new information from *Ishmael*... information that provides the very basis for *Soft Landing*.

But here is the thing... You can wait to read Ishmael until you have finished reading *Soft Landing*.

Trust me on this... In terms of how it relates to what I am saying in *Soft Landing*, I will tell you what you need to know about *Ishmael* in the Introduction and in Chapters 1 and 2. After that, you will not see so many references to *Ishmael*.

Don Shepherd

Introduction

◊

Twenty-five years ago, I read a novel that began with the narrator reading a newspaper ad.

Teacher Seeking Pupil
Must have an earnest desire to
save the world.

The novel was *Ishmael, An Adventure of the Mind and Spirit*, by Daniel Quinn. I read it, and then I read it again. And then I read it again. For me, the message conveyed through the story in the novel was fantastic news. It appeared to me that all that was necessary in order to save the world was for enough people to read Ishmael!

Over the next six or eight months, I gave away probably forty copies of *Ishmael*. I gave them to all of my friends, and to anyone I met who showed the slightest interest in what I was so excited about.

Then, the results started coming in... "Sorry, Don. I just couldn't get into it."

And, "Here is your book back, Don. I tried to read it several times, but the telepathic gorilla just didn't interest me."

Of the forty or more people I gave books to, few even read it, and of those who did read it, only a handful understood its message as I did.

I couldn't believe it. The explanation for how things came to be this way, even if told by a telepathic gorilla, was clear and succinct. The book had won awards, including the $500,000 Turner Tomorrow award, given by Ted Turner for the work of fiction judged to be the most influential in helping to save the planet. Of course, there were thousands of people who understood and appreciated it... Apparently, though, there were not very many from my particular group of friends.

It was a terrible blow.... I was forced to admit that saving the world was not going to be as easy as I had naively thought it would be. Upon reflection, I realized that many of my friends were in the oil and gas exploration business as I was... a fact that was certainly a big factor with the lack of success in people "getting it". Most of my friends, even those who were not in the oil business, were relatively affluent. They were completely invested in our culture, and totally unwilling to question whether or not our culture might be doomed to failure. Most of them had gone to college, graduated, and were in the process of carving out their little piece of the pie. They had worked hard. They had done what they were supposed to in order to be successful. And now, they were ready to reap their financial rewards and enjoy the security that came with their success. According to their reaction to Ishmael, they were most certainly NOT willing to consider that our culture was fatally flawed at its most basic level. Apparently, they had invested way too heavily in making this culture work for them, and they were not willing to just give up on it. And especially, they were not willing to help to bring an end to it.

Eventually, I came to realize that another reason many people did not understand *Ishmael*, was that they were not accustomed to thinking for themselves... at least not about the big questions. For those, they preferred to depend upon the "experts", being the recognized governmental and religious leaders.

This unwillingness on the part of many of us to think for ourselves about the big questions is a huge problem. The result is that the rich and powerful get to answer those questions on our behalf.... Which is really not a good idea. Hopefully, *Soft Landing* will help many of us begin to fix this terrible situation. Many of those big questions that each of us, as individuals, need to start tackling instead of abdicating, are going to be addressed herein. If you are one who, up to this point, has been abdicating instead of thinking, I encourage you to be brave and read on…. Your bravery may ultimately provide a big contribution to helping save our world from devastation. At the very least, you will find your own life to have been enriched by the process of beginning to think a little bit more for yourself.

Despite my frustrations with having shared *Ishmael* with so many people who didn't appreciate it, I remain extremely grateful for the truths I learned within those pages. In my own case, the result of my finding out the truth about our culture was that it set me free. It turned out that the truths I learned from reading *Ishmael* were the exact truths I had been searching for my entire life, without even realizing that I was searching for them. I have thanked the powers of the Universe each and every day since first reading *Ishmael* for allowing me to have this fantastic knowledge. Now I know why I have had a lifelong problem accepting authority. Now I understand what bothered me about religion. Now I can visualize a world free of war, hunger and strife… a world I can proudly pass along to my son and to the generations that follow him. Now I can spend the rest of my life working towards a goal that really matters to me… helping to save our planet from destruction.

Well… here I am again. Twenty-five years later… giving the creation of that world I can proudly pass along to my son another shot. But instead of giving away copies of *Ishmael*… which I have continued doing all along… this time, I'm putting out my own work… the book you are holding in your hands. Unlike *Ishmael*, this is a non-fiction work, which will allow me to delve a little deeper than Daniel Quinn was able to do in his fictional format.

For twenty-five years now, I've lived with the following truths, most of which I learned directly from reading *Ishmael*, and the others from reasoning forward from what *Ishmael* taught me. And, I can report to you that after twenty-five years of examination and re-examination, they remain as firm and solid as they did when I first came to understand them. Here they are:

- ❖ Our worldwide culture, which includes every person on this planet who is not a member of an indigenous tribe not yet assimilated, is flawed at its most basic level. For this reason, it is doomed. In fact, it is failing.

- ❖ The reason our culture is flawed is because it is based on the false premise that everything is separate. This fosters a false sense of separation. Separation between man and nature... Separation between man and the rest of the Community of Life... Separation between the weak and the powerful... Separation between the rich and the poor... Separation between you and me.

- ❖ The reality is that man is just another species that evolved on this planet as one of millions of life forms.

- ❖ This means that man is a part of the Community of Life... not separate from it.

- ❖ Our flawed and doomed culture must be replaced with a new culture that is based upon the truth that everything is connected.

- ❖ Humans must resume their role as Responsible Members of the Community of Life.

- ❖ If we continue down this road, riding on our flawed and doomed culture, then one day, perhaps one day very soon, we will arrive at our destination... a terrible crash.

❖ The only way the monumental task of replacing our flawed and doomed culture can be achieved is through the establishment of a Critical Mass of people who understand the problem and want to fix it.

❖ Helping people to understand how things came to be this way will be a main key to the successful creation of the Critical Mass.

❖ Not everyone is conscientious enough, or conscious enough, or emotionally stable enough to be capable of making the saving of the planet a personal goal. Many of us are just not ready to take on that task. As people grow and mature, many become capable of taking on these truths and joining the Critical Mass.

❖ The majority of the rich and powerful people currently living on this planet like things the way they are. They love their comfort. They love their luxurious lifestyle. They love their conveniences. And they love their security. Many of these comfortable, rich, and powerful people will ultimately become a part of the Critical Mass, but because it works so well for them, many will be slow to recognize the need for change.

❖ The rich and powerful will very likely some day realize that they also should have loved their polar icecaps.

❖ The quality and strength of the Critical Mass is very important. The more people it includes, the stronger it will be.... And the stronger it is, the more capable it will be of effecting change in the face of adversity. Also, the more people the Critical Mass has in it who are rich and powerful, the better.

❖ Without question, there are some very twisted and sick people in this world who wield a lot of wealth and power. Also, without question, many of these people will be extremely opposed to the cultural shift. For this reason, there is a chance that things might get very messy.

I will choose messy over insane every time. We can work through messy. There is no cure for the type of insanity represented by our present, insane culture. And besides... things are already pretty messy.

Here is a final truth that is crucial for us to understand if we are ever going to succeed in transforming our flawed and doomed culture to a responsible, sane one...

❖ **The Critical Mass may only be added to one person at a time. This is because nobody can think for another person.**

As the Critical Mass grows from where it is today, it will get easier and easier to add more people to it. This is because as time goes along, and more and more people come out in favor of the ideas set out herein, people like me will not be considered so crazy and radical as we are today.

I recently read Naomi Klein's book, *This Changes Everything*. Given that when I read it, I was in the process of finishing the writing of this book wherein I am advocating for replacing our flawed and doomed culture, I was very glad to find that the title to Naomi Klein's book, *This Changes Everything*, refers to the fact that the only way the looming disaster represented by global warming may be averted, or even its consequences mitigated, is through the achievement of a cultural shift. And she is correct. Global warming may not be dealt with by winning the argument that global warming is real. The only reason we are having that argument in the first place is because the huge corporations that are responsible for continuing to add to the accumulation of greenhouse gasses have hired their own pseudo-scientists to dispute the findings of the real scientists.

In *This Changes Everything*, Klein tells us the battle over global warming and climate change may only be won by taking the power back from the corporations, and forcing them to either operate in a manner that benefits our connected world, or terminating their right to exist. Klein correctly points out that the right-wing conservatives understand very well how deeply their way of life and their ideologies are threatened by global warming. That is why they are fighting so hard and also so unfairly. It is the liberal progressives who do not understand this very important point. The liberal progressives are still wasting their time arguing the facts. They do not realize that global warming is orchestrating a battle to the death between the two ideologies.

Of course, I agree with Naomi Klein. Twenty-five years ago, after first reading *Ishmael*, I realized what a waste of time most of the activists' causes are. It is not that their causes are not important or worthy…. They are very important and very worthy of our attention…. But the problem is, using our finite energy to fight battle after battle involving the complete spectrum of the activists' issues divides and dilutes the power of the progressive forces. In general, the progressives have truth and justice on their side, along with a finite amount of people with limited resources who understand those truths and are willing to fight for justice. The rich and the powerful have wealth and power, along with a relatively equal amount of people, but much greater economic resources and also much greater governmental clout. Wealth and power cannot defeat a divided force represented by truth and justice every time. But money and power does enable the other side to prevail in way too many of the clashes. The point is… these battles are never going to end until the progressives learn they need to concentrate their resources and join together to fight the only battle that will ever make any difference: The battle over whether our culture should be based upon a false myth that our world is separate, or the truth that everything that exists is connected.

When we win this main battle over whether our culture should be based upon a world that is separate or a world that is connected, we will never have to fight any of those lesser battles ever again.

Consider this a call to all activists everywhere. Whether you are an environmental activist, a civil rights activist, a peace activist, a human rights activist, a gay rights activist, an indigenous rights activist, a women's rights activist, a labor rights activist, an immigrant's rights activist, a right-to-privacy activist, an activist for veteran's causes, or an activist for any other progressive issue... let's get together and work on growing this all-important Critical Mass of people who understand how things came to be this way. Let's discard this flawed, doomed, and insane culture for a new culture based upon the reality that everything is connected, and we are all one. If we join forces and win this one, then we will also win all of those other activist's battles at the same time. All we have to do is grow our numbers until we achieve the Critical Mass of people necessary to effect changes, even when opposed by those who remain satisfied with the status quo. Then, when that Critical Mass is achieved, by definition, we will have won.

After reading *Ishmael*, another epiphany occurred when I realized the truths set out above are not only logical, rational truths, but spiritual ones as well. The spiritual masters have told us for thousands of years that "We are One," and "Everything is connected."

The spiritual masters who have told us these truths beginning thousands of years ago, and the spiritual masters who are still telling us these things today did not just pull "Everything is Connected", and "We are all One" out of thin air. They learned these truths through their own, direct experience... by going within.

There is a scale of consciousness that progresses from highly unconscious people, who are almost constantly consumed by shame, guilt, anger, grief and fear, to higher and higher levels of consciousness wherein people become more and more present, aware, accepting, loving, joyous, and peaceful, until finally they achieve a level of consciousness where the truth of "Everything is Connected", and "We are One", is a certainty for them. They have achieved enlightenment.

Of the many thousands of spiritual masters who have achieved these very high states of consciousness, certainly the most famous is Gautama Buddha. Not only did Buddha achieve enlightenment while still a young man, he lived to be 80 years old. Before he died, he taught hundreds of disciples how to achieve enlightenment for themselves, and he also taught them how to teach others.

Today, there are somewhere between half a billion and 1.5 billion practicing Buddhists. Most Buddhists would not consider themselves to be religious. Instead, they consider themselves to be practitioners of a proven and much utilized method of raising consciousness. The same would be true for most Hindus.

There are many paths to spiritual enlightenment. Also, there are many degrees of enlightenment as well. A person who has achieved an egoless state of consciousness and who lives totally in the present moment, without the need to label and judge those present-moments, could certainly be considered enlightened, especially in relation to the rest of us who have not yet achieved that level of consciousness. Next, a person who has achieved a state of Samadhi where he or she feels a connection to and a love for everything that exists, would be even further down the path towards true enlightenment. A third, even deeper stage of enlightenment involves achieving a state of consciousness wherein that person merges into the Oneness and the individual is no longer distinguishable from All That Is. According to what I have read, once a person achieves one of these higher states of consciousness, a certain vigilance or dedication is required for that person to maintain that state. Apparently, many people get glimpses, but then fall back into normal, everyday reality. In the many accounts I have read by those who have achieved this state, all agree there are no words that could possibly describe it. I imagine that almost every person who achieves any of these states of enlightenment has that experience locked into their memory and is forever transformed by the experience. Probably, there has never been a person who has regretted attaining one of these higher states of consciousness.

Buddha left a detailed map for his students and practitioners, based upon self-reflection and a dedication to the practice of meditation. Hinduism also has a rich tradition of raising consciousness with the goal of achieving enlightenment through meditation, yoga, and even through tantric sexual practices. Taoism tells us that enlightenment is the natural state of a human. The process of enlightenment for Taoism appears to be about awareness of the Tao, (all that is) and achieving a functioning, Tao mind through living the teachings. I believe that many tribal people who have not had their consciousness corrupted by our culture live naturally in a "present moment" state of awareness. Many Native American traditions, as well as other ancient cultures around the world, have traditions aimed at furthering the spiritual enlightenment of their tribal members that involve fasting, sleep deprivation, intentional pain, sweat lodges, and ingestion of natural psychedelics. Many of my own contemporaries who grew up in the sixties and seventies, got their first glimpse of higher states of consciousness through psychedelic drugs like LSD, mescaline, peyote, and psilocybin mushrooms. Millions of people throughout history, as well as millions of people living now, have been awakened to the existence of higher states of consciousness by a near death experience or a spontaneous out of body experience. When a person finds oneself out of his or her body, but still thinking and functioning, they come back with the certainty that life will continue after death. Other people have had spontaneous awakening experiences brought on by depression or feelings of deep despair... otherwise known as the "dark night of the soul". Two famous examples of this from present time are Eckhart Tolle and Byron Katie. Michael Singer, the renowned author of *The Untethered Soul*, and *The Surrender Experiment*, spontaneously "woke up" to the reality of the unwanted dialogue going on in his own head while sitting on his couch.

Many scholars think that Jesus of Nazareth may have traveled to India and spent a few years practicing Buddhism. Unfortunately, there are no historical records to support this theory. Historical records do seem to support that Jesus actually traveled in Galilee performing miracles and healings and preaching to throngs of people. The fact that Jesus could perform these miracles and healings, along with the fact that written accounts of his sermons indicate an extremely high level of attained wisdom, would support the hypothesis that Jesus was a spiritual master.

I spent a few years in my early adulthood being fairly pissed off at Jesus. My thinking was... If Jesus was such an enlightened Master who was so devoted to transforming our world, then why would he have allowed himself to be crucified by the Romans when he was such a young man? Couldn't he have at least got his followers a little more organized before allowing himself to be martyred? In my way of thinking, he had really messed up. And the result of this too early martyrdom was the terrible religion called Christianity our world is saddled with today.

Eventually, I got over blaming Jesus for Christianity. After all, there are very few enlightened masters who choose to address the masses. Most don't even attempt it. I ended up giving Jesus a lot of credit for at least trying. I do think, however, that Jesus was much more of a revolutionary than people understand. He was undoubtedly very devoted to kicking the Romans out of his homeland. And I believe that is the main reason he was crucified.

As stated earlier... Christianity is a terrible religion. Rather than providing a proven method of raising consciousness, Christianity tells its flock that all that is necessary is a belief in God and an acceptance of Jesus Christ as your Lord and Savior. The Protestant concept of salvation by faith is probably one of the worst contrivances I have ever heard of. The result is a world full of millions of judgmental Christians who are too lazy to think for themselves.

When compared to the higher consciousness and spiritual mastery achieved by participants of the Eastern mystical traditions, very few spiritual masters come out of Christianity, Islam, or Judaism. All three of these religions promote a make-believe story about a Creator-God who is separate from us and will judge us when we die. And that is why organized religion is such a problem. I do not think it will be possible to achieve the necessary Critical Mass of people who understand the truth about how things came to be this way without first stripping Christianity and also Islam of a very significant portion of their adherents.

The reason for this is because the truth that "Everything is connected" simply does not jive with the Creator-God story of Christianity and Islam. The creation stories of these religions are basically about a fairy-tale God who created the world especially for man, so He could utilize our material world as a test to see whether or not each of us who are born into this world is worthy of joining Him in Heaven. The billions of people who buy into these fairytales end up believing there is no need for them to worry if things appear screwed up here on earth. After all, they are only going to be here in the physical realm for a few short years. Never mind if those years entail a lot of suffering. The important thing... according to these religions... is that each of us needs to jump through the necessary hoops in our time here on Earth, so that when we die, God will grant us the privilege of spending eternity with Him in Heaven. And if the positive incentive of being able to spend eternity with the Father in blissful pleasantness is not sufficient motivation, then there is the negative motivation provided by these religions... eternal damnation in Hell for failing to recognize and acknowledge the supremacy of God and to do as He requires of us.

It is the existence of these religions that are based upon their creation stories involving a God who is separate from us… who will judge us when we die… that foster and reinforce the same false sense of separation as the one on which our culture is based. Roughly half of the world's population considers themselves to be a member of one of these three religions.

Most people, including most people who belong to these religions, don't realize it, but Christians, Jews, and Muslims, all pray to the same God. As you can imagine, I am extremely dubious about this, but ancient scriptures say that the God who supposedly first revealed himself to the patriarch Abraham was the same God who was responsible for creating this little planet as a gift, just for man to conquer and rule. Of course, at the time that little fairy tale was first told, people didn't realize what an insignificant rock we are all standing on. Today, we have a much different understanding of the cosmos, and of our place in it.

Also, considering the foundational myth of our culture is based upon this off-planet God who is separate from us, I find it extremely significant that this God chose to reveal himself to a patriarch, and patriarchy is such a continuing problem for us today. This God of Abraham first became the Almighty God worshiped in Judaism. Then, one thousand years later, Christianity took a slightly different tack, keeping the God of Abraham, and adding God's only begotten Son to the story. Seven hundred years after that, the Prophet Muhammad prescribed another way to worship the same God, who he preferred to call Allah.

So… From the standpoint of helping to transform our flawed and doomed culture by fostering and promoting the reality of the connectedness of all things…

Reason and logic… Good!

Spirituality... Good!

Abrahamic Religions... Bad!

But, in addition to reason, logic, and spiritual truths, there is also modern physics. Most people's understanding of the three pillars of modern physics – relativity, special relativity, and quantum mechanics, do not go very deep. I can say this because in preparation of writing this little piece about modern physics, I have been studying like crazy for the past month, and I am still struggling to wrap my head around the concepts. My contention is, that science, especially modern physics, provides a third route for people to arrive at the truth of the connectedness of all things. And apparently, the only way to achieve this intellectual knowing as a physicist is through many years of study and hard work. If you have a doctorate in physics, then you have been through a rigorous academic program, one that probably took you at least seven years to complete. And that is after you received your undergraduate degree. Obviously then, if you are a PhD physicist, then you have looked very deeply into what is known about your particular field of study. My contention is that this deep understanding of modern physics will lead people who attain that knowledge towards a deep understanding, and a deep knowing, of the connectedness of all things.

This is because our modern physicists have come to understand that the sub-atomic particles, which are the building blocks of matter, are composed of pure energy. If everything is composed of energy, then everything in the universe including you, me, the earth, and everything on it and in it, the sun, the stars, the galaxies, and even all of the vast space in between all of these things, is made of energy. And, all of it is connected.

To re-cap... According to our present, insane culture... Everything is separate and the world was made for man to conquer, rule, and to exploit as he sees fit. And, that is why it is okay for a tiny minority of us to accumulate most of the wealth and resources, while billions of us struggle to provide ourselves with our most basic of needs pertaining to our very survival. And, that is also why it is okay for countries to wage war against each other over things like territorial disputes, racial, religious, or ideological differences, economic considerations, or a need to exploit resources. And, that is also why it is okay for corporations to reap insane profits from the exploitation of desperate and poor workers, and from the destruction of our precious forests and our other natural resources. And, that is also why it is okay to make the providing of health care all about profit, and to withhold it from those unable to pay the exorbitant prices. And, that is also why it is okay for huge multi-national corporations to make all of the most important decisions about how our world is to be ordered, utilizing profit as their main decision-making criteria.

Yet, according to reason and logic... And according to universally recognized spiritual truths... And now, according to modern physics... Everything is connected. What would a culture look like if it were based upon this reasonable, logical, spiritual, and scientific truth that everything is connected? Well, for one thing, it wouldn't have the problems set out in the preceding paragraph. Nor would we be on the verge of planetary devastation through global warming and climate change. Our atmosphere, and our oceans, rivers and streams, would not be so terribly polluted. Our people would not have to worry about their basic needs being met. Our prisons would not be crowded to overflowing. And, our population would not be robbing and killing and sexually assaulting each other and anesthetizing itself with drugs and alcohol. Most of our problems would magically go away.

Why can I say this? Because, if our culture was based upon the truth that everything is connected, then each of our actions as individuals would arise from that basic reality. Our world would be re-ordered so that it mirrored our basic understanding of the connectedness of all things. All of a sudden, we would all become Responsible Members of the Community of Life on this planet.

The measuring stick I have devised which can be utilized to ascertain whether or not we have achieved our cultural shift is that we need to measure our progress in the following three areas…

FIRST… If we have succeeded in providing basic needs to all of the people on this planet.

SECOND… If we have stopped cutting down our last remaining forests.

And

THIRD… If we have at least made a serious effort to begin the process of ceasing to pollute.

Then, we will have successfully transformed out culture from an insane one to a rational, sane culture where humans have become Responsible Members of the Community of Life.

Please understand, I am not advocating that we give up our technological advances, or that we return to a primitive, hunter-gatherer lifestyle. On the contrary, I see plenty of potential for technology and innovation in a new, post-soft-landing connected culture where everyone understands the reality of the connectedness of all things.

The achievement of the providing of basic needs to all people everywhere, and the stopping of the cutting down of our precious forests could be achieved very easily. After we have achieved that all-important Critical Mass of people who understand, then all we would have to do is commit to doing these things. Pollution is the hard one. But, with a Critical Mass behind us, we could make real progress on the effort to stop pollution very quickly. It just might take a little while to succeed completely.

Think about it... Would it be possible for us to achieve these things within the framework of our present, insane culture that is based upon the premise that everything is separate? Absolutely not. The only way that any of these things is ever going to happen is as a result of a cultural revolution.

Don't you feel a deep sense of responsibility to this beautiful little planet and to all of its diverse life forms, including our own?

Let's make it happen! Let's save the world!

This is a call to intelligent people everywhere to examine the facts and choose to see the truth. This is a call to reasonable people everywhere to embrace the truth and replace our flawed and doomed culture before it crashes on its own. This is a call to responsible people everywhere to step up and do what we have to do to save this planet. Other than greed and selfishness, there is no reason for us to continue down this path that leads to our destruction.

I believe that achieving this Critical Mass through helping people understand how things came to be this way represents our best hope for saving the planet and the rest of the Community of Life from destruction by our insane culture. The other possibilities are achieving the Critical Mass through either spiritual enlightenment or an understanding of modern physics. The key is for people to understand the truth about the connectedness of everything that exists. By whatever means he or she achieves that understanding, whenever a person comes to know the truth that everything is connected, then that person will also see the need to transform our culture, which is based upon the false premise that everything is separate.

It is totally within our power to change this situation. First, we must assemble a Critical Mass of people who understand that everything is connected, and our present, insane culture does not recognize this reality. Then we make changes.

After achieving the Critical Mass, the easiest way to effect a worldwide change would be for the people here in the United States to wake up and take their government back from the huge corporations that have stolen it from us. All that is required is for us to replace our current, mostly corrupt batch of legislators with new Senators and Congressmen who understand the truths I am advocating herein and stand ready to implement the necessary changes via our legislative process and our U. S. Constitution. In this case, the Critical Mass would be achieved when there are enough voters available to win elections for enough of our candidates, so that changes may be implemented via Congress. Of course, we would also need to elect a President who is on our side.

Then, once the United States has been rescued from the huge corporations and their bought and paid for politicians, the rest of the world should fall in line rather easily. Why? Because the United States is the richest and most powerful nation on the planet. If the United States began acting responsibly, then I believe the other developed nations would fall in line rather easily. The developing nations wouldn't be a problem either. I imagine that these countries would very much appreciate receiving "true" aid, rather than the "pseudo" aid we have been doling out to them since the end of World War II.

That is my blueprint for change. However, please know that I am totally willing to deviate from the script as warranted by new developments. (Forgive the mixed metaphor, but you know what I mean.) And again… nothing can be accomplished until the Critical Mass is assembled. That is a given.

As I see it… The key to my being able to contribute to the effort to attain a Critical Mass is for this book to be successful. Therefore, I am trying to do the best job I possibly can of organizing, and researching, and writing, and explaining, and persuading, and convincing. If this book is successful, then, as I see it, there will be a place for my company, Save the World, Inc., to have an impact as well. My plan for Save the World, Inc. is for it to utilize video and the Internet, and any other means available to continue the effort of growing the Critical Mass. Another task I would like for Save the World, Inc. to take on would involve helping to coordinate efforts with the electing of our own representatives to Congress. If we are to succeed in replacing this flawed and doomed culture with a viable sane one, then we are going to need not only a sufficient amount of people, but a sufficient amount of money and resources as well. The rich and the powerful who will oppose us will not go quietly.

As stated previously, a huge key to convincing people that our culture is insane and must be replaced is for people to understand how things came to be this way. Part One of this book is called "How Things Came to Be This Way", and it describes the journey of humanity from its evolutionary beginning millions of years ago to the present time and shows us the time and place where our culture of today was born. You will find out in Part One what the basis for our present worldwide culture is and why it is fatally flawed. And you may be surprised to find out that the grandest lie of all, which is the cause of so much destruction, misery, pain, and suffering, can be set out in a simple, innocent looking, declaratory sentence... a sentence that is the very basis for our culture. The rest of Part One lays the groundwork, which will prepare you to be able to understand the terrible significance of this simple declaratory statement.

Oh, what a tangled web we weave when first we practice to deceive! Part Two will explore the myriad ways in which our culture must deceive us in order to cover up the fact that it is based on a fallacy. All of the biggest problems that plague our world of today will be addressed. By the time you finish reading Part Two, you will have all the information you need in order to become fully awakened and totally free!

In Part Three, I will present a workable plan under which this flawed and doomed culture could be discarded and replaced with one that actually works. The good news is that the Critical Mass we need to begin implementing the plan is not even close to fifty percent.   The bad news is that many of the richest and most powerful among us, and the huge corporations and governments that are managed and run by them, will not want to see any changes. And, all that wealth and power gives these individuals and their organizations the ability to assert some control. But those few young souls will not be able to stop progress forever. When we are contemplating the implementation of these changes, you and I must keep in mind that these rich and powerful individuals represent only a teeny, tiny minority of us. With the right effort, we will be able to bring this flawed and doomed culture in for a soft landing before it crashes on its own. Then, once we get it safely on the ground, we can rebuild it.

We can save the world!

Part One

How Things Came to Be This Way

1

The Great Forgetting and The Peacekeeping Law

◊

Our world has serious problems... problems that we can't seem to do anything about.

Here is a partial list of some of the bigger ones:

❖ The top 1% of the richest individuals control half of the world's wealth, while the bottom 50% live in poverty, struggling to provide themselves with their basic needs of food, shelter, clothing, health care, safe drinking water, and sanitary living conditions.

❖ All the big decisions as to how our world should be ordered are made by huge corporations whose only criteria for making any decision is how it will affect their own growth and profit.

❖ Nine countries own enough nuclear weapons to destroy all life on this planet 100 times over.

❖ More than 160 million people were killed as a result of wars in the twentieth century. Today, people are still dying in more than twenty-five armed conflicts around the globe. In this century, somewhere around 1 million people have died in wars in Syria, Iraq, and Afghanistan alone.

❖ The richest and most powerful nation on the planet considers health care to be a commodity that should only be provided to those who can afford to pay the exorbitant costs.

❖ The cause of global warming and climate change, being a growing accumulation of human-generated greenhouse gases in the upper atmosphere, has been identified for more than thirty years, and yet no meaningful progress has been made on the effort to stem it.

❖ The human population has grown from 1 billion to more almost 8 billion in the past 200 years, and it continues to rise, despite the fact that we all know what a serious a problem this represents for all of us… and also to all of the other members of the Community of Life on this planet.

❖ Deforestation due to natural resource exploitation, and farming and ranching operations, as well as human overpopulation in general, is causing the biggest species die-off since the dinosaurs went extinct 65 million years ago.

❖ Pollution of the air we breathe and of our rivers, streams, and oceans is at critical levels and continues to get worse with no end in sight.

But there is good news… For the first time in the ten-thousand-year history of our culture, because of Daniel Quinn, we finally have the ability to address all of our biggest problems at their most basic level. Everyone knows… If you want to rid your garden of weeds, then you need to pull them out by the roots. Likewise, if you want to solve our problems, then you must address the root cause of those problems. Until Ishmael, nobody had ever given us the tools that would allow us to do that. Here is what I learned by reading *Ishmael, An Adventure of the Mind and Spirit:*

The very root of our problems is that we all live in an insane culture. Our culture is insane because it is based upon a fallacy. Our culture is telling us that we live in a world that was made especially for man to conquer and rule, which is not true. The problems we are experiencing are happening because we are enacting our cultural story. We are actually conquering the world, just as our cultural story commands us.

If we want to save the world, then we must change our cultural story to the reality-based story that tells us, "Man is a part of the world." We must re-make our world so that man can return to his original role as a Responsible Member of the Community of Life on this planet.

This was the knowledge I was so excited about when I read *Ishmael.* The reality of that statement is so powerful, that I just could not contain my relief, and my joy, and my excitement. Finally! Somebody had figured out what was wrong! Daniel Quinn had actually provided us with a recipe for saving the world! And, even better... It was going to be easy! All we had to do was to get enough people to read *Ishmael!* The solution was there in the pages of the novel. Any reasonably intelligent person who read it could not help but understand it!

As I reported in the Introduction, I was so excited about the potential of *Ishmael* for saving the world, that I gave away something like forty copies of the book in the first six months after first reading it. Then, slowly, as the results came in, I was forced to face the harsh reality... Most of my friends were apparently not ready to hear these truths. Saving the world was not going to be as easy as I had naively thought.

It has been more than twenty-five years since I first read *Ishmael*. I've had more than twenty-five years to let these truths percolate around in my brain. And, I am happy to report... I'm every bit as grateful today as I was upon first learning of them. While it is true that saving the world is going to be harder than I first thought it would, at least I know what has to be done. And, thankfully, I no longer have to wonder about why our world is saddled with such seemingly insurmountable problems.

With *Ishmael*, and its follow-up novel, *The Story of B,* Daniel Quinn made some very significant contributions to our knowledge and understanding about ourselves. The first, and most important of which was described above.

As I found out the hard way, if you are going to try to tell someone that our problems exist only because our culture is insane, then you better have some pretty good bullshit ready to back you up. If you simply make the statement, then you will most likely be dismissed as a fringe lunatic. If you try to explain, then your explanation better be short and succinct and bullet proof, because you are not going to have anyone's attention for very long... especially if you say something you can't back up to their satisfaction. I have found it is usually pretty difficult to persuade someone that our problems exist only because our culture is insane in a conversational format. The problem is one of credibility. After all, who am I to try to tell you our philosophers, and our religious authorities, and our governmental leaders have all had their heads up their butts for millennia? Even if every statement I make in a conversation is irrefutable, I still am likely to have my arguments fall on deaf ears... simply because of the credibility problem.

The reason a book format can be effective in reaching people is because if you can get your book published, then that automatically provides a certain level of credibility, especially if the publishing company is well known and well respected. Then, if the reviews are positive, that provides a whole other level of credibility. Finally, if you are able to establish a base of people who are recommending the book to their friends, then that is where things can really take off.

Ishmael accomplished all of this and more. Quinn tells us in his autobiography, *Providence, The Story of a Fifty-Year Vision Quest,* how he had been working on different versions of the book that became Ishmael for many years. When he heard about Ted Turner's Tomorrow Award, which was famously going to give a $500,000 prize to the work of fiction judged to be the most influential towards the goal of saving the planet, he decided to take one last stab at getting it right. He was able to finish *Ishmael* just prior to the deadline for submittals, and he won first prize. Today, *Ishmael* is a classic novel that is taught in schools all over the world. While it is true that I have had a considerable amount of trouble getting my friends interested, there is no question that the book has positively affected many thousands in the same way it inspired me.

In order for Daniel Quinn to be able to state definitively that the basic cause of our problems is because our culture is flawed at its very foundational level. Quinn had to lay some groundwork. He had to build his case. In Ishmael, he began with a review of what we know about the history of our Universe, with an emphasis on the history of humans. Out of that review came the next of Quinn's original contributions to what we know about ourselves, an event in our human history that Quinn called the Great Forgetting.

For this, Quinn pointed out that man has been around on this planet for a period of time approaching three million years, and that people of our species have been here for more than two hundred fifty thousand years. But until recently, this wasn't known or understood, because it had been forgotten. Our civilized ancestors had somehow lost this critical piece of information about ourselves. A few generations after leaving the hunter-gathering lifestyle to become agriculturalists and herders living in settlements, our ancestors simply lost contact with the fact that their ancestors had ever existed as hunter-gatherers. If you think about it, this Great Forgetting probably occurred more than five thousand years before writing was invented. You probably know quite a lot about what life was like here on Earth two hundred years ago, but that is because of our written historical records. How much do you know about your own family from ten generations ago? Unless you are a dedicated genealogist, probably not much. And, even if you are a genealogist, then what you know about your family from ten generations ago was assembled from written records, and not from oral accounts passed down to you through the generations.

At some point, thousands of years ago, our ancestors simply forgot their ancestors used to be hunter-gatherers. It was an examination and evaluation of the fossil records during the past two hundred years that enabled us to finally re-connect with this very important fact about ourselves. Until the fossil records told us otherwise, we actually thought man had simply come into existence only a few thousand years ago and immediately began building towns and villages and eventually cities. We even thought tribal people had previously been civilized, but had somehow either regressed to their primitive states, or possibly had been outcast. Then, when we finally did piece together the reality of this earlier existence, our reaction was to lump everything that took place earlier than the beginning of written history into a grand and totally unimportant category called pre-history. In other words, the fact that humans were three million years old instead of five thousand years old was considered to be an inconvenient new piece of knowledge, and so, was simply swept under the rug. When this new information came to light roughly two hundred years ago, our cultural foundation thinkers should have been hugely impacted and motivated to re-think a lot of religion, philosophy, and history that were developed in ignorance of the real facts... But instead, they ignored it.

As a part of the effort to help people to understand that we are living in an insane culture, we need to recognize the fact that our culture was founded upon faulty information that was not understood to be wrong until very recently. It might have seemed reasonable to a foundational thinker who was a victim of the Great Forgetting, and thought that man had always lived within civilizations, that God must have created the world especially for man to conquer and rule, but once such a person is privileged to have the correct information telling us that man is actually millions of years old and evolved from the same, simple origins as all other life on this planet... Then such a cultural premise would not seem so valid.

The next significant contribution Quinn made to our understanding about ourselves was that he established there is a law governing evolution that nobody else before him had ever been able to reason out. And the law is not the "Kill or be Killed Law of the Jungle -Only the Strongest Survive" law that many of us think must be controlling things in nature. That law, Quinn tells us, is complete bunk. The natural world does not operate that way.

The evolutionary law I am referring to is called the law of limited competition, which is also known as the peacekeeping law. This law states that a species may compete to the best of its abilities for food or other resources, but it may not wage war, or kill indiscriminately, or set out to eradicate another species just because that species might be in competition with it for food or other resources. And the penalty for violating this law is a harsh one... Extinction.

It is because we are in violation of this law that we can say with certainty that our way of living is not sustainable. Our culture is operating outside of this law, and therefore it is doomed to fail. It does not function properly and it cannot be fixed.

It is important to note, not every human who is alive today is in violation of this law. Only each and every one of us who are members of our culture is guilty of this. Indigenous tribal people who are still living on their ancestral lands in their ancient and proven ways are exempted from this culpability. They remain as

Responsible Members of the Community of Life, just as they always have. At the beginning of Part Three, we will examine the significance of this fact that not every human being is in violation of the peacekeeping law in a chapter titled "We Are Not Humanity".

Quinn used an allegorical story to bring out the truth and the undeniable impact of the ultimate result of our culture being in violation of the law of limited competition. His tool in this case was the story of the Hapless Airman.

Our culture, Quinn argued, can be compared to the people who wanted to build flying machines before anyone understood the law of aerodynamics. Since nobody understood the law of aerodynamics, the design and construction of flying machines was a "hit or miss" enterprise that mostly missed. The fact that nobody understood there was a law governing what would fly and what wouldn't fly did not serve to diminish in any way whatsoever the fact that the law did exist. Although the people of that time didn't understand it yet, it was an irrefutable fact that any flying machine, which was not constructed in accordance with the law of aerodynamics, would not fly.

And likewise, any culture, which is not designed in accordance with the law of limited competition, is doomed to failure.

Once we understood the law of aerodynamics, we were able to build successful flying machine after successful flying machine. And likewise, once enough of us come to understand the law of limited competition, we will be able to build successful culture after successful and sustainable culture. And perhaps more importantly, we will realize that we must abandon the one we are presently living in… Before all of us experience that terrible crash landing together.

Here again, are the three pieces of the puzzle provided by Daniel Quinn in Ishmael, that explain how our world came to be such a mess:

First: We live in an insane culture that is based upon a fallacy. The world was NOT made for man to conquer and rule.

Second: Until recently, we all thought humans were only a few thousand years old. We had no idea that we were actually millions of years old and fit into the branch of mammals classified as primates. Nor, did we understand that until 10,000 years ago, we had all been hunter-gatherers. This is what Quinn called the Great Forgetting.

Third: There is a law called the peacekeeping law, or the law of limited competition, that governs evolution. Our worldwide culture is in violation of that law.

To some degree, Quinn may have relied upon earlier thinkers. But as far as I can tell, he did most of the heavy lifting for these three things on his own. I don't think anyone before him had ever pieced all of this together, and it took a tremendous amount of intellectual sleuthing in order for Quinn to accomplish it.

Thank you, Daniel Quinn... from the bottom of my heart. I am eternally grateful to you for what you have done for our planet. And, also for what you have done for my peace of mind. I sleep much better now that I know where to place the blame for our troubles. But most importantly, thank you for showing us how to fix what is wrong with our world.

After more than twenty years of being grateful for this knowledge and understanding, it is my turn to give back. What follows is my effort to comply with the recommendation for action set out at the end of Ishmael. Please enjoy the rest of *Soft Landing*. And, if after reading *Soft Landing*, you find that you have become a part of the growing group of people who understand the root cause of our problems is a result of our culture being based upon a falsehood, then it will be your turn to teach a hundred people what I have taught you. If you are able to reach even more than one hundred people, so much the better.

It is my wish for you that the knowledge and understanding contained herein will provide you with the same peace of mind that it has given to me. Enjoy.

2

How Things Came to Be This Way

Through his novels, Daniel Quinn explained to us how our culture began roughly ten thousand years ago when some early adopters of agriculture decided to lock up the food. But until recently, nobody understood that. Ten thousand years ago, the culture that became our present culture was one of thousands of cultures that existed here on earth. Now, ten thousand years later, our culture covers the entire planet, and it has either conquered and destroyed, or assimilated all but a very few of those thousands of other cultures.

Another important concept we didn't understand until recently was evolution. It was Charles Darwin who enlightened us about the process of evolution and how it explains our existence here. And in the century and a half since then, archaeologists have assembled fossil evidence and other scientific proof telling us that our particular animal species, homo sapiens, has been walking on this earth for at least 250,000 years. Our species evolved out of a branch of warm-blooded mammals called primates. Six to eight million years ago, the branch that ultimately leads to us, split into two branches, and one of these branches leads to us, and the other to chimpanzees. One big point from Chapter 1 that needs to be repeated here to help people understand how things came to be this way, is that until recently (about 200 years ago), everyone thought humans had only been around for perhaps five thousand years.

Before that time, people actually thought man's appearance on this world roughly coincided with the onset of our written history and the beginning of civilization. Other misconceptions included thinking our world was a stationary object around which the moon and the sun and the stars and everything in the sky rotated. (At least they were right about the moon.) Also, we had no idea of the spherical shape of our world. We presumed it to be flat. Otherwise, how could it have been possible for us to be standing on it? Of course, we had no idea that the stars we saw in the night sky were actually similar to our own Sun. Likewise, we didn't have the slightest clue that many of the points of light we called "stars" were actually distant galaxies containing hundreds of billions of stars. We didn't have the slightest clue that our world and everything we saw when we looked up at night was actually billions of years old.

These misconceptions shared by people of our culture until science was able to enlighten us, served as the very foundation of the flawed and doomed culture that we are all a part of today. We thought man was only a few thousand years old, and when he arrived, he immediately set about to build civilization. Many people even assumed that tribal people had somehow tragically regressed into a savage and brutal existence from a civilized way of life practiced by their ancestors. We thought God created this world especially for humans to conquer and rule, and that the sun and the stars and everything in the Universe revolved around us.

Now, however, we know our Universe is billions of years old, and that our planet Earth revolves around the Sun, as do all of our other sister planets in our Solar System, which resides in the outer reaches of the Milky Way Galaxy, which is one of hundreds of billions of similar galaxies containing hundreds of billions of stars in this vast Universe. And that all life on this planet has evolved from the same, simple beginning, slowly, over billions of years. And, we know that humans, just like us, have been walking on this planet for the past 250,000 years.

Maybe, as a result of having this new information at our disposal... information that contradicts the facts on which our present culture is based... it is time we made some adjustments in the way our culture is structured. Besides, as evidenced by the list of problems from Chapter 1, something definitely needs changing.

People who are alive today have the great privilege of understanding a whole myriad of facts about our natural world that people born previously did not have access to. For instance, have you ever stopped to consider how remarkable it is that almost eight billion of us are all standing on this tiny, little rock called Planet Earth, which we now know is one of eight (or nine, depending upon whether you want to count Pluto) planets orbiting our Sun, which we now know is one of hundreds of billions of stars in our Milky Way Galaxy, which we now know is one of hundreds of billions of similar galaxies in our Universe. And, we can now explain with relative certainty to each other, remarkable facts about our existence, which we know because our scientists have figured them out for us.

For instance,

Our Universe is approximately 13.8 billion years old. 13.8 billion years ago, our Universe was actually very small. Then, with a Big Bang, it began expanding very rapidly. Now it is so immense, we cannot possibly imagine how far it is from one side to the other.

Then, there is this...

The periodic table of elements contains 118 elements. Our children learn in their school chemistry classes that everything in our physical world is comprised of some combination of these elements. We now know that only three of these elements were present in our Universe immediately after the Big Bang... these being lots of hydrogen, some helium, and trace amounts of lithium. We also know that all of the 115 other elements that make up our world of today were formed as a part of nuclear reactions within stars, and then dispersed across the Universe when those stars exploded as supernovae. Certainly, one of the most remarkable facts any person could ever wrap their head around is that everything in our world, including even our own physical bodies, is made of stardust.

The first stars in our Milky Way Galaxy formed shortly after the Big Bang, and our particular star was a second or third or possibly even a fourth-generation star that formed approximately 4.6 billion years ago, mostly utilizing debris from earlier generation stars that had gone supernova. Our Planet Earth, which orbits around this star, is around 4.54 billion years old, and is also composed mostly out of the same leftover debris. Simple single-cell life began here on Earth about 3 to 4 billion years ago. Although we don't know the exact process by which life first began, we have identified several ways in which it could have occurred. If the origin of life did begin here, perhaps it could have been the result of a lucky lightning strike on some primordial soup that contained the right constituents in the necessary proportions.

Another popular theory is the deep-sea vent theory that tells us life could have begun at submarine hydrothermal vents. At this time, there are several other plausible scientific theories out there setting out how life might have begun here on Earth. Many have tried, but so far no one has been able to create life out of inanimate materials in a laboratory setting.

Then, there is the possibility that life began somewhere else. If life came from elsewhere in the Cosmos, then certainly, it is possible that early life on our planet hitchhiked its way here on a meteor, or maybe a comet. However, whether or not life "just happened" here or even somewhere else, or whether the origin of life can be attributed to Divine creation, or to extra-terrestrial intelligences from elsewhere in the Cosmos, is not really important to the discussion herein about our culture. The important point for this discussion is that once life got its foothold here, the fossil record, and all other evidence, supports Darwin's theory of evolution. I do think it is important to state that I don't see any aspect of this scientific creation story that tells us our planet or our solar system or our galaxy is unique within this vast universe, although I must assume that planets like ours, with our extremely diverse and beautiful, carbon-based life forms, are rare, and would most certainly be prized discoveries to any intelligent beings who happened upon this precious blue jewel called Planet Earth in their travels.

Also, when considering this question of the origin of life, I think it is important for us to keep in mind the age of our solar system relative to the age of our galaxy, and also relative to the wider Universe. Whether life began here or elsewhere through an accidental chemical reaction, or whether life began here through the active intervention of a higher consciousness from somewhere else, there are certainly a lot of other places within this vast Universe, where the same thing could have occurred billions of years earlier than it did here on Earth. And, assuming those ancient beings were able to figure out the things we are addressing in this book, and thus avoid the problem of going extinct through their own ignorance, these extra-terrestrial life forms might have quite a head start on us in terms of their understanding of the true nature of our shared reality.

Charles Darwin demonstrated with his *On the Origin of Species*, which was published in 1859, that life has evolved here on Earth, over time, from simple to more complex organisms. Historians tell us he already knew it many years before his book was published, but Darwin was reluctant to take the ridicule he knew would come if he stated in his book that humans and apes have common ancestors, so he did not make that case in *Origin*. However, the fact that man, along with every other living thing on Earth, has evolved from earlier and simpler iterations of themselves, can be easily reasoned out of Darwin's work by anyone who reads it. Of course, this fact did cause considerable controversy within the religious community, who were heavily invested in their fairy-tale story about God having created the world especially for man in only seven days. If it was not evident from the Introduction, I want to state here and now that I have no qualms whatsoever about the possibility of this book causing some controversy within the religious community. To be fair... If Darwin was alive today, I'm sure he would no longer be concerned about it either.

Since Darwin's book was first published, two years before the beginning of the American Civil War, a lot has happened in regard to the quest to understand the evolution of humans. Much of the progress in this area involves the discovery of thousands of fossil records, some of which have been demonstrated to be more than 4 million years old. Other major developments are the discovery of DNA, which has resulted in the development of an entirely new scientific field of study called genetics. Also very important has been the development of more and more sophisticated dating techniques, with some of the most relied upon and apparently some of the most accurate of those, coming out of genetics.

Today, scientists are able to compare dating estimates made by archaeologists and paleontologists with estimates made by molecular biologists, and they are finding a lot of agreement. DNA analysis gives molecular biologists the ability to estimate with relative certainty that chimpanzees and our human forefathers diverged from each other about six to eight million years ago. We now know from genetics that chimpanzees are more closely related to humans than they are to any of the other primates. By the way... The separation in sub-species that occurred immediately prior to the human and the chimpanzee line was the one between our line and the line that leads to gorillas.

The main trait that distinguished early man from early chimpanzees and from all other primates was man's bipedalism. Advantages to humans arising from this development included the freeing up of the hands for other tasks, the ability to travel longer distances in less time, and an enhanced field of vision. In the first one to three million years after the two species diverged, our ancestors were probably not much more advanced than their chimpanzee cousins. However, as time passed, fossil records show that our brains grew larger and larger. Archaeological evidence indicates early humans began been using crude stone tools at least 3.3 million years ago, and our ancestors probably controlled the use of fire for warmth and cooking more than a million years ago.

According to the fossil record, as confirmed by DNA analysis, anatomically modern humans first appeared 250,000 to 400,000 years ago. However, archaeological evidence indicates these early anatomically modern humans may have existed as little more than smart, bipedal chimpanzees who could cook, from the time they first evolved until some unknown event caused the "Great Leap Forward" about 50,000 years ago. Humans after that time are considered to be both anatomically modern, and also behaviorally modern. Archaeological evidence of the Cro-Magnon man from 43,000 years ago found in France, are the earliest records found to date of anatomically modern humans with more sophisticated stone tools, including hafted axes and knives, awls, needles, and even spear throwers. Also significant to the Great Leap Forward is the fact that cave paintings dating back to around this period have been located in Spain and France, as well as Indonesia and Australia.

The particular development that enabled this Great Leap Forward is much debated. Many scientists hypothesize the reason may have been the development of complex language. There are good reasons supporting this school of thought. For instance, logic and abstract reasoning may have developed, or at the very least been greatly enhanced, when humans first began to utilize complex language. Without a doubt, collaboration on hunting strategy and brainstorming on potential tool making improvements, as well as tribal debates about where to locate, and other important matters, would have certainly been enhanced whenever spoken language was developed.

Piecing the story of humanity together from the available evidence, it appears that after reaching the behaviorally modern plateau 50,000 years ago, our best guess is that for the next 35,000 years, humans continued living as hunter-gatherers in small bands of less than 100 members. I say this is our best guess, because, other than the stone tools we have found from this period, we really don't have a lot of tangible evidence telling us what, exactly, was going on. There is no physical evidence of villages or settlements dating back farther than 12,000 years ago, and such evidence from earlier than 9,000 years ago is extremely rare. And remember... we are talking about more than 35,000 years of pre-history involving human beings who were just like us. That is a period of time that is more than five times longer than all of recorded history... a very long time, indeed.

As a mental exercise to help you wrap your head around the significance of a missing 35,000 years of human pre-history, just consider how closely you identify your current existence with the people who were alive during the height of the Roman Empire, which, by comparison, was a mere 2,000 years ago. When you think about everything that happened within the last 2,000 years, you realize that a lot could have happened both culturally and otherwise during this 35,000 yearlong stretch of pre-historical time. And, unless someone would invent a time machine that could take us backwards in time, we would have no way of knowing about it. The stone tool archaeological evidence indicates that during this time there were people living pretty much everywhere on the planet that was not covered in ice, with the only possible exception being the Western Hemisphere, which many experts believe was not inhabited by humans until around 14,000 years ago.

One of the competitive advantages that humans have over many other species is the fact that we are omnivores, meaning our bodies are capable of processing either meat or plant-based foods to provide nourishment for our sustenance. That is why humans are able to live as hunter–gatherers (carnivores-herbivores). Fifty thousand years ago, when behaviorally modern humans finally started down the road that led to improvements in stone tools, etc., they must have had a real zeal for figuring out other ways in addition to better stone tools that could make their lives even easier. I imagine it would not have been too great of a leap for some of the members of some of these hunter-gatherer tribes, who were enjoying better hunting successes with their improved stone tools, to also decide to attempt to improve the gathering side of their hunter-gatherer lifestyle by beginning to practice some limited forms of agriculture.

Eventually, these agricultural efforts resulted in very tangible agricultural innovations. For many pre-historic people, this meant the end of hunter-gathering, and the beginning of agricultural based settlements. This is a hugely significant innovation in the way of life of certain humans. For the first time in the entire 250,000-year history of Homo sapiens, people were beginning to live in settlements and procured their food in a manner other than as hunter-gatherers.

As it turned out, this was also a hugely significant innovation for not only everyone who is alive today, but for the entire planet, and every living thing on it. If you have read *Ishmael*, or if you have read *Guns, Germs, and Steel*, by Jared Diamond, then you know how significant the appearance of these first settlements were. They lead directly to us… And to everything that is good and bad about us, including all of those terrible problems outlined in the beginning of Chapter 1.

Most experts believe the earliest of these agricultural-based settlements was the one in ancient Mesopotamia, between the Tigris and Euphrates rivers in an area occupied by present day Iraq. The big breakthrough for these people happened when they discovered wheat and barley could be cultivated, harvested and then stored safely for long periods, leading to surpluses and increased food security. Archaeological evidence indicates that wheat, barley, and cotton were also cultivated very early in the Nile River valley in present-day Egypt. Rice, barley, beans, and other crops were cultivated in the Indus River valley in present-day India. And rice, wheat, and lentils were cultivated in the Yellow River valley and the Yangtze River valleys in present-day China.

Additionally, there were at least two early centers of agricultural development in the Americas, these being Mesoamerica, where maize was successfully bred in a generations-long process from a grain called tesotine, and eventually grown in fields called milpas, along with beans, squash, melons, tomatoes, chilis, sweet potatoes, yuccas, and avocados. The final agricultural center, Norte Chico, sometimes referred to as Caral-Supe, was located in coastal and near-coastal present-day northern Peru. Because of its use for fishing nets, cotton was one of the most important early crops there. Other edible crops grown there included squash, beans, and sweet potatoes. The food surpluses, which were the result of these agricultural innovations, were extremely significant and led to increased populations and many changes in the way these previously hunter-gatherer people lived.

Jared Diamond, like Daniel Quinn, and Charles Darwin, is a hero to me for all of his thought, and effort... and his success... in figuring out how things came to be this way. Like Quinn, he believes our worldwide culture got its start ten thousand years ago, when formerly hunter-gathering people living in ancient Mesopotamia, learned how to create food surpluses for themselves by farming wheat and barley. The grains could be stored for long periods without spoiling, and the resulting food surpluses opened up many new possibilities, including specialization of skills, division of labor, and ultimately, a stratified class society with an elite ruling class. The next big step for these hunter-gatherers turned agriculturalists was the domestication of goats, sheep, and eventually, cattle, pigs, and the rest.

The increased food supply soon led to an increased population. As things turned out, these improvements gave these early farmers and herders such an advantage over their hunter-gatherer neighbors that, this new, innovative culture never stopped expanding until it had gobbled up the entire planet by either conquering or assimilating neighbor after neighbor, until finally, there were no more neighbors left. Today, with very few exceptions, you and I and almost every other person on the planet, are members of the culture that began in this manner, in ancient Mesopotamia. But, as we shall see... It didn't have to turn out this way.

As Diamond tells it... his quest to understand how things came to be this way began forty years ago when a New Guinea native asked him why the white men had so much "cargo", and the New Guinea people so little. Ultimately, after many years of thought and research, Diamond was finally able to answer that question in a book titled *Guns, Germs, and Steel*, which won the Pulitzer Prize. And, the answer was... It all came down to geography. The white man was not smarter or more capable in any way than the primitive New Guinean people Diamond came to know on his travels there. There was no genetic or racial component whatsoever to the answer of why the white man had so much cargo. The answer, according to Diamond, was the luck of geography... pure and simple.

When that ancient tribe of hunter-gatherers in Mesopotamia figured out how to cultivate wheat and barley and domesticate animals, they did so on Eurasia, which is a huge, east-west trending landmass that is also connected to North Africa. Once they figured out this new way of living, there were thousands of miles of similar land lying on the same geographical latitude, both to the east and to the west, where the climate and the growing seasons were similar, and where their new form of agriculture could be copied simply by taking the seeds, the animals, and the know-how to those sites.

Diamond did some research on domesticated animals and discovered that of the fourteen large mammals that man has successfully domesticated, only the relatively insignificant llama/alpaca came from the Western Hemisphere. The five most important ones, being sheep, goats, cattle, pigs, and horses, as well as all of the others except the llama, all originated on Eurasia. The fact that all of the domesticated animals came from Eurasia gave the people living there huge advantages over people living elsewhere. Among them were increased food security, help with transport, an ability to till more land, and to plow deeper into the soil, all of which led to increased populations. Eventually, these increased populations led to technological advances, two of which were the Guns and Steel from the title of Diamond's Pulitzer Prize winning book.

It turns out that the other word in the title… Germs… also had much to do with domesticated animals. Certainly, the guns and the steel gave the Spaniards and the other Europeans some advantages over the Native Americans when they arrived here. And, similarly, the Europeans that colonized South Africa and Australia had the advantage of those inventions over the native populations there as well. But if it wasn't for the germs, the colonizers and conquerors would have undoubtedly had a much harder time getting their way.

The reason the transfer of germs was so one-sided was because the diseases had been present in Europe and Asia for thousands of years. These diseases were originally present in cattle, pigs, ducks, chickens and other domesticated animals, and because of the domesticated animal's proximity to people, the disease was able to "jump" over to humans. The European advantage in this unintended and unplanned transfer of germs by the Europeans to the Native Americans was due to the fact that the diseases had been present in Europe for many generations. This meant that over time, those Europeans possessing a genetic resistance to these diseases tended to be more likely to survive and reproduce, passing on those disease resisting genes to their offspring. Hence, statistically speaking, Europeans were much more likely to be able to survive these diseases than the Native Americans, whose entire population consisted of people who had never been exposed to any of them. Also, the European invaders were all adults, and many had already survived exposure to these diseases earlier in their lives. Generally speaking, you only have to survive chicken pox, measles, pertussis, mumps, or smallpox once. After that, you have a lifetime of immunity.

The Europeans that came to the Western Hemisphere, beginning in 1492 with Columbus, came here with the intention of colonizing, exploiting, and conquering whoever and whatever they found. When I was learning about this in public school, we were told the Western Hemisphere was largely empty and unoccupied when the Europeans arrived here. Now, new research is not only saying there were more than 100 million Native Americans thriving here when Columbus arrived, but that they were much more advanced, civilized, and sophisticated than previously understood. It was the smallpox, measles, influenza, and typhus, along with the diphtheria, malaria, mumps, pertussis, plague, tuberculosis, and yellow fever that infected and killed the native population, and really turned the tide for the conquerors. It is now being speculated that these diseases spread out across the two continents ahead of the conquerors, and decimated the native populations in advance of actual, physical contact. For the most part, the Europeans were unaware that it had even occurred.

Diamond has much to say about this subject in Guns, Germs, and Steel... And rightfully so. If this unintended and unplanned transfer of germs by the colonizers and conquerors to the native populations had not been so one-sided, the outcome would certainly have been different. Without it, the Europeans may have prevailed in the end, but most definitely, they would have had a much harder time doing so. And, if the Native Americans had developed their own genetic resistance to similar diseases originating from their own domesticated animals that the Europeans had never been exposed to, then the outcome might have been very different indeed. Imagine if Columbus had brought back germs on his return to Spain from his initial voyage to the New World... and those germs ended up wiping out more than 90% of the European and the Asian populations. Certainly, if that had occurred, we would be living in a much different world today. If there had been more domesticatable animals in the Americas, that might very well have been the outcome.

It goes back to his basic premise... After thirty years of cogitating on it... Diamond's answer to his New Guinea friend was that the white man has so much cargo because of pure luck. The lucky white man's ancestors had resided in Eurasia. Wheat and barley originated there, as did the wild ancestors of the animals they domesticated. Eurasia was a large land mass oriented on an East to West axis. Once the farming techniques were developed and those animals domesticated, there was a lot of room for the increased populations to do the same thing on other lands with similar climate and growing conditions. Those increased populations eventually led to the technological advances that included the smelting of steel from iron, and the invention of gunpowder, which was then used in guns to fire projectiles to kill game in hunting, and to kill enemies in war.

Of course, this is a somewhat simplistic explanation of Jared Diamond's Pulitzer Prize winning book. However, for the most part it is an accurate account of what he says occurred. For instance, a lot of formerly tribal people adopted the new farming and animal domestication innovations on their own, without any coercion. Afterwards, they became de-facto members of our culture, even though they might have considered themselves and their ways separate. An example of this would be the Oriental people who have always, throughout history, remained somewhat separate, culturally, from the rest of the world. Never having been conquered from the outside, they have developed a rich culture that is a part of ours... yet separate. Still, there is no question that China, and her 1.4 billion citizens, are a part of our worldwide culture of today... At least in every way that matters to this discussion of how things came to be this way.

Also, it needs to be said that the process involving the conquest and assimilation of all of the world's other cultures into our culture of today took thousands of years to accomplish. For instance, the American Indian wars ended here in the U. S. only about 135 years ago. Plus, there are a few indigenous people scattered around the world in remote areas today who are still living tribally as hunter-gatherers, who have not been conquered by or assimilated into this worldwide culture that you and I are a part of. However, I think it is pretty safe to say, as well as very sad to think about, that one way or the other, it does not appear they will be doing so for much longer.

On the face of it, learning how to cultivate wheat and barley, and learning how to domesticate goats, sheep and cattle, and pigs seems like excellent progress over hand to mouth hunting and gathering ways. And, to be sure, adding these farming and animal husbandry tools to our survival toolkit was certainly a big plus. However, as we shall see, the progress had a huge price.

Archaeological evidence indicates that, give or take a thousand years or so, the first civilizations arose around 5,000 to 7,000 years ago in each of these six agricultural centers as a direct result of the increased agricultural bounty supporting denser populations, leading to specialized labor and class-based societal structures. For the purposes of this examination of how things came to be this way, we are especially interested in the cultures that humans were a part of during this time period... or we would be interested in them, if it were possible to know them. While we do not have specific data, we can speculate on the existence of thousands of relatively small, tribal, hunter-gatherer cultures that we imagine were present around the world during this time, some of which were located near these early civilizations. Probably, these tribal cultures, being based as they were, on their hunter-gatherer lifestyles, were similar to cultures of tribal peoples encountered and studied in our own time.

Unfortunately, we don't know enough about these ancient civilizations to be able to judge whether the basis of their culture was "Everything is separate", or "Everything is connected." I, for one, would love to know the answer to that one. All we can say for sure is that at some point, the ruling class must have become corrupt and began exploiting their powerful positions for their own personal benefit. Whether it happened at the time our culture first developed, or at some later point in time, the oppressed and exploited people within our culture, along with the rest of the Community of Life, have suffered the consequences ever since.

Ten thousand years ago, when our culture got its start, there were maybe 10 million people alive on this planet, and most were living tribally in bands of no more than 100 to 150 people, just as they had ever since humans evolved from their primate cousins millions of years previously. To be sure, a world occupied solely by tribal people was no utopia either. For instance, even though there were certainly situations where neighboring tribes regularly interacted peacefully with each other, inter-tribal relations were often quite problematic. And, as demonstrated by Quinn, each tribe represented its own, unique culture. I imagine that many of these tribes provided settings for their tribal members that were quite idyllic. However, there is no doubt that many of those unique cultures were also quite flawed to the point that they did not work well for their tribal members, or even for the landbase on which they were located, or with the Community of Life within that landbase.

Eventually, though... given enough time... those problems would have been worked out in the evolutionary process that includes Quinn's peacekeeping law, through which the tribe either made the necessary adjustments or ceased to exist. In terms of our discussion of how things came to be this way, it is important to understand that for the most part, it has been demonstrated by anthropologists that people within tribes took care of each other. In most tribes, no member was cold or hungry unless every member of that tribe was cold or hungry. In general terms, tribal people also had extremely light footprints on the ecological systems in which they existed. Plus, without question, they were more in touch with the natural world, and had a much closer sense of connection with nature and also their fellow tribesmen. To quote Daniel Quinn...

The Leavers' (tribal people's) cultural story told the tribal members, "Man belongs to the world."

Imagine if you can, our beautiful planet as it existed ten thousand years ago, in the time just before that tribe in Mesopotamia began practicing totalitarian agriculture. Ten thousand years ago, planet earth was populated by maybe 10 million humans, all of them living sustainably on their own landbases as hunter-gatherers, many of who were also practicing limited and sustainable forms of agriculture. But whatever their particular lifestyles consisted of, and whatever methods they were utilizing to secure food and shelter, and however they chose to relate to their particular environment and to the Community of Life that surrounded them... all of these things had evolved over many generations, through an interaction between themselves and their particular landbase and everything on it and in it. And for many of these tribal peoples, this process had been ongoing for millennia.

Except for the fact that today's population is much more racially mixed than were the people of ten thousand years ago, those people were just like us in every way. Each of our present physical characteristics had evolved and had been present for more than two hundred thousand years already. And this includes our brains and our mental capabilities as well. The individuals who made up the human population ten thousand years ago were each born into an environment where customs and processes were in place to care for and to nurture them and to instruct them in regard to their way of life, just as our children of today are born into environments that provide customs and processes to nurture and care for and instruct them also.

Ten thousand years ago there were no cities, no towns, not even any villages. Ten thousand years ago, humans had a presence on every continent that wasn't completely covered in ice. North and South America, two of the last of these ice-free continents to be inhabited by humans, had a population that had been there for at least 4,000 years.

With very few exceptions, these ten million inhabitants of ten thousand years ago were all living tribally in groups of no more than one hundred or so. Their "technology" consisted of bows and arrows and spears and spear throwers, and fire-starting tools, and knives made of stone, and other tools and implements made of stone or bone or antlers, in combination with animal skins or twine or rope made from other handy materials.

Ten thousand years ago there was no significant man-made degradation of the environment anywhere on earth. All of earth's life forms and all of earth's ecosystems had evolved to their then present state without any interference whatsoever by man. A possible exception to this could be the many species of large mammals, as well as other species, in many areas around the globe, that may have been hunted to extinction by man. Today, we see this man-made environmental destruction almost everywhere we look.

Can you imagine how beautiful our planet was before the people of our culture began destroying it? Ten thousand years ago, people drank water from the stream. Ten thousand years ago habitat for game and for all forms of life throughout the planet was undisturbed by man.

Ten thousand years… It really wasn't that long ago. When viewed either from the perspective of the three million plus year history of man, or even from the perspective of the two hundred fifty-thousand-year history of our particular species of man, it was only the blink of an eye ago. Think about it… Ten thousand years ago man had existed on the planet for more than three million years already. And our particular species of man had been here for more than two hundred fifty thousand years. Yet the earth and her ecosystems and her millions of life forms were still completely and totally unmolested by our presence.

Fast-forward now, ten thousand years to the present time. Think for a moment about the present state of our planet. Instead of ten million people all living sustainably on their own landbases, we have almost eight billion people living mostly in cities, and the only ones who are living sustainably are those few tribal peoples who are still living on their ancestral lands in their ancient and proven ways as members of indigenous tribes. By now, tribal people across the globe have almost all been completely wiped out. But there are still a few who are lucky enough to have not been killed or assimilated into our culture only because they live on lands so remote or inhospitable that some of us have not yet figured out a way to profit by stealing their land... at least not so far. I think each of us realize by now that there is no real mechanism in place which will prevent these last few tribal people from eventually being killed or assimilated in just the same manner as all of those who preceded them.

Today, there are several cities whose population is more than double the entire world's population of ten thousand years ago. In fact, there are twenty-two cities around the globe with more than ten million inhabitants. The very air we breathe around these cities is terribly polluted, mostly from the exhaust from our automobiles, but also from industrial activities. In Los Angeles and in many other cities, this air quality situation is monitored daily, and it is not at all uncommon for the city officials to issue air quality warnings and to advise the population that it would be better if they remained indoors at least as much as possible on certain days. Is this really how we want to live?

Most of man's destruction of the planet's ecosystems has been the result of the cutting down of ancient forests. In Europe and Asia, where civilization is older, this process began long ago, but was speeded up by the inventions and necessities brought on by the Industrial Revolution of the past one hundred fifty years. Now, as a result of new technology, namely chainsaws and bulldozers, etc., the other continents have caught up very quickly. The forests were cut down, the timber was sold for profit, and the land that had once represented an ancient ecosystem was put to use for some other profitable purpose. Today, our last remaining ancient forests, our tropical rainforests, are being quickly cut down and replaced by pasturelands mostly so Americans, Europeans, and Asians can enjoy eating hamburgers from fast food restaurant chains which can be found in any city or even in many small towns across the globe. With the cutting down of these last remaining forests, we are not only losing precious ecosystems and all of the ancient life forms within them, we are losing the very capability of these tropical forests to convert carbon dioxide to oxygen. This is beyond pollution. This is beyond even the thoughtless destruction of ecosystems resulting in the extinction of whole species. This is the destruction of the last remnants of a system we absolutely cannot live without.

In his first sequel to *Ishmael*, another novel called *The Story of B,* Quinn wrote a piece he called The Boiling Frog, in which he told the history of our civilization from the standpoint of population doublings and their effects. Again, all credit goes to Quinn for shining a light on the story that was right in front of us, but so hidden behind cultural myths that nobody else before him had been able to see through them. The connection Quinn is able to establish between overcrowding, as the cities first appear and then get larger over time, and problems that arise like war, famine, plague, crime, and so on, is undeniably real.

In the piece, Quinn effectively showed how dramatically and consistently each doubling of the population of our culture happened in less and less time and also how new problems arose with every doubling. When our culture was just beginning, the first doubling from 10 million to 20 million people took five thousand years. The last doubling from 3.9 billion to our present population of 7.8 billion people has occurred since 1974. Are there any of us out there who actually thinks that having 12 billion of us crowded onto this struggling globe is going to be a good thing?

Showing us where we came from, showing us how we came to be here, and enlightening us about the events that caused this to happen. This was Quinn's first great accomplishment with Ishmael. With the novel as his vehicle, he showed us how things came to be this way. He explained to us how our culture was born ten thousand years ago when that one tribe in ancient Mesopotamia threw away their ancient tribal ways, rejected their position as a responsible member of the Community of Life, and began practicing totalitarian agriculture. And he explained to us how just prior to that time there were ten million of us living here sustainably and tribally on a planet that was totally and completely free of damage by human activity. He pointed out the cultural myths that controlled the behaviors of the people who lived tribally, and also the cultural myths of the people of the new culture (ours).

For this, I am and will always remain grateful to Daniel Quinn, a man who is undoubtedly one of the greatest thinkers to ever set foot on our planet. By the way... Here are those cultural myths that are the basis of the two types of cultures.

For the tribal peoples who preceded us and for those tribal peoples who are still hanging on against all odds...

We are a part of the world and a part of the Community of Life.

And for the rest of us...

The world was made for man to conquer and rule.

As evidenced by this cultural myth that is the very basis for our culture... Our culture is insane. It is flawed at its most basic level because its very basis is a fallacy. It cannot succeed and it cannot be fixed. We must return our culture to one based upon the truth that everything is connected and we are a part of the Community of Life.

Are you ready to do your part to save the world? If so, then you need to become a part of the growing group of people who understand that our culture is flawed and doomed and must be replaced with a new culture that actually functions well for humans, as well as all other living things. Once your consciousness joins mine, and all of the others who have already reached this understanding, the task for all of us is to do everything we can to influence others to make the intellectual leap that enables them to join as well. That all-important Critical Mass must be achieved so that changes can be made before this flawed and doomed and insane culture comes crashing down on its own.

3

Tribal Living

◊

Before we leave the opening section of this book which is dedicated to describing how things came to be this way, let's look at what was discarded when that particular tribe of people in ancient Mesopotamia began practicing totalitarian agriculture. Ten thousand years ago, the original members of what has become our modern culture rejected their position as Responsible Members of the Community of Life and threw away their ancient tribal ways. And in the ensuing years, tribal living was also what our culture has eradicated every time we have killed or assimilated a neighboring tribe in order to appropriate their land. As we have established in the preceding chapters, that process has been going on for ten thousand years, and at this point, there are not a lot of tribal people left on the planet for the people of our culture to kill or assimilate in order to take their lands.

The United States of today is a country of approximately 319 million inhabitants. Although some of the descendants of the Native American tribal people we conquered in order to steal their lands are still living together on reservation land that has been allotted to them by our government, these people are no longer living tribally as hunter-gatherers. But those of us residing here on this hemisphere only have to look back a little more than five hundred years to the time just before the Americas were discovered by Christopher

Columbus in order to see two entire continents populated mostly by tribal people. I say "mostly" because the Aztecs of present-day Mexico and the Incas of present-day Peru were not living tribally and had not been living tribally for thousands of years. Additionally, there were other civilizations present in the Americas in 1492, about which we know even less. Some of these may have returned to tribal living and hunter-gatherer ways after being decimated by the European diseases brought by Columbus and those who came after him.

The Indian wars here in the United States ended about one hundred forty years ago. That means in a mere four hundred years after the arrival of Columbus, our culture had completed its takeover of the lands formerly inhabited by two whole continents full of tribal people. In Chapter Two, I made the point that ten thousand years was the blink of an eye when compared with either the three-million-year history of humanity or the two hundred-fifty thousand-year history of our particular species of humans. How about five hundred years? When the Spanish arrived here in 1492, the various ecosystems that make up this hemisphere were totally undisturbed by the people who lived here. In terms of human impact on the environment, a lot has happened here in this hemisphere during those five hundred years. For instance, can you estimate how far you would have to travel from where you are right now to find some undisturbed habitat? If you went there, would you drink water from the stream that runs through it? Do you think the stream would even be flowing? Or would the upstream dams prevent the water from even reaching you?

As we have established, tribal people live in accordance with the Peacekeeping Law. They know themselves to be a part of the world and a part of the Community of Life... a knowing that is the very basis of their culture. For each of these tribes, the way they secure their food and the manner in which they take shelter from the elements and their entire way of living has evolved over many hundreds, if not many thousands, of years. And that process of evolution has taken place through an interaction between those tribal people and their particular landbase and everything on it and in it. Invariably, this evolution and interaction between many generations of an intelligent tribe of people and their world resulted in a way of living that worked well not only for the tribal members, but also for every other living thing that existed on that landbase. This is because over time they kept what worked and they discarded what didn't. …. And they did so while adhering to the Peacekeeping Law.

Can you imagine what it would be like to be a member of a tribe of hunter-gatherers? Most of us are probably hesitant to try such an exercise, even from a purely mental standpoint. We have all become so dependent on modern technology, and also so impressed by it, that we are reluctant to even consider what it would be like to live so close to nature. And besides, even if we could imagine it, where would we go on this earth to find a landbase undamaged enough by our modern culture so that a tribe of people could live as hunter-gatherers in the manner of the Native Americans as they did before our arrival? Regrettably, just about the only places still remaining where this might still be done in the U. S. are in protected parks and designated wilderness areas, and even most of those are too small for a group of tribal people to provide for themselves as hunter-gatherers, at least not sustainably.

But the question of practicality aside, let's examine some of the differences that stand out between a group of people living tribally and a group of people living as members of our present culture. Remember, our culture is based upon the premise that our world and everything in it was made for man to conquer and rule. In stark contrast, the tribal cultures believe themselves to be a part of the world and a part of the Community of Life.

All of us who read these words are members of our modern culture. We all live in a world that is defined by the basic cultural myth that the world was made for man to conquer and rule. If you examine this cultural myth closely, you will see that adherence to it causes separation between ourselves and the natural world. And separation between ourselves and the whole Community of Life.

But this separation does not stop there. In the end, this basic cultural myth results in the separation even between ourselves as individuals. For once we begin the process of defining who shall be the conqueror and who or what shall be the conquered, then where does the separation cease? Obviously, when you look at our culture, we have a world with humans on one side and all the rest of the Community of Life on the other.

But in addition to that, we have also ended up with a very small group of humans on the top who live in luxury and make important decisions, etc., and the rest of the human members of our culture, along with the rest of the Community of Life, trying to make do with limited resources on the bottom. Any cursory look through the recorded history of our culture will confirm this. Or, if you would rather look at the present, that is easily done as well. For instance, in 2013, there were four hundred individual or joint tax returns filed here in the U. S. that reported income of more than $100,000,000, and the average adjusted gross income for those four hundred tax returns was more than $213,000,000. Remember, a tax return reflects income for one year, not an accumulation of a lifetime of wealth.

Of course, for the other component of disparity of wealth, we need to examine the resources controlled by those on the bottom. According to the U. S. Census Bureau, the median household income is less than $50,000 per year, and 12.6% of the population lives in poverty. Keep in mind that in our culture, the food is locked up. And here in the United States, the medical services are as well. People who don't have any money don't eat, and they don't get to see the doctor, and they don't receive medical treatment. Shelter, in the form of rent for apartments and houses, costs money as does clothing. There are millions of Americans who struggle to provide these basic needs for themselves and their families, and many are cold, hungry, sick and even homeless.

Contrast that with the many cultures represented by the tribal people who used to populate our world. These are people who lived by the basic cultural myth that says "We are a part of the world and a part of the Community of Life." If you examine this cultural myth closely, you will see that it does not cause isolation or separation, but instead, it fosters and confirms a sense of connection... a connection between themselves and everything that exists. The result of this is that tribal people did not destroy their landbases. They did not cut down their forests or dam up their rivers, or pollute their streams, or hunt entire species to extinction. All of life and everything that existed was sacred to them. And as diverse as were the customs of these thousands of tribes, which formerly populated our world, this sacredness with which they viewed their world and everything that existed within it was the one universal constant for all of these various tribal cultures.

And what is the result of this sense of connection as it pertains to relationships between individuals? Again, a close examination of the cultural myth indicates that this sense of connection would apply to relations between individuals as well. Tribal members take care of each other. In our culture, if your mother has Alzheimer's disease, then you are the one who is responsible for taking care of her. Never mind if the care is too expensive or time consuming.... Her care is your responsibility. Similar situations within a tribe do not burden just one person with caring for a sick parent. Help comes from everywhere because each member of the tribe enjoys the riches of tribal living, which are represented by cradle-to-grave security. Nobody in a tribe is hungry or cold unless everyone is hungry or cold. And as we have established, tribal ways and customs evolved over millennia, and almost invariably resulted in a way of living that worked well for the tribal people and for everything else that existed on their particular landbase. So, at least until the people of our culture came along to eradicate them and to steal their land, it was very rare for a tribe of people to not have their basic needs adequately provided for.

Until recently, my favorite movie of all time has been *Dances with Wolves*. It is the one movie, out of the hundreds of movies based on themes from the old American West, where the Indians are fairly and accurately portrayed as the competent, rational, moral and caring group. And in stark contrast, the people of our culture are shown to be mostly insane, immoral, and incompetent. The dilemma faced by the Sioux Indian tribe as they wrestle with how to handle the encroachment of the white men onto their lands is very poignant and very well done. This is the real story of the old West, and thanks to Kevin Costner and to Michael Blake, the author of the screenplay, for finally showing it to us as it really was.

Now a new favorite movie has emerged for me. Basically, though, it is the same story as *Dances With Wolves* told in a different setting... Pandora. This movie, of course, is *Avatar*. I love it when Neytiri's mother, Mo'at, tells Jake Sully, "It is hard to fill a cup that is already full." And a little bit later, "We will see if your insanity can be cured." Thank you, James Cameron. If the truth wasn't so dangerous to the people running our insane culture, Avatar certainly would have won the Oscar for best picture in 2009. Hopefully, the 2.7 billion dollars, and counting, you brought in worldwide from moviegoers eased the pain of this loss a little for you.

On our planet, and evidently on the fictional moon called Pandora as well, tribal cultures evolved over time through an interaction between the tribal people and everything else that existed on the landbases they lived on. Over time, a way of providing food and shelter for the tribe was devised that worked well, not only for the people in the tribe, but for everything else that existed on that land. Then, every time our culture came along and decided to kill or assimilate the tribal people who occupied some land we wanted for ourselves, one of the things we destroyed was a time-tested and sustainable way of living on a particular landbase.

But we destroyed more than that. Ways of living for tribal people evolved differently in different areas of the world, mostly due to the differences encountered by each particular tribe as they got to know their respective landbases. But there was one universal constant among all tribal people everywhere: a knowledge of the sacred. Tribal people everywhere knew that everything that exists has a spirit and is alive. This animation includes not only plants and animals, but even supposedly inanimate objects like stones, fire, wind, and water. Our culture tries to tell us that these "primitive" people we have chosen to kill and assimilate so that we could steal their lands were "child-like", or "naïve" and it was only right and natural that our superior culture would appropriate these lands and put them to a better use.

Our culture tries to tell us that the shamans we found in tribes all over the globe were doing nothing but "hocus pocus" silly play-like healings and rituals. After all… our culture tells us… there is no invisible world for these shamanic practitioners to be interacting with. If there were, then certainly a superior people like us would have known about it before these ignorant savages could have possibly figured it out. Most of these shamans, we are told, probably knew there really is no invisible world and were just putting on an elaborate ruse to raise their standing with the naïve members of their tribes. Other shamans… our culture tells us… may actually believe in this "make believe" existence…. But they are like innocent children… fooled into thinking they see and hear things that are not actually there. Any trained scientist or investigator, our culture tells us, could easily debunk these supposed experiences with just a little bit of the right effort.

As with any other subject, one can read about Shamanism and endeavor to understand what others are saying about it. As we do so, then if we are wise, we will understand that some of the authors we might read from are telling us that they are speaking and writing from direct experience. Others take the more scholarly approach and assemble all the available research and then they reason out for us the way things must be. When judging the validity of any work on this subject, I would think that one certainly must give more weight to someone who speaks from actual, direct experience, than from someone who is simply reasoning out how things must be.

For the record, I have a little direct experience on the subject of an unseen world. I have seen a ghost. I have actually lived in a haunted house. I have left my body and traveled to an astral plane. I have had numerous lucid dreams, some of which even correctly predicted future events. I see auras every day, not only around people, but even around other living things like trees. Often, I think of a person just before the phone rings and it is that person calling me. These things I have experienced directly tell me not to dismiss too easily the possible existence of an entire unseen world that I am only just beginning to understand and explore. I also have quite a lot of reading and research under my belt. And I am far enough down the path at this point where I can say to you with confidence.... One doesn't really know anything until you experience it personally. You can speculate and conjecture all you want about the true nature of reality. And you can reason it out with a series of "sounds true" conjectures. But you don't really know anything until you have experienced it for yourself.

We should not dismiss the tribal person's view of the nature of reality just because our culture and our organized religions tell us to. After all… as I have already argued… these tribal cultures are all based upon the true nature of reality, which is…. **We are a part of the world and a member of the Community of Life**. While our own culture is based upon a fairy-tale myth that tells us … **The world was made for man to conquer and rule.**

If you would like to read a wonderful book on this subject that is based upon direct experience, then I would highly recommend *Original Wisdom,* by Robert Wolff. This book is Wolff's autobiographical account of his experience as a young man in Malaysia with an indigenous tribe called the Sng'oi. In 1961, after many months of spending time off and on with them, he was actually able to access their way of knowing which definitely included what we would term an "unseen world". Once he "got it" "it" was his to keep, and his life has been totally transformed ever since. One of the best passages came as he was describing the scene as he was leaving the Sng'oi to go live in a city. Everyone in the band knew how difficult it was going to be for him to go and live in the smack dab middle of our culture given his new consciousness and understanding.

"Be strong," they told him with great concern. "You are alone."

I believe I have a fairly good understanding of what Wolff is describing, but I have yet to experience it for myself... at least for an extended period of time like he apparently has done.

In the following passage, Wolff describes the moment when he "woke up" in the jungle of Malaysia.

The jungle was suddenly dense with sounds, smells, little puffs of air here and there. I became aware of things I had largely ignored before. It was as if all this time I had been walking with dirty eyeglasses—and then someone washed them for me; or as if I were watching a blurry home movie—and then someone turned the focusing knob. But it was more than that—much more. I could smell things I had no name for. I heard little sounds that could be anything at all. I saw a leaf shivering. I saw a line of insects crawling up a tree.

Then... continuing on the next page...

My perception opened further. I no longer saw water—what I felt with my whole being was a leaf-with-water-in-it, attached to a plant that grew in soil, which was also part of a larger living skin around the earth. And nothing was separate; all was one, the same thing; water—leaf—plant—trees—soil—animals—earth—air—sunlight and little wisps of wind. The all-ness was everywhere, and I was a part of it.

Shamans and shamanism has been a popular subject lately. There is a wide range of current books available on the subject if you would care to look into it. I recommend a recently published one, *Awakening to the Spirit World, The Shamanic Path of Direct Revelation,* by Sandra Ingerman and Hank Wesselman. The words, "direct revelation" in the title should tell you whether this is a strict, scholarly work, or whether these authors are speaking from their own experience. Actually, Wesselman, as well as some of the other contributors, do have PhD's, just in case that matters to you.

Here is a pertinent excerpt…

The shaman's practice of direct revelation is the ancient precursor of all of our religious and philosophical traditions, both ancient and modern. This is a given, and while some may consider this to be an extraordinary claim, the great antiquity of the shaman's path is confirmed by what we know from the archeological evidence of rock art and cave art from Ice Age Europe and elsewhere in the ancient world.

And another…

There are certain commonalities in a shaman's worldview and practice across the world that allow us to make certain broad generalizations about shamanism. In the majority of indigenous cultures, the universe is viewed as being made up of two distinct realities; a world of things seen and a world of things hidden, yet no distinction is drawn between them. A shaman understands that those two worlds present themselves together as two halves of a whole. The shaman is the inspired visionary, a man or a woman who learns through practice how to enter into this "world of things hidden," and once there, he or she typically encounters extra-mundane personalities or archetypal forces that the indigenous peoples refer to as spirits, ancestors, and even gods.

All true shamans—and by association all authentic modern visionaries—discover, often by accident, that they possess the ability to go into trance very easily, which allows them to make contact with this hidden world. Trance in this sense is not an unconscious state, but rather a state of expanded consciousness in which the individual intentionally dissociates his or her focused awareness away from the everyday world and enters into an alternate or parallel reality that the indigenous peoples regard as "the spirit world."

Through practice, shamans develop relationships with these spirits, allowing them to do various things, initially on behalf of themselves, and then increasingly on behalf of others.

As stated previously, I am not advocating herein for a return to hunter-gathering. I am, however, suggesting as strongly as possible that we should endeavor to re-connect with the sacred... With the sacred that was a part of the every-day life of the millions of people belonging to the thousands of tribes that our culture has destroyed during its ten-thousand-year reign.

In Part Two we are going to dig a little deeper into our culture and examine the many ways in which our culture must lie to us in order to keep us all consuming the world as mandated by our basic cultural myth.

Part Two

Our World of Today

4

The Outlaw's World

I was born in Bartlesville, Oklahoma in 1954, and I grew up there. Back then; Bartlesville was the headquarters for two large, well-known oil companies, Phillips Petroleum and Cities Service Oil Company. My father worked in the geophysical department of Cities Service, and my mother was a homemaker. The 1950's and early 1960's were an idyllic time to grow up, and Bartlesville was an idyllic place as well. It seemed that the two oil companies provided well-paying office jobs for most of the men in the town of fifty thousand inhabitants. Compared to other cities of similar size, I am sure there were significantly fewer poor people in Bartlesville than in other places. I didn't grow up with a bunch of rich kids, but the families of all of my friends certainly had enough income to pay for all of their basic needs with money left over.

I think the first event in my life that prepared me to be awakened to the lies our culture tells us (which didn't happen until I read Ishmael in 1995) happened in December of 1960. It was a week or so before Christmas and I was walking home from the Will Rogers Elementary School where I was attending the first grade. On this particular day, another boy who lived a block away fell in with me as I walked. Although we lived relatively close to each other, Johnnie Wolf and I were not friends, and we did not usually spend time together. There were kids everywhere in our neighborhood, and I had probably ten or twelve friends who lived in the block between him and me. But it didn't take long to figure out why he wanted to walk with me…. He wanted to tease me because he had learned in school that day that I still believed in Santa Claus.

And I did believe in Santa Claus. After all, I was only six years old. Young enough to still remember some of the magical things a small child knows about, like Santa Claus, that I didn't have to pretend about or imagine. Admittedly, like all of us do, I was quickly forgetting about the magical world of small children. But I still remembered some of what it was like to live for the moment and to be aware of the things that go away when our egos start running the show. So, it wasn't much of a stretch for me to believe in Santa Claus. After all, it was my mother and father who had told me the story of Santa Claus. I was confident they would never lie to me about something so important. Besides, he showed up every Christmas just like they said he would, didn't he?

So, as we walked, Johnnie Wolf teased me and I told him to shut up and leave me alone. "Maybe Santa Claus doesn't come to your house because you are naughty," I told him. But he kept after me all the way home. And when we got close to his house, he really turned it up a notch. He started dancing around and calling me a little baby.

And that was Johnnie Wolf's big mistake. I might have been immature enough to still believe in Santa Claus, but I was far from being a frail or helpless child. I got Johnnie Wolf down on the ground and began to beat the shit out of him.

But after I got him down and he could see how mad I was, and how he was about to get a real pounding, Johnnie Wolf realized he better stop teasing me and start reasoning with me. So, in between blows he started saying. "Really, Don. I know what I'm talking about. Think about this…." And he would tell me something to help me to understand that Santa Claus was really pretend. I guess he got in about three or four good reasons before I decided he was sufficiently subdued and adequately punished enough for me to quit hitting him. He wasn't hurt badly, but he did have a bloody nose and some pretty good bruises. I left him lying there and I continued up the street towards my house. As I walked, though, I started thinking about what Johnnie Wolf had told me there at the end. And before I got home, I realized he was right.... There really was no Santa Claus.

At first, I was angry with my parents for lying to me... very angry as a matter of fact. But they explained to me they didn't mean any harm. They only wanted me to enjoy the holiday like all the other children. So, I got over my anger and disappointment with my parents fairly easily. After that, however, I had to deal with the fact that the magical world I had believed in, of which Santa Claus was a part, did not exist. It was a terrible blow.

Looking back on that experience, I can see now that our culture uses the Santa Claus story very well for its devious purposes. It goes like this.... As a small child, you are told by your parents, and by everyone else, that Santa Claus exists. You are told that Santa Claus is a wonderful and jolly old man who loves all children everywhere and he lives at the North Pole where a bunch of elves work all year under his direction making toys for all the good little girls and boys. You are told that Santa Claus has magical powers, which enable him to watch you from afar to determine if you have been a good boy or girl. And he has other magical powers that enable him to travel the entire planet visiting every house around the globe on Christmas Eve, riding in a magical sleigh pulled by eight flying reindeer. So, if you are good, then Santa will deliver presents to you and all the other good little girls and boys.

Eventually, we all reach an age where we are old enough to be able to see through this farcical tale. And when we do, we learn a very important lesson... at least from our culture's standpoint.

That lesson our culture wants to teach us is:

There is no such thing as real magic. Only a foolish and very young child would even think such a thing. You made that

mistake once with your naive and foolish belief in Santa Claus. But that's okay. You were just a little child. You are older now. Don't do it again.

Fortunately, many of us know enough not to fall for this terrible lie our culture tries to tell us. I foresee a time when things we would call "magic" today will have scientific and/or practical explanations. In fact, I am fairly certain there are spiritual masters alive today who have these answers already. There is no doubt that the quantum physicists are edging closer as well. The quest to understand the true nature of reality is pursued by way too few of us, and one big reason for that is our experience as little children with Santa Claus. While it is true that Santa Claus does not exist, it is not true that the unseen world of the shaman does not exist.

Let's look now at some of the other big lies our culture must tell us in order to keep us sleeping, and to keep itself in power. Here is a look at the world of our insane culture... the world of the people who do not adhere to the Peacekeeping Law.... The Outlaw's World.

Here is a big one....

There is not enough.

That's right. Our culture tells us not enough resources are available so that people everywhere can have their basic needs met. What do you think would happen if everyone on the planet decided one day to take a real hard look at the validity of that one? Do you think it would hold up under that kind of intense scrutiny? Of course it wouldn't, because it is not true. That lie is told by the people who have too much to the people who don't have enough as a reason for the people who don't have enough to accept not having enough without too much complaint. That's it. In actuality, there is absolutely no good reason why basic needs cannot be met for every person on this planet. Basic needs are food, water, clothing, shelter, health care, and sanitary living conditions. This can be done even though there are way more people on this planet than should reasonably be here. That this can be done is beyond questioning. Why is it not being done? Greed. And also because those of us who don't have enough have not yet woken up to the lie contained in the cultural myth that there is not enough. This is one important cultural myth that still has a very strong grip on the people of our culture. Something needs to be done about this one.

Here is another. Success in this world is based upon....

Survival of the fittest.

Here is a cultural myth that is losing its grip on us. This is the one that has resulted in white men owning all the wealth and controlling all the power. This, thankfully, is breaking down. It still needs work, but consciousness is being raised and we are making progress. It is the dawning of the Age of Aquarius and women are regaining some power. And racial prejudice is waning and civil rights for minorities of all kinds are being implemented. Here in the United States, a black man was elected President. Unfortunately, though, our next succeeding President was a blatant racist. There is still much work to be done with this cultural myth, but a lot more progress has been made with this one than with the "There is not Enough" one.

Here Is a big one....

Something will save us.

This one is actually very important.... At least it is important if you are someone who wants to keep our insane culture operating. Basically, this cultural myth acknowledges that we are facing some very real problems. But we should have confidence because technology is advancing rapidly, and there are very smart people working very hard on all of these problems. Someone will come up with an answer for each of them before it is too late. After all... God is on our side. So how could anything ever go wrong under His watchful eye? He made the world just for man... didn't He? Haven't we conquered it just as He commanded we should? Are we not ruling over every other life form just as God planned for us to do?

Running out of oil? Don't worry. Cold fusion is just around the corner. And when that comes, we'll have a world like George Jetson's futuristic cartoon world. There will be flying cars, floating houses, and conveniences everywhere for everyone. And if the answer is not cold fusion, then some smart person will invent something else to satisfy our energy needs.

Worried about the hole in the ozone layer? Don't worry. Somebody will invent a way to patch it before it is too late.

Too many people on the planet? Don't worry. If we fill this planet up, we can start putting some of our people on the moon and then on other planets also. After all, this world was made for us, right? By extension, that must mean that all worlds everywhere were made for us. (Better watch out... you blue people on Pandora.... We are coming!) We just need to figure out how to get there and then our overcrowding problem will be solved. That is why we have NASA. But if NASA wants to be the hero, then they better hurry up. Many corporations are already working on this. And other countries, also.

Worried about crime? Don't worry. We just need to step up our law enforcement efforts a little. When our police and our judicial system get more efficient and, when we finally build enough prisons, then all the bad guys will finally be caught and punished, and the rest of us will be able to live in peace.

What about pollution? Don't worry. We are close to getting that one straightened out. All we need is some tougher laws and some better enforcement. New technologies will also help. A pristine planet with clean air and water is just around the corner.

Worried about the loss of our forests? Don't. We are planting trees to replace all those we cut down. We are very smart and responsible about this. This process of cutting down forests and replacing them with newly planted trees can go on forever.

What about cancer, AIDS, bird flu, etc? Again, smart people are working very hard on these things. They will come up with something to save us.

Terrorism? Those guys can't last forever. Our intelligence services are aiding our armed forces, and other allied nations are helping as well. Eventually, we will find and punish them all, and then there will be peace.

What about hunger? Simple. We just need to grow some more food. We are working hard on this. Soon there will be no more starving people anywhere.

Global warming? Maybe this one is just a ploy by the tree huggers. If not, then we will figure something out. Don't we always?

War? Well, that is a tough one. But one thing is for sure... The answer lies in preparedness. If we are strong enough, then no other nation would be crazy enough to challenge us. And eventually, we will even be strong enough so that we can tell other nations that they can't fight each other either. Then when everyone realizes that we are too strong to be challenged, we will have a world at peace.

I think you get the picture.... Given enough time, there is nothing this fabulous culture can't handle. After all, wasn't the world made for man to conquer and rule? And isn't that what we have been doing? Just look at the progress we have made in the past one hundred years alone. One hundred years ago, most people walked or rode horses or maybe rode the train. Now we all drive our own cars and fly around in planes and jets and helicopters. With the

Creator on our side, we can do no wrong. Everything will work out. Just give us a little more time.

You see…. Our culture is insane. It is insane because it is based upon a fallacy and it has to work very hard to cover up that fact. It is founded upon a cultural myth that tells us that the world was made for man to conquer and rule, which is a myth that fosters a false sense of separation.

In reality, man is just one member of the Community of Life, and everything is connected. The tribal people we have killed and assimilated had it right. They said, "We are a part of the world and a part of the Community of Life." This, actually, is reality. The foundation of the cultures for all of the tribal people that we have eradicated was not a myth. That is why those tribal people were able to exist upon this beautiful planet for more than three million years without destroying it. In contrast, our culture began only ten thousand years ago, and really didn't represent a threat to the planet until it had grown like a cancerous cell for five thousand years. To continue that analogy… The cancer has now metastasized.

All of these secondary cultural myths we have addressed in this chapter arise out of that basic one. And the result of our culture's being based upon this false cultural myth is that we do not adhere to the Law of Limited Competition. As explained in Part One, our not adhering to this very important evolutionary law means that our culture cannot succeed. Like the hapless airman who was riding a creation that was not constructed in accordance with the law of aerodynamics, our culture cannot fly. But until it crashes and burns, or until a Critical Mass of people understands this fact and decides to strap on their parachutes and jump, it is pretty obvious that our culture is running things here on Planet Earth.

I hope that most of you who read this are already capable of seeing the absurdity behind all of the issues detailed under the heading "Something Will Save Us". My feeling is that most of you will be able to do this, although many of you probably have never thought of these issues in this manner. Also, for those of you who are unable to see the absurdity, I'm afraid the reason is probably due to your very strong identification with our culture and with your unwillingness to challenge it. I understand very well that it is difficult for people to consider the possibility that their whole lives may have been based upon a lie. Remember, I am the guy who gave away forty copies of Ishmael and only had three people appreciate it. Not everyone is ready for these difficult truths. But thankfully, some of us are. That all-important Critical Mass of people who understand the need for change is growing... one changed mind at a time.

In the next chapter, we are going to look at another secondary cultural myth.... A really strong one that is directly responsible for much pain and suffering. This one has a firm grip on a huge part of our culture, a grip that is going to have to be loosened before meaningful changes can be made. Throughout history, there has always been a small minority who saw through it. And today, it appears the relative numbers of that small minority may be growing. In order for meaningful changes to be made, we are going to have to help many others to see through it as well.

5

God Will Judge Us

◊

Have you ever stopped to consider that the people of today are the first people who have had access to a reliable, scientific explanation to questions like….

How big is our universe? When and how was it created? How many galaxies and how many stars are there within our universe? How many different types of stars are there? What is at the center of every galaxy? Where, exactly, is our Milky Way Galaxy located within the universe? Where, exactly, is our solar system located within the Milky Way Galaxy? How old is our solar system? And, how old is our planet Earth?

As well as other questions like…

What are the components of our material world, and how were they created? What do we know about the processes involved when those components combine to form other, more complex substances?

And…

How long have living things been present on this planet and what is the process through which they have changed and evolved? What do we know about our particular species of life? How many years ago did the first homo sapien evolve?

Today, we can chronicle the entire history of the natural world beginning with the singularity that existed just prior to the Big Bang. For instance, we know that 13.8 billion years ago our universe began its rapid expansion, leading to the formation of the more than one hundred billion galaxies, containing hundreds of billions of stars each. We know that our own galaxy, the Milky Way, began forming 12 to 13 billion years ago, and today contains around three hundred billion stars. One of these stars, our own sun, began to coalesce around 4.6 billion years ago. Earth gained its spherical shape about 4.54 billion years ago, and it took another billion years after that before the first, single-cell life forms made their appearance here. Evolution, the process through which all of life including our particular species, was created, is still continuing. And we understand, not only the time frames, but also the mechanisms through which all of these events came into being. (Except for how life itself got started. We still don't know that one.) Thousands of extremely intelligent, well-trained, and well-equipped scientists are working every day to add to this body of knowledge.... And they are succeeding. For instance, as I write this, a piece has flashed across my Google News page explaining that new evidence has emerged supporting the theory that our moon was formed when the earth collided with a sister planet approximately 400 million years after both planets formed.

Compare this with the knowledge available to the people of one hundred years ago... How about 200 years? 500? 1,000? A mere five hundred years ago, I'm quite sure that heated arguments were still raging all over Europe about what causes the sun to rise and set, and whether the earth is round or flat.

Clearly, we have access to a truly immense amount of information that was not available even for our grandparents. How, then, do we justify our reliance on fairy-tale creation stories made up by men living three thousand years ago during a period when nobody had any idea what they were looking at when they gazed at the night sky?

When I was a little boy growing up in Bartlesville, I was very interested in spiritual matters. My parents didn't go to church, but when I was about five, because of my obvious interest, they embarked upon a mission to find the right church for our family. Eventually, after trying several, we settled on the big Methodist church located downtown.

I was an active participant in that church until I was thirteen, and old enough to join as a full-fledged member. The church had a course of study for kids my age who wanted to formally join. There were other kids like me who had been active in Sunday school and choir and the Methodist Youth Foundation, and a few of us were ready and eager to take the next step. The course consisted of studying all the things that Methodists believed in, and while we were attending, we also had responsibilities for helping out around the church.

One day, as I was nearing the end of the course, I was in the sanctuary working on my assigned job of arranging the hymnals, pledge cards, pencils, and other material in the pews, and our youth minister Jerry Perryman came in. He greeted me and asked how I was doing. I told him I had a question that had been bothering me and could I please ask him to help me with it?

I told Jerry that we have been spending a lot of time during the past few weeks learning about the process of salvation. It seemed to me that what we had been learning was very specific to Methodists. What, I wondered, was going to happen to my other Christian friends who are Catholics, or Baptists, or Episcopalians or even to my non-Christian, Jewish friends? Obviously, they were not proceeding down the same road I was towards salvation. Were they going to make it to heaven?

I have always been grateful for the honest answer I received from Reverend Jerry Perryman that day. Without my being aware of it, my question had gone right to the heart of one of the biggest flaws with organized religion, and Jerry knew that. But rather than try to put me off or deflect the question or bullshit me in some other way, he answered that yes, he would be concerned about the prospects of anyone getting to heaven who didn't proceed in the Methodist way as I had been learning it.

Of course I was not pleased with the answer. I was only thirteen and not yet very learned or worldly, but I was pretty sure that God wasn't like that. It made no sense to me that we could come to church every Sunday and learn about the love of God, and then find out that it didn't apply to my friends who were in another church singing similar hymns as members of the choir there, thinking they were doing the right thing and looking forward to making it to heaven also.

But by that time, I was almost finished with the program and I went ahead and became a church member. However, I did stop attending church shortly thereafter. Much like losing Santa Claus, it was a big loss for me. Afterward, I had no mentor to turn to for guidance, and I knew of no other way to satisfy my spiritual yearnings. At that time I was in the seventh grade in school. Then, just a few weeks later, I started seeing notices about a big event that was going to happen soon. There were going to be picnics and other activities for all the kids my age and older. Many of the popular girls I was interested in would be there.

The big event was a week-long Baptist revival led by a young, evangelistic preacher named Richard Hogue. He was traveling all over the country with the goal of bringing as many kids as possible into the Baptist church. I had only recently been through the bad experience with the Methodists, and I was pretty sure the Baptists were not going to be any better in that regard. But I think it was the chance to spend some time with some interesting girls, along with the social aspect of the event, that attracted me more than anything.

I went to a couple of events and they were very well attended and a lot of fun. After the second one, they got all of us kids into the sanctuary of the big Baptist church downtown, and then Richard Hogue stood up at the podium and started preaching about Revelations. I remember he would tell us in his big, booming voice that in Revelations such and such, it says that the world is going to come to an end when so and so happens.... "And brothers and sisters! Did you know, that very thing happened in such and such a place just last year!" And after a dramatic pause he would continue... "And let me tell you something, my brothers and sisters!... When the world comes to an end... if you have not already gotten down on your knees and accepted Jesus Christ as your Lord and Savior, then YOU ARE GOING TO BE DOOMED TO ETERNAL HELL AND DAMNATION!"... And then he spent some time basically trying his best to scare the shit out of all of the poor kids in that big sanctuary. I'm quite sure most of them were probably there like me, just to have some fun. And then he told us all that the only way we could be sure that we would make it to heaven when the world comes to an end would be for us to get up out of our seats, and come down to the front of the sanctuary, and get down on our knees, and be saved.

During that service, he went through several more examples from Revelations about prophecies that portended the end of the world, always followed by stories about how that very thing had happened just recently. And after each new example, he demanded that each of us should come up and be saved before it was too late. Richard Hogue was very persuasive, and very charismatic, and he had a lot of success with the kids in the big sanctuary that night. If memory serves, at least eighty to ninety percent of the kids went up to the front of the church and got saved. Even the ones who had already been saved figured they better do it again, just to be sure. I sat there fuming that God wasn't like that, and wondering what does that say about a church when apparently they must stoop to using scare tactics to get people to join? But in the end, even I decided, "What the Hell can it hurt? Maybe I should do it, just in case."

But, of course, the experience didn't sit well with me. And the result of having two such horrible experiences back to back left me basically without anywhere to go for my spiritual needs. At that age, I wasn't aware of the spiritual practices that are available to seekers of enlightenment from outside of organized religion. All I knew was that organized religion appeared to be total bullshit, and I wanted no part of it. Given my interest in spiritual matters from a very early age, it was a very disappointing realization. But I didn't know what else I could do, or where else I could turn for help.

I have never, even for a moment, ever regretted leaving organized religion. Spirituality is very important to me, though. I have read extensively on the subject ever since I was twenty years old. And over the years I have read numerous books by many different authors who all resonated very deeply with me. As I move my body, mind and spirit down the path, the road has become much clearer… and I am extremely grateful for that.

So… without further adieu, here is the cultural myth for this chapter….

God will judge us.

At least that is the cultural myth for the one in every two of the inhabitants of this planet who adheres to the Christian, the Muslim, or the Jewish faiths.

This cultural myth tells us that although this world may be full of pain and suffering, we shouldn't worry. It is the next world, which we will enter in our afterlife that is important. We are here in this world only for a few short years, and then we will die. But our next life… our afterlife… lasts forever. The important thing for us to understand is that when we take our departure from this life, **God will judge us**. And it is very important that we should make the right choices while we are here so that our next life, which lasts forever, can be spent with God (or Allah) in Heaven and not with

Satan in Hell. You never know.... Having Richard Hogue put his hand on your head and tell you that you are saved may just be your ticket to everlasting pleasantness.

Does it seem a little bit fishy to you that our world is full of these organized religions who are all telling us not to worry if things are kind of shitty down here on earth?

Of course it is this cultural myth that is the very basis for these religions. Who else but the Pope, or the cardinals or the bishops or the priests, or the preachers, or the ministers, or the Grand Ayatollah or the other Ayatollahs, or the imams, or the rabbis would ever be able to advise us about such matters? And, considering the un-testability of their claims, why do so many people even listen to them? Certainly, the actual experience of the real nature of the afterlife is not something most of us have ever experienced for ourselves. And for that matter, neither have these authorities from organized religion.

My concern here is with the Abrahamic religions, namely Christianity, Islam, and Judaism, because each of them has the following as their basis.... They are each here to explain the true nature of life and death, and to intervene for us with the one true God who created the universe just for us, and will judge us when we die.

Approximately one of every two inhabitants of this planet are members of one of these Abrahamic religions. But also significant, is that everywhere in the world except for India, China, and Southeast Asia, one or more of these Abrahamic religions is the prevalent religion. The prevalent religions in India, China, and Southeast Asia are Hinduism, Buddhism, Confucianism and Taoism, practices that some religious scholars don't even classify as religions. These religions, or practices, depending upon how you view them, involve consciousness-raising practices dedicated to achieving mystical experiences in this lifetime. These people, unfortunately, still have to live in an insane world, where the basic cultural myth fosters a false sense of separation, but at least, their religions do not require devotion to a judgmental God.

I have learned a lot since those terrible few months when I was thirteen and I realized Christianity was not for me. These days, I meet regularly with a group of friends on Friday nights, and every week three of us from the group enjoy spending some time talking about spiritual matters. Recently, another friend and member of the group who does not usually join us in the spiritual discussions asked me to tell him about my spiritual beliefs. After talking with him for a few minutes, I suggested that it might be time for him to consider leaving the Catholic Church.

Think of it this way, I suggested.... I'll give you two scenarios and you choose which is the most likely to be the true one. First... There is a God who sits in Heaven watching over us. And two thousand years ago he decided to send his only son to earth in order to save us from our sins.... Or Second... Jesus of Nazareth was a normal human being who was not born of a virgin mother. Like many men and women before and since, he achieved a high state of consciousness and chose to teach others about it. Then, three hundred years after he had been crucified by the Roman government for being a disruptive force in regard to the Roman occupation of Jerusalem, that same Roman government decided to co-opt his life story, add their own embellishments, and utilize many of his teachings in order to establish their own religion which they could use for profit and control.

My friend told me he understood, but unfortunately for him, breaking with the Catholic Church would be too big of a deal. As he explained it to me, his entire extended family is so dedicated and involved in it that he could not or would not do it.... And this comes from a gay man who has already taken the huge and courageous step of telling them all he was gay!

Yes... this cultural myth has a very strong hold on our culture. Think about it this way.... The secondary cultural myth we are discussing in this chapter is "**God will judge us**". It is a secondary cultural myth because it has its basis in our culture's basic cultural myth that tells us "**The world was made (by God) for man to conquer and rule**". As we discussed in previous chapters, this cultural myth, which is the very basis for our culture, creates a false sense of separation.

It is this false sense of separation that enables the secondary cultural myth we are discussing in this chapter, where a God who is separate from us will judge us. And it is this false sense of separation that tells the members of each of these organized religions.... "Ours is the only path to God." And it is this false sense of separation that tells the members of each of these organized religions.... "We are God's only chosen people." And it is this false sense of separation which results in a struggle for power between the various organized religions that is the very cause of so much pain and suffering and war and death and destruction.... How many wars are you aware of which were fought over religious differences? I assure you... there have been many more that you do not know about. And I assure you also... people will die today as a result of disagreements in their religious views.... And more people will die tomorrow, as well.

According to the CIA's *The World Factbook,* there are approximately 2.2 billion Christians, and 1.6 billion Muslims in our world of today. The Jews also believe in the same judgmental God, but since there are only an estimated 16 million Jews alive today, I'm not going to say much about them. Anyway, whether they are Christian, or Muslim, or Jewish, I think everyone would agree that the majority of these religious participants are moderate in regard to their religious viewpoints. They take part in these religions by going to their church, or their Sunday school, or their mosques, or their synagogues, with an emphasis on making their own way to Heaven. For the most part, they aren't concerned with converting everyone they meet to their faith, or judging everyone who doesn't believe the way they believe. Most of these moderates realize they don't have all the answers, and most of them probably believe there may be more than one path to Heaven. In fact, I'm sure there are more than a few who have some serious questions about what their holy books and their religious leaders are telling them to believe about God and the afterlife. For the most part, these moderates respect that other people may be following a different path, and they make no attempt to judge them for it.

The Christian and Moslem fundamentalists, along with the Christian evangelicals, however, are a different story. It is this group who are most affected by the **God Will Judge Us** cultural myth of this chapter. And, likewise, it is these religious fundamentalists who most adversely affect our world by their religious beliefs and practices. These are the ones who strongly believe in a judgmental God. And it is this belief in a judgmental God that gives them license to judge others.

I don't think there is any question that it is the Muslim fundamentalists who are having the most adverse effect on our world. For the moderate Muslim, the term "jihad" simply means "struggle". But for many Muslim fundamentalists, the term "jihad" means "holy war". They read passages in the Quran, and they see a directive by Allah to kill infidels. They read the Quran and believe they will serve Allah by flying hijacked airplanes into the World Trade Center, or by strapping bombs to their bodies and blowing themselves up in a market, or a restaurant, or a bus filled with non-believers. In fact, they believe Allah will be so pleased with them if they do this, that He will reward them by sending them straight to paradise where, upon their arrival, they will receive lavish treatment and sexual favors from a bevy of beautiful, young virgin girls.

Can you believe we live in a world where this can happen? Can it be possible that we live in a world where deluded young fanatics will actually blow themselves up just to kill infidels in the promise of receiving favor from this fictional deity? Since I have only three friends who are Muslim, this means that these fanatical imbeciles want to kill me, and everyone I know, except for three people!

Fortunately, here in the United States, I don't have to worry too much about getting blown up by Muslim wackos while shopping for groceries or dining out. Hopefully, the suicide bombers will not begin operations here anytime soon. I do, however, have to live in a country whose legislative bodies, as well as many other important governmental functions, have been hijacked by the activist Christian conservatives comprising the religious right.

As most people are aware, conservative Christians have aligned themselves with the Republican party. Ronald Regan bears a big part of the responsibility for this "unholy" alliance. He courted the religious right in order to win election in his first presidential run, and the Republican party has not been the same ever since.

The religious right in the United States is not a rigidly defined entity, so please allow me to tell you how I see it. I would say that most are Protestants, though some are Catholics. They are mostly white. Most are either evangelical or fundamentalist. All members of the religious right, are by definition, socially conservative, with the vast majority being economically conservative as well. But, here is the main thing... Basically, the religious right in this country is made up of a bunch of power-hungry believers in a fairytale, judgmental God who want to make America into a church state. Although this country was founded on the principle of separation of church and state, the religious right has succeeded in gaining tremendous power and influence in our political arena. The main reason for their success is because the aging Republican party didn't have enough rich, white guys left in order to accomplish anything without allying themselves with the Christian conservatives.

The main issues on the agenda of the religious right appear to be as follows. First.... They want abortion banned under all circumstances, because, even though we never hear from them in regard to gun control or the death penalty, they want to protect the sanctity of life. Second... They want to see their fairy-tale bullshit taught in our schools. They don't want evolution or sexual education taught in school, but they do want creationism and abstinence-only sex education taught there. And Third... The religious right is fighting to restrict the rights of gays and lesbians. Their war cry is "Protect the sanctity of marriage!" Oh... And they don't seem to have much to say about caring for the poor, the sick, or the homeless.

Can we get any sicker than this? Religious tolerance is largely to blame for this outrageous situation. It is high time that reasonable and rational people who can see through this bullshit stopped saying nothing about the obvious insanity of religious beliefs out of respect for those religious beliefs. People have been dying for millennia because of ridiculous and insane religious beliefs. And they will continue to do so until a sufficient number of the well-meaning but misguided people among us decide the time for religious tolerance is past, and it is time to speak out.

The problem with this is that it will do no good for a mainstream Christian or Jew to speak out about the insanity of Muslim beliefs, or vice versa either. The only way anyone can have any credibility on this subject is if they have already rejected the notion of a judgmental God, and that includes the judgmental God of their own religion.

Sam Harris wrote a book called *The End of Faith*, in which he makes the point very well that it is the presence of the religious moderates that enables the religious extremists to continue to exist. If it were not for the religious moderates propping up the religious extremists and making an attack of their ridiculous claims and beliefs out of bounds for the rest of us, we could easily disarm these silly claims regarding a judgmental God. However, it is the respect granted to the religious moderates, which keeps the rest of us from attacking the beliefs of the fundamentalists. Harris argues that the moderates, who are vast in number, participate in these various religions by picking and choosing the parts they want to believe in, which makes no sense either. Harris goes on to recommend that the rest of us should cease respecting the feelings of the religious moderates and take every opportunity to point out the fallacies of their beliefs as well. It's the only way we can affect the behavior of the fundamentalists like the Moslem suicide bombers, and the members of the religious right who are attempting to hijack this country. I agree.

Please understand that when I say I agree with Sam Harris that the time for religious tolerance is past, I am speaking about the religious tolerance for the Abrahamic religions ruled by their judgmental God. I have no problem with the estimated 1.1 billion Hindus or the 500 million to 1.5 billion Buddhists. The men and women involved in these religions are not so much religious followers as they are practitioners of yoga, meditation, and other proven methods of achieving higher states of consciousness. And, though they are not based upon yoga or meditation, at least the hundreds of millions of followers of the Chinese religions of Taoism and Confucianism are not burdened by a belief in an off-planet, judgmental God who is separate from us. While I concede that many of the countries where these religions are the prevalent ones do have a lot of problems, I contend that those problems have more to do with economic concerns that are either brought about or magnified by corrupt, authoritarian governments, and/or through the exploitation of their poor citizens and their natural resources by the developed countries. If they were predominantly Christian or Moslem, then their problems would be much worse.

The reality is... everything is connected. In reality, the tribal people we have eradicated had it right.... Even as we were killing them and stealing their lands, they tried to tell us "We are a part of the world and a part of the Community of Life.... And so are you."

Everything that exists is a part of The Great Spirit of the Native Americans... If there is a God then we are a part of Him. There is no separation. So, why do we need an ancient and obviously flawed organization to intervene for us between ourselves and something that we are already a part of?

This cultural myth of **God Will Judge Us**, is a cultural myth we need to work on right away. Adherence to one of these Abrahamic religions promotes belief in a judgmental God, which creates judgmental people, which fosters and confirms the false sense of separation on which our flawed and doomed culture is based. This is a secondary cultural myth that wreaks havoc on our world.

6

We Have Big Problems

◊

I would like to begin this chapter by mentioning a few things with which our modern society is all too familiar...

> Hunger, famine, starvation, poverty, homeless people, the lack of affordable health care, pollution of our air, land, and water, the loss of our rainforests and other precious timberlands, overpopulation, ozone depletion, global warming and climate change, war, terrorism, the threat of nuclear war, rampant crime, overcrowded prisons, police brutality, governmental corruption, alcoholism and drug addiction, racism, sexism, physical, emotional, and sexual abuse, suicide, depression, gun violence, and mass shootings.

Certainly, our world contains plenty of positive things as well. Many of us are fortunate enough to know truth, beauty, and love through our interactions with our world and our fellow inhabitants. But the point I want to make from the outset is.... Whatever good there is in our world exists in spite of all of the problems set out above. Very few of us escape unscathed mentally, emotionally, or often even physically, from the insanity represented by these well-known problems.

That is the world we live in. Is it really okay for our world to be so full of such terrible problems? Although some of these problems are more recognized than others, I think we can agree that separately, each of these things is recognized by the collective society as a problem that has its own specific causes, and its own potential cure. But lumped together? I think the only general comment our collective society would make concerning all of these problems when lumped together might be that these problems represent the price of progress. And when we consider the fantastic progress we have made, our collective society might try to suggest that it is not too high a price to pay. After all, just think how far we have come from the horse and buggy days of a mere one hundred years ago... not to mention how far we have come from the caveman days when much of nature itself was a threat to us.

Not only have we conquered nature to the point that wild animals are no longer a threat, but we have tamed the elements as well. Plus, we have utilized our magnificent minds to invent and manufacture incredible, modern conveniences that make our lives much easier and more productive. Sure, we are aware of the problems set out above, although many of us believe some of them to be highly exaggerated. But whatever their validity, it is an undeniable fact that we have smart people working very hard to solve these problems. We are told that things will get better when our technological expertise and our regulatory laws and our ability to enforce those laws improves. We are told that right now, we are doing our best, but there are simply not enough resources to address all of these concerns at the same time.

My question to you is this.... What do you think? Do you accept the answer of our collective society? Or, are you willing to explore the possibility that the answer lies someplace else? Would you be willing to consider the possibility that all of these problems are the result of a single cause? How about a single cause that we can do something about?

This book has only one purpose... And that is to serve as a tool to help awaken people to the undeniable truth that our worldwide culture is fatally flawed at its very foundational level. For this reason, it does not function properly and it cannot be fixed. That is why all of the problems set out above are never going to go away. That is... they are not going to go away until we get rid of our flawed and doomed culture and replace it with one based upon the reality that everything is connected and actually works well, not only for ourselves and our fellow human beings, but also for all other living things on this beautiful planet.

Keeping that assertion in mind, let's take a closer look at each of these issues.

HUNGER, FAMINE AND STARVATION

Here is a set of issues that can easily be connected to the secondary cultural myth of "There Is Not Enough". And, as we have discussed, this cultural myth follows directly out of our basic cultural myth of "The World Was Made for Man to Conquer and Rule", which fosters separation. In a tribal culture based upon the premise that "Man is a Part of the World and the Community of Life", which fosters a sense of connection, a situation where "There Is Not Enough" would mean that the entire tribe would be hungry. In our culture, it simply provides an excuse for some to be hungry while others have more than enough.

In our culture, the food is locked up, and this is supposedly a good thing, because it provides motivation for people to work. Tribal people lived in a world where everyone knew that everything was connected and nobody was hungry unless the entire tribe was hungry. Another of our prevalent cultural myths which also contributes significantly to these issues is "Survival of the Fittest". According to this one, these people who are hungry are either too lazy or too ignorant to feed themselves, and therefore our culture says it might be best if we just let them starve. If they die before reproducing, then our culture's gene pool should be improved as a result.

In our culture, cheap labor provides wealth and riches for the privileged. The more desperate a person is, the less money he or she will work for, and the more profit the big corporations and their stockholders can make from their labors.

Actually, there is enough for everyone. And this is true even though there are way too many humans on this planet. Except for greed, there is no good reason why the basic needs of every person on this planet cannot be provided for. Basic needs are food, shelter, clothing, clean water, sanitary conditions, and health care. In fact, the only reason there are people on this planet who struggle to provide basic needs for themselves and their families is because of our culture's secondary cultural myth of "Survival of the Fittest", which provides the excuse for those in power to ignore the basic needs of the world's impoverished masses.

The real logic of the rich and powerful is that if the basic needs of these poor people were provided for, then they would have no motivation to work in sweatshop factories for subsistence wages. Sweatshop laborers and others around the world who toil for subsistence wages are being exploited. Many of those companies who employ these people used to make their products in the United States and in other developed countries. But a few years ago these companies figured out that developing countries are full of desperate, hungry people who can be exploited for subsistence wages, which translates into more profits for these big corporations. And as we have discussed, profit considerations provide the basis for all decisions made by these huge corporations.

It's high time we stopped bullshitting ourselves by accepting the "There is Not Enough" myth as being true. Certainly, there are great numbers of us alive today who are capable of seeing through this one. When enough of us do see the truth, then changes can be made. Ten thousand years ago, when our culture was born, the individuals in power decided to take control of the food supply and allow access to the other members only if they contributed their labors. That practice still continues today. In fact, it is one of the defining characteristics of our culture. Our culture tries to bullshit us by saying "There is Not Enough". But in reality, there is plenty. In reality, some people go hungry simply because the food is locked up and they don't have the means to pay for it.

Here is a telling fact about famines…. There has never been a famine in a modern functioning democracy.

There have, however, been countless famines throughout history in which millions of people have starved to death. The earliest I have seen from recorded history happened in Upper Egypt circa 2250 BC. It was caused by a decades long drought and it is said to have been a major cause for the demise of the Old Kingdom.

There are also records of other early famines in Ancient Rome and China dating back more than 2,000 years ago. Then, as our culture's world population increased, resulting in regional populations in various locations which exceeded the carrying capacity, famines became more and more common. Overpopulation and oppression by authoritarian rule seem to be the two most important factors leading to famine. When those conditions are met by stress caused by crop failure, drought, flooding, war, or some similar situation, which negatively affects the food supply, then conditions are ripe for a famine to take place. A good example of the importance of oppression as related to famine is the famous potato famine of Ireland in 1845 and 1846 when more than 1 million people starved to death, and many more escaped starvation by immigrating to America. During that time, food was being shipped **from** Ireland **to** England, because only the English could afford to pay the high prices being demanded.

There are serious famines right now in Nigeria, South Sudan, Somalia, and Yemen. The presence of ongoing armed conflicts within these countries with authoritarian rulers are most certainly factors in these famines.

I am lucky. I was born in the richest and most powerful nation in the world. My parents were not wealthy, but they were not poor either. I was able to attend college. Never in my life have I ever been hungry because there was not enough food available for me. I know this may not have been true for my father who grew up in West Texas during the Great Depression. Mostly, my father and his family had enough food, although I'm sure many of the common people like my grandparent's might have been concerned about food availability at times during the Depression. I know the hobos from the train used to come to my grandparent's house for handouts, so my Dad's situation could not have been too desperate. The 1930's were certainly lean years for many, though from what I have read, hunger was common, starvation, less so, and nothing approaching a famine materialized.

And hard times are here again for many of us. I know there are people right here in Austin today who do not have enough to eat. I see the people holding signs at traffic lights as I drive around the city saying "Will Work For Food", and I almost always give them money.

I hope I live to see our culture transformed into a culture where everyone understands that everything is connected and each of us know ourselves to be Responsible Members of the Community of Life. That is the only way problems like "hunger, famine and starvation" are ever going to go away.

POVERTY

Any guesses about what I'm going to say about this issue?

Of course I'm going to blame poverty on our secondary cultural myth of "There Is Not Enough". And fortunately, as we have seen, "There Is Not Enough" is only a myth. In reality, there is plenty. This secondary cultural myth arises out of our culture's primary myth about the world being made for man to conquer and rule which fosters separation. The result of this myth is that a small percentage of our culture's population enjoys the benefits of most of our world's comforts and conveniences, while most of us make do with much less. "There Is Not Enough" is used as an excuse by the people who have too much for the people who don't have enough so they will accept their condition of not having enough without too much complaint. In reality, ample resources are available so that adequate food, shelter and clothing as well as clean water, sanitary living conditions, and yes... even health care could be provided for every person alive on this planet today. This is true even though there are way more people on this planet than should be here.

Think about it this way.... If every member of our culture had adequate money to pay for their basic needs, do you think those needs would be met? Of course they would. These basic needs are not provided to everyone only because many people don't have the resources to pay for those things. And in our culture, if you can't pay for these things, then you can't have them.

As Quinn pointed out.... The food in our culture is locked up. This situation began ten thousand years ago when our culture's original exploiters of the weak and disadvantaged locked up the food and refused to let anyone have access to it unless they either worked for it, or traded something else of value for it. The food is still locked up today. And money, or some other form of payment, must be made for people to receive other basic needs as well. Some of the governments of our more developed countries do a very good job of funding and administering welfare programs charged with providing for the needs of their poorest people. However, there are other developed countries that don't do such a good job taking care of their poor.

In many developed countries and most of the developing countries, the most underprivileged members of our culture find themselves in dire situations with very little support. These impoverished billions have very little alternative but to figure out some way to provide food and other basic needs for themselves and their families. Many people fall short. A large percentage of the world's population are hungry and prone to disease and illness arising from lack of sanitary conditions and other inadequate living conditions, such as lack of access to clean water or adequate shelter from the elements.

Here are some facts about world poverty.

❖ According to UNICEF, 3 billion people around the world live on less than $2.50 per day. This represents 40% of our total world population. 1.3 billion of those 3 billion make do with less than $1.25 per day. 71% of the world's population, or more than 5 billion people, live on less than $10 per day.

❖ One billion people lack reasonable access to safe drinking water and, largely as a direct result of this, 1,000 children die every day from diarrhea.

❖ 1.2 billion people around the world do not have electricity.

❖ More than half a million women die each year from easily treatable complications of pregnancy and birth.

❖ Depending upon the study cited, and the criteria utilized in the various studies, there are somewhere between 15 million and 55 million millionaires worldwide. The United States has more millionaires than any other country.

There are many sides to this huge issue. We will begin this discussion by looking at how poverty is addressed in the United States and then we will compare it to how poverty is treated in other developed nations. Later, we will also look at poverty in the poorer, developing countries and examine the type of aid the developed nations give them. For this issue, I'm going to skip looking at the history. Just looking at the present state of poverty is a big enough job. And besides, everyone knows poverty has been around since the beginning of our culture. Remember, in a tribe, nobody is hungry unless everyone is.

Poverty in the United States

Here in the United States we have more than 80 federal welfare programs as well as many other state-run and privately-run programs, which are all geared towards alleviating poverty. Welfare spending by the federal government and our fifty state governments totaled more than $1 trillion in 2016.

The U. S. Census Bureau is charged with keeping track of poverty in the United States. They tell us that in 2015 we had 43.1 million people living in poverty in this country. This represents 13.5% of our inhabitants. The Census Bureau defines poverty according to income and differentiates between single individuals and families or households containing more than one person. Generally speaking, a single person who makes less than $10,000 annually is considered impoverished. A family of five would be living in poverty if their income is below $25,000. The poverty line was developed in 1963 and was keyed to three times the cost at that time of "an economy food plan". Since then, the "poverty line" has been revised and updated each year according to inflation.

Looking at this situation regarding poverty in the United States from a "separate versus connected" standpoint provides conflicting results. On the one hand, the situation we find ourselves in here, the richest and most powerful nation on earth with one out of every eight of our citizens living in poverty, was obviously created by our culture and its basic and secondary cultural myths which foster separation. But on the other hand, it is also obvious that we have recognized the need to alleviate the pain and suffering of the poorest among us, and it is certainly commendable that we are expending so much effort to try to make things better, even if we have been somewhat ineffective.

Over the years, these welfare programs have been the subject of much debate and the target of intense scrutiny. Basically, the conservatives oppose welfare and the liberals are in favor of it. Again, the conservatives who oppose welfare seem to mirror much more closely the "separate" viewpoint of our culture. Their main objection seems to be that in order to fund welfare, which they oppose, the government unfairly taxes their incomes at a much higher level than would be necessary if there were no welfare programs. Many of them view this taxation in order to fund welfare programs they oppose as "theft". Recently, during a time when we had a conservative President and conservative majorities in both houses of Congress, legislation was passed for a huge tax cut for the rich, even though we were involved at the same time in two very costly wars, and the tax cut therefore resulted in a record deficit.

It sure appears to me that the conservatives may have given up on ever getting rid of the welfare programs and also the hated entitlement programs like social security and Medicare, through legislation. Bankrupting the government may be their new tactic. I certainly don't see any other way to make sense of these Bush era tax cuts during a time when we were spending so much money in Iraq and Afghanistan.

The United States is the richest and most powerful nation on earth. According to the IMF rankings, in terms of GDP per capita, we ranked 11th in 2016, with an average of $57,436. It should be noted, that most of the countries ranked ahead of the U. S. were much smaller. Of the countries belonging to the Organization for Economic Cooperation and Development, (OECD countries) only Switzerland ($59,561), Norway ($69,249), Ireland ($69,231) and Luxembourg ($104,003) ranked higher. As compared to the rest of the developed nations, our manner of managing and administering the welfare programs here in the United States is highly bureaucratic, and therefore more costly to administer. Our goal here seems to be to identify those people who are most in need and to dole out the aid very carefully so that nobody who is not in dire need receives any. This causes the recipients to jump through a lot of hoops that are apparently designed to weed out the cheaters. Evidently, in the United States we will help out if we absolutely have to, but in doing so, we will endeavor to make our welfare recipients either feel guilty because they need the help, or mad and frustrated because the help is so hard to get. I guess you could say we want to try to keep the food locked up as much as possible here while doing all we can to motivate the poor to help themselves.

As I reported earlier in this section, in 2016 in the United States, we spent over $1 trillion on poverty. Also, our U. S. Census Bureau reports that there are 43.1 million or 13.5% of all U. S. citizens living in poverty. This means that in 2016 we spent the equivalent of over $23,200 on each impoverished citizen. Of course there are administrative costs involved, but do you think each impoverished citizen received relief or services valued at anywhere close to a reasonable percentage of that $23,200?

Poverty in Other Developed Countries

European countries utilize a different method, which involves fewer hoops for the needy to jump through. Accordingly, the cost of implementation and administration is much lower. This results in more aid going to people in need and less money going to the bureaucracy administering the aid. Also, all of the European countries we will discuss provide health care for their people. In fact, the United States is the only industrialized nation that does not.

The Nordic model of welfare, used in Norway, Sweden, Denmark, Iceland and Finland, is the most socially conscious welfare model used anywhere. It results in the highest taxes and the lowest poverty rates, but critics call it pure socialism and cite a reduction in productivity. However, these five countries are all ranked within the top nine countries on the Economist's Democracy Index list for 2016. Additionally, they all rank within the top twenty-six nations in the world in terms of GDP per capita per the IMF report covering 2016. Again, the IMF's GDP ranking includes many smaller countries. Other than Norway, Sweden, Denmark, and Iceland, only twelve other OECD nations rank ahead of Finland. This model of welfare is achieved by imposing a higher tax rate on the highest income levels. As a result, Sweden, Denmark and Norway have the lowest income disparity in the world. The local governments are more responsible than the federal governments for the administration of welfare in the Nordic model.

The Anglo-Saxon model of welfare is practiced by England, Ireland, and Canada. Ireland is the number 7 country in the world in terms of GDP per capita, and the United Kingdom and Canada are #'s 24 and 22 respectively. All three countries provide for health care and guarantee a subsistence level of income for their people. Generally, this model results in a lower unemployment rate, higher poverty rates, and more income inequality than the Nordic model.

France, Germany, Belgium, and Luxembourg practice the Continental model which can be said to occupy the middle ground between the types of welfare practiced in the Nordic and Anglo-Saxon models. This model emphasizes job protection, generous unemployment benefits, and high-quality health care. These countries impose a large amount of regulation on their industries and also have strict rules regarding job protection, which empowers their labor forces. Critics say their labor force wields too much power and that negatively affects their productivity. In terms of GDP per capita, Luxembourg is #1 with an average of $104,003. Germany, Belgium, and France, come in 18, 23, and 25 respectively.

Another model of European welfare is the Mediterranean model. This one is practiced in Italy, Spain, Greece, and Portugal, and it is considered similar to the Continental model because there is a focus on regulations for job protection, resulting in a powerful labor force. Also, these countries have more poverty than the countries practicing the Continental model. In the Mediterranean model, there is more of a focus on generous state pensions. These countries are all well down on the list of countries with the highest GDP per capita averages. Their rankings are Italy (32), Spain (33), Portugal (42), and Greece (47).

The Japanese are number 27 in these GDP per capita rankings with an average of $41,275. They have a complicated social welfare system involving government, business, and families, which has worked very well for them and resulted in a very low poverty rate. Recently, though, in the past twenty years their marginal income tax rate for the rich has been reduced from 70% to 45%. Predictably, this is resulting in more stratification of the rich and poor. Eventually, this stratification will affect their social welfare system. If this situation continues, time will tell what will happen to the poor in Japan.

One thing is certain. Each developed country around the world practices a system of social welfare that is the result of a constant tug of war between opposing forces. Each individual within each developed country either believes we should provide an adequate safety net for the underprivileged among us, or they don't. Also, in many countries like the United States, big business has a big influence on politics and on issues like social welfare, so the issue is not entirely up to the people. Whatever the dynamics, each new election brings changes, and sometimes they are big ones. Many would say that nothing defines a country and its government so much as this issue of social welfare and how it is handled.

Poverty in Latin America

Let's begin the discussion of worldwide poverty in developing nations with someplace I know a little about from personal experience… Latin America. In 1998, when I was researching which of the Latin American countries I would choose to spend a few months in, I knew I didn't want to be in a country where a few families owned everything and the rest of the population got by on very little. Whichever community I ended up in, I knew I didn't want to have next door neighbors living in dirt floor hovels, struggling to provide the basic needs for their families, and looking at me and my possessions and obvious resources with resentment. Unfortunately, as I looked into it, this turned out to be the situation in almost all of the Latin American countries. I can see now that this situation is a continuation of the exploitation begun by the Spanish and Portuguese colonists, which was carried forward by the corrupt authoritarian governments set up after each country obtained their independence.

According to *The Economist's* Democracy Index, the little country of Uruguay (19) is the only fully democratic country in Latin America. Costa Rica (23) just misses the full democracy cutoff. I have never been to Uruguay, but I can tell you from personal experience that the government of Costa Rica is quite corrupt. In fact, having lived there, I will tell you that I doubt whether it would be possible to have a successful import/export business there if you didn't pay some sort of bribes to someone. And from what I have seen, Costa Rica's judicial system appears to favor cronyism a lot more than it does truth and justice.

But Costa Rica does have a significant middle class, which is more than we can say for most of the rest of the Latin American countries. If you go to the capitol city of San Jose, which has a population of approximately 1.5 million, you will see the desperate type of urban poverty associated with crime and drugs. But outside of that one sprawling urban center, the temperate climate and abundance of fruit trees and other food sources seems to make Costa Rica an excellent place to be for people with little resources. Of course, the fact that Costa Rica provides health care for everyone is also significant.

The rest of the Latin American countries in Central and South America in order of their appearance on The Economist's

Democracy Index list are: Chile (34), Panama (45), Argentina (49), Brazil (51), Colombia (57), Peru (59), El Salvador (60), Mexico (67), and Paraguay (72). These countries are all considered by The Economist to be flawed democracies. Guatemala (79), Honduras (79) (tie), Ecuador (82), Nicaragua (104), and Venezuela (107) are the other Latin American countries. All of them are considered by the Democracy Index to be hybrid regimes, meaning they contain elements of democracy while also being very authoritarian.

I spent the better part of five years living in Costa Rica. My son, John Paul, was born there in the year 2000. (He was named after the Beatles, not the Pope!) Our family of three was able to live there very comfortably for about $1,500 per month. We had an old car that was paid for. Mayela had built her house on the cheap and it was also pretty much already paid for. After getting married, we shipped a container of my stuff down there, so our house had a lot of books and artwork and knick-knacks and nice kitchen stuff, and it was plenty comfortable. On this small monthly allowance, we were able to afford to have a lady come in three days a week to clean and do our laundry and ironing. We also paid very reasonable rates for others to perform many of our lawn and gardening chores. We were even able to make occasional trips to the beach and elsewhere.

I think most of you who live here in the United States would be impressed that we were able to live so well in Costa Rica on so little money. The cost of living there is just that much lower than it is here. Phone, electricity and water bills are very inexpensive, although the frequent interruptions in water and electric service do make those prices more realistic. During that time, laborers in Costa Rica were making about a dollar and a half an hour, and they were able to support their families on that amount. Mayela was making about $700 a month as a public high school music teacher, and that was certainly sufficient income for many families in Costa Rica to live on.

In contrast, I spent some time in Nicaragua where the middle class is almost non-existent. I met a schoolteacher on one of my trips there who told me he made $40 per month. Obviously, if a public schoolteacher can survive on $40 per month, then the cost of living must be even lower in Nicaragua and in most of the other Latin American countries than it is in Costa Rica.

World Bank Statistics on Poverty

According to the most recent World Bank statistics, 1.2 billion of the 7.4 billion inhabitants of this planet are living on an income of less than $1.25 per day. I have been researching this issue off and on for several weeks now, and I must say there are so many statistics and so many sides to this huge issue that it is a little difficult to get a real handle on the situation. But from what I understand, the World Bank is now saying $1.25 per day per person is the threshold for extreme poverty because this would be extreme poverty even in our poorest developing countries where the cost of living is the lowest.

Another significant statistic from the World Bank is there are a total of 2.8 billion people out of our world population of 7.4 billion who live on less than $2 per day. These 1.6 billion people with incomes between $1.25 and $2 per day are considered by the World Bank to be moderately impoverished. These statistics tell us that 38% of the world's population lives on less than $2 per day. And keep in mind, this figure does not represent the total number of people on our planet living in poverty. In order to figure out the total percentage of the world's population that lives in poverty, you would need to add in the number of people living in poverty in the United States and other developed countries who are impoverished, yet make more than $2 per day.

Also relevant and important to this discussion, I know many people question these thresholds which define poverty levels in developing countries and wonder if they are not set way too low.

When you look at the poverty threshold in the United States, it is set at around $10,000 per year for an individual or $25,000 per year for a family of five. These numbers would convert to $27 per day for an individual or $14 per day for each individual within a family of five. Without question, the cost of living is higher in the United States than it is in any developing country, so it makes sense that these poverty thresholds based upon income would be different in the United States as compared to developing countries.

Let's go back to Costa Rica and look at how we lived as a family of three for $1,500 per month. This would convert to $16 per day for each of us. And... as I described above, we were living pretty well for that amount. There was absolutely no problem providing our basic needs and we even had money left over for traveling, etc. Yet, if we tried to live on that same income in the United States, we would be very close to the poverty line. Let's take the examination of Costa Rica a step farther and imagine that Mayela was supporting a family of five on her $700 per month salary as a high school music teacher. This would translate to less than $5 per day for each individual within the family of five. I can tell you that many schoolteachers do support their families on salaries like that in Costa Rica, and I would not say they live in extreme poverty, although I would probably consider them at least very close to the threshold for moderate poverty. Yet, if they tried to live in the United States on that same income they would be living well below the official poverty line.

How about the laborers in Costa Rica who were making $1.50 per hour? If they worked a 40-hour week, and supported a family of five, that would convert to $240 per month, or $2,880 per year of total income for the family. Converting this to the World Bank type of figures, you get that each individual within that family was living on $1.60 per day, an income level that would classify them as living in moderate poverty according the World Bank. Based upon my experience living there, I would say that "moderate poverty" would be an appropriate designation for a situation like this. Also, I think it is significant to realize that an honest and hardworking semi-skilled laborer in Costa Rica, which is certainly one of the more developed of the developing countries, could be working every day and still not have enough income so that his family of five would be existing above the World Bank's official $2 per day poverty line.

As we have seen, even if you draw the line for individual income that defines poverty at a low number like $2 per day in developing countries, and $10 per day in developed countries, billions of our fellow inhabitants of this planet are impoverished. Africa is especially hard hit. According to the CIA Factbook, there are 28 countries around the world with 50% or more of their population living below the poverty line and 20 of those countries are African. Also, according to the same source, 44.2% of the 1.25 billion people of India live on less than $1 per day. Surprisingly, only 18.8% of China's 1.36 billion people are similarly impoverished. Together, more than 63% of the world's poor people live in either India (41.01%) or China (22.12%). India and China have both made huge progress in recent years in developing their economies. Of the two countries, China has come farther. China's GDP per capita is $7,990 as compared to India's $1,617.

Foreign Aid and Poverty

Another side to this issue of poverty is foreign aid, which is itself a huge, multi-faceted topic containing many obscure and murky facts. Here is what I have been able to figure out. Foreign aid can take the form of either humanitarian aid or developmental aid. The funding of humanitarian aid has many sources, including governments, individuals and private organizations. Usually, humanitarian aid is given to relieve human suffering in the short term resulting from natural disasters like hurricanes, earthquakes, tsunamis, famines, droughts, floods, tornadoes, wars, genocides, and other similar crisis situations.

Additionally, the governments of all of the industrialized nations give development aid to support the economic, social and political development of developing countries. Although somewhat controversial as we shall see in a minute, this development aid is supposedly geared to facilitating long term solutions and is distinguished from humanitarian aid which is given to alleviate human suffering in the short term. This development aid has an official name, which is Official Development Assistance, and it is known by its acronym of ODA. In terms of the amount of ODA given, the United States is the largest donor, averaging about $50 to $60 billion per year. However, in terms of a percentage of GDP, the United States donates the smallest of any developed nation. This amount was 0.14% in 2003. The United Nations suggests that developed countries should donate 0.7%, but currently only Sweden and four other nations do so.

This ODA money is given by the governments of developed countries to the International Monetary Fund and the World Bank which are charged with loaning it to developing countries ostensibly to help the development of their economies. However, there is a huge amount of controversy surrounding these institutions. Many allege that although the World Bank and the IMF claim their goal is to relieve poverty in developing countries, their actual purpose is exploitation. This is, of course, a very serious charge, and if true, would represent the epitome of any Machiavellian schemes ever concocted. Unfortunately, as incredible as it sounds, there does appear to be a lot of truth to these charges.

The World Bank and the International Monetary Fund came into existence at the end of World War II as a result of a conference in New Hampshire called the Bretton Woods Conference. The purpose of the conference was to agree on a post-war framework for international economic cooperation and to provide funding for the rebuilding of the war-ravaged countries. The first loan went to France, and other loans followed, which helped other countries get back on their feet after the terrible destruction from the war.

Significantly, the last G7 or European country to borrow money from these institutions was Italy, and this was in 1977. Since that time, these loans have all been made to developing countries.

The World Bank and the IMF are owned by their member countries in proportion to the amount they are funded by each country. The United States owns the largest share of any member country, being an 18% share of the IMF and a 15% share of the World Bank. These organizations are set up much like corporations. Each member country has voting rights corresponding to its ownership share. Since their inception, the president of the World Bank has always been a U. S. citizen and the president of the IMF has always been a European. The constitution of the IMF provides that no action may be taken without the agreement of 85% interest of the member countries according to their ownership share. So the 18% share of the United States gives it the ability to unilaterally veto any loan or other business brought before the board.

Allegations by John Perkins

As a part of my research into the World Bank and the IMF, I watched an hour and a half long interview of the author of *Confessions of an Economic Hit Man*, John Perkins. In the interview, Perkins came across as so earnest, credible, and likeable that after watching it, I felt compelled to read his book. Perkins says he was recruited right out of college in the late Sixties by an international consulting firm and trained by them to go into developing countries and get them to accept World Bank loans. On the face of it, making loans to poor countries doesn't sound so sinister. But the money came with strings. It had to be used to build infrastructure like port facilities, airports, and dams, which would benefit mostly the wealthy elite within the country. Additionally, contracts to build the infrastructure were required to be given to international corporations like Halliburton and Bechtel and the lesser known firm Perkins worked for that no longer exists, Charles T. Main and Associates.

Additional conditions for the loan typically included a requirement to devalue their currency and to privatize public infrastructure like power generation plants, water purification plants, telephone companies, pipelines, etc. The currency devaluations conveniently made the purchase of natural resources and infrastructure cheaper for the multi-national corporations who gobbled up the bargains. International corporations also benefited because they used this new infrastructure built with the World Bank loans to exploit the country's cheap labor and/or natural resources, as well as the country's presumed lack of regulation in regard to pollution. Adding insult to injury, these loans were always made for more money than was necessary and servicing the interest on the debt invariably crippled the ability of those countries to provide basic services like education, health care and other social services for their citizens.

Perkins says he was actually told that he was being trained to be an Economic Hit Man, (EHM) and that his job was to go into these developing countries and facilitate all of this. Additionally, he says he was told that if he was not successful in his duties as an EHM, then often, the next step would be to send in the Jackals to deal with the situation. According to Perkins, the Jackals were mostly ex-CIA or ex-military intelligence people now employed in the private sector as highly trained and well-paid assassins. If the Jackals failed, then the next step was often a military invasion. Perkins says that Iraq is a good example of a country where the EHM's and the Jackals both failed, resulting in the necessity to send in the troops.

These are, of course, very serious allegations. Hundreds of billions of dollars of public money has already been spent and is continuing to be spent by the World Bank and the IMF, with the stated goal of helping these developing nations to alleviate poverty. But according to Perkins, the actual goal of these programs is so sinister, it is almost beyond belief. Perkins says he was assigned to projects in Panama and Ecuador during the 1970's. As a result, he developed deep friendships with the presidents of both of these countries, Omar Torrijos of Panama and Jaime Roldos of Ecuador. Neither of these leaders wanted the World Bank loans, at least not with the conditions that came along with them. According to Perkins, neither Torrijos nor Roldos could be corrupted. Both wanted only the best for their people and both had made the determination that their countries would be better off without the World Bank loans and their conditions. But there was a critical issue in Panama with the canal, and Ecuador held huge oil reserves, so Perkins alleges that someone higher up the chain of command decided stronger measures were warranted. Victor Torrijos and Jaime Roldos both died in 1981, when their planes exploded and fell out of the sky. Perkins says he is sure the Jackals were to blame in both cases, but unfortunately, he has no evidence to back his claim.

One of the biggest problems we face in making difficult issues like poverty better is that the governments of so many of the developing nations around the world are so full of corrupt authoritarian leaders and other governmental officials, that the money which is spent to alleviate the situation often either gets stolen before it can do any good, or is used for programs that benefit the wealthy few rather than the impoverished general population. Then, according to Perkins, two honest and capable leaders come along and because they would not accept bribes or play ball with the powerful forces whose goal is to profit from the continued exploitation of their country's people and their natural resources, they both were simply murdered. And worse, according to Perkins, this was all done with the knowledge of governmental organizations run by the United States and other developed nations in collusion with corporations.

This story goes a step farther than what I have been saying about big corporations making decisions based solely on the profit motive. Perkins calls the collusion between governments and corporations a corporatocracy. Undoubtedly, there is exploitation. Given that these developing countries are being exploited, the question becomes whether or not there is collusion between the IMF, the World Bank, and the corporations doing the exploitation. Obviously, given the situation, either there is collusion, or there is incompetence on behalf of the IMF and the World Bank in regard to their implementation of these poverty-alleviating programs.

To me, it appears the answer appears to be collusion, but it all starts with the corporations, and I assert that we need to be mindful of that fact so that we can do something about it. I think this story of John Perkins also points out how cynical and disconnected an individual must be in order to carry out the plans of the corporatocracy. Fortunately for Perkins personally and for the rest of us as well, Perkins was apparently not cynical enough.

Whether this story is true or not... Do you think this is something that could possibly happen in a world where everyone understands that each of us are a part of the world and each of us knows that everything is connected and we are each Responsible Members of the Community of Life?

Unfortunately, I cannot tell you how much of this is true. The research required to corroborate Perkins allegations would require a huge effort that is beyond the scope of this book. However, the veracity of these allegations is not the point. Because if you will even concede that it might be possible for them to be true, then I think we all must admit there is something terribly wrong here. I'll tell you this, though.... Making loans to poor countries with the conditions that are required by the World Bank and IMF do not make sense if your goal is poverty reduction. However, they do make sense if your goal is exploitation.

Also, Perkins is playing the role of a whistle blower, which would seem to add credibility to the story. Perkins is the classic inside guy who initially played along, then had a change of heart, and that makes his allegations harder to refute. Certainly, if what Perkins says is true, then the exploitation must be stopped and the people responsible should be forced to face justice for their incredibly sinister actions, which have resulted in the death and suffering of millions. Hopefully, someone is already working on this.

It is an incredible story and Perkins comes off as extremely likeable in spite of all of the misery and pain, which have evidently resulted from his actions while carrying out his duties as an EHM. Apparently, he got pretty rich doing all of this stuff. Now he regrets it and feels it is his obligation to tell the story, despite the very real personal danger coming forward represents to him. He said he resigned his job as an economic hit man in 1980. He first started the book in the 80's but word got out that he was writing it, and he was persuaded by a bribe to drop the project. During the ensuing years, there were other attempts to write it, which were always thwarted by either bribery or threats. Then, he was so affected by the September 11th terrorist attack that he felt compelled to finish the book and publish it, no matter what risk the project posed to his personal safety.

And John Perkins is not the only person complaining about the World Bank and the IMF. Many others are saying basically the same thing. The protestors who attend the meetings seem to be an especially dedicated bunch. The World Bank and the IMF tell us their purpose is to relieve poverty in developing nations. But when you look closely as I have, the result of their "help" seems to track more with the scenario depicted by Perkins and the protesters than by the relief achieved according to the supporters of these organizations.

Conclusions on the Poverty Issue

For as long as anyone in our culture has had a social conscience, well-meaning people have been trying to fix problems like poverty with tactics like education or job training, food stamps or housing projects, or other "band aid" type approaches. I say if you want to effectively remove a weed from your garden, then you need to pull it out along with its roots. Otherwise, it will quickly grow back. Problems like poverty, hunger, famine, and starvation are never going to go away as long as we all live in a culture based upon the cultural myth of "The World Was Made For Man To Conquer and Rule", which fosters a false sense of separation... Separation between humans and the rest of the Community of Life... and separation also between ourselves as individuals. Ultimately, the only fix available is for us to abandon this flawed and doomed culture which is based upon the illusion that everything is separate and replace it with one based upon the reality that we are a part of the world, and the Community of Life... **and everything is connected**.

In the previous section on hunger, famine, and starvation I talked about our culture's need for cheap labor. I think cheap labor is also very pertinent to the present issue of poverty. The rich and powerful individuals and corporations who make all of the important decisions for our world like the fact that cheap labor is available and would oppose anything that would change this situation. For instance, goods like clothing and steel and virtually everything you find outside of the food section in your local Wal-Mart store used to be made in factories right here in the United States. Then, about thirty years ago, corporations decided our labor force here had become too affluent. Our workers were no longer satisfied living on subsistence wages.

Therefore, the corporations decided to move many of the factories oversees to places where the people were very poor so they could be put to work for a small fraction of the wages demanded by our workers here. Once again, this decision was made by huge corporations with the sole consideration for making the decision being increased profit. No thought was given to the lives of the people here in the United States who no longer had jobs. And no thought was given to the quality of life of the exploited workers in the poor countries where the factories were relocated.

In many cases, before the arrival of the factories and sweat shops, those poor people were living in a subsistence economy where they had no money for luxuries, but they had no trouble in meeting their basic needs of food, shelter, clothing, clean water, and sanitary conditions. Then, the factories came in, and all of a sudden, the people were required to toil long hours for a little bit of money they hadn't seemed to need before. Inevitably, their subsistence economy and their simple way of living were destroyed when the factories came in. In many cases, after a few years the big corporations decided there was another source of better and cheaper labor elsewhere, so they abruptly left.

Something else that is pertinent to this discussion is the fact that a group of Asian countries including South Korea, Vietnam, Thailand, and Malaysia has received notoriety for economic growth and poverty reduction in recent years. And guess what? Apparently, they have done so because their governments have made decisions based upon what is best for their countries and their citizens while resisting the corruption and the crippling conditions that usually go along with loans from the World Bank. And unlike Panama and Ecuador, these governments were strong enough so that the murder of one of their leaders would not have made any difference.

The huge corporations who are running this show called our worldwide culture do not have the same needs as "we the people". We have to wake up to the fact that we have allowed these artificial entities called corporations to take over our world. Huge, multi-national corporations rule our world because of their wealth and the influence it buys them. Their only goals are continued growth and more profits. Corporations have no need for breathable air or drinkable water. They make hugely important decisions that affect our planet every day, based solely upon their bottom lines, without due consideration for the needs of either people or the environment. They consider poverty "good" because they know that desperate people who live in poverty can be exploited. It is imperative that we take our world back from these huge, multi-national corporations so that problems like poverty, hunger, starvation, famine, war, governmental corruption, pollution, global warming, destruction of our ancient forests, and health care, can be dealt with in a rational and reasonable manner by "we the people".

Is there an evil corporatocracy running things like John Perkins alleges? Incredibly, it does appear that it actually exists. But if the corporatocracy is really out there spinning its evil and sinister webs, then the easy fix is to take away the ability of the corporations to profit from the exploitation. As powerful as these corporations are, they are still only artificial entities whose continued existence relies upon the continued permission of "we the people." And whether the corporatocracy is out there or not, the corporations need to be dealt with anyway.

HOMELESS PEOPLE

People have basic needs. And shelter from the elements is one of them. If we don't have a warm, dry place to sleep, then death from hypothermia is a real possibility. If a person is wet and exposed to a mild wind, hypothermia can occur within an hour even with temperatures in the 50's. Usually, our media judges the death of a homeless person to be not all that newsworthy. But here in Austin, where the winters are fairly mild, we lost a homeless lady one cold night last winter when she froze to death. Her death made the news because she had been active in local politics as a homeless person for years.

Then, aside from the dangers of exposure to the elements, there is our stuff, and the need to have someplace for it. George Carlin's famous riff on stuff says it all about this. He said our houses are simply big boxes with a lid to keep all our stuff. When we get too much stuff, then we are forced to buy bigger and bigger houses to keep it all.

Without question, a lot of us in this consumerist society have more stuff than we need. But can you imagine what it must be like for the hundreds of thousands of homeless people in this country who have no place to put their stuff? How would it feel to be in a position where you had to take all of your possessions with you everywhere you went? Would you opt for a small backpack or a shopping cart? Clearly, some tough choices must be made when faced with this decision.

If you are a homeless person, then where do you use the toilet? How do you prepare your meals? Where do you take your showers and clean your clothes? How do you receive mail? Is there a way for prospective employers or anyone else to call you on the phone? Where can you go to relax?

Clearly, being without a place to live presents a person with a whole series of problems.

I think most of us who are reasonably affluent like me, view their homes as more than a place to keep their stuff and give them shelter from the elements. I am divorced now, but when I was married, our family had not one, but two houses. Neither place is the least bit fancy or ostentatious, or even very expensive, but both are plenty comfortable. Both are full of books, and artwork, and knick-knacks, and music, and televisions, and computers and clothes, and stuff to cook with, and eat with, and plenty of things to keep John Paul entertained.

But perhaps more importantly, both are nice places for us to be able to spend time. Our private deck in the back of our house in Austin is full of beautiful plants and flowers. We can sit out there in the shade of the trees anytime we want and watch the swan and the ducks swim around in the lake which adjoins our property, and listen to the birds sing, while we contemplate whatever is occupying our minds at the moment. Or, if we were in Costa Rica, our house there was just as comfortable in terms of books and artwork and knick-knacks and kitchen stuff and televisions and stereos and computers and toys. Plus, if we wanted to sit outside and relax, we had the choice of sitting in the back and enjoying our plants and garden and the visiting birds in privacy and solitude, or of sitting in the front and enjoying the great views while we watch and greet all the people passing by.

Yes, we were very fortunate to have not one, but two comfortable abodes to call home. But an estimated 100 million people around the world are not so lucky. They are homeless. Do you think this is something that could possibly happen in a world where everyone understands that everything is connected and each of us are a part of the world and the Community of Life?

And yes... Of course I am also going to blame this one on our secondary cultural myth of "There Is Not Enough". Once again, the resources are there. This problem could be solved if we wanted to solve it. The biggest reason these people are homeless is because they lack resources. In our culture, if you can't pay for something, then you can't have it. The food is locked up along with everything else.

As we saw in the previous discussion about poverty, most of the other developed nations are doing a better job of taking care of the poor and disadvantaged than we do here in the United States. For simplicity's sake, let's acknowledge that homelessness is a problem around the world, including even other developed nations with more enlightened methods of administering social services. But rather than taking a lot of time and energy to write about specific situations within other developed nations, let's just concentrate on the situation here in the United States. Homelessness in developing countries is another story as well. I believe it is safe to say that homeless people are going to be found anywhere there is extreme poverty.

Here are some statistics about Homelessness in the United States taken from the Wikipedia article by the same name. The article reports that the United States Department of Housing and Urban Development estimates that 640,000 people are either on the street, in temporary shelters, or in a transitional housing program on any given night, and as many as 3.5 million people experience homelessness at least for one night in any given year. Obviously, according to these statistics, most people are only homeless temporarily. The article reports that the number of chronically homeless people, defined as people who are homeless most of the time, is falling, and is now down to around 120,000.

As to the estimated 3.5 million people who experience homelessness in any given year...

23% are families with children
51.3% are single males
24.7% are single females
5% are minors unaccompanied by adults

The biggest ethnic group of the homeless population is African American (42%), with Caucasians a close second (38%), and Hispanics a distant third (20%). Of course, these statistics are affected by the relative make-up of these ethnicities within the general population. For instance, considering they comprise only 13% of the general population, the African Americans are seriously over-represented in the homeless population. And, because they comprise 72% of the general population, Caucasians are very under-represented. The 20% of the homeless population that is Hispanic is more in line with their percentage of the general population, which is 16%.

Of the estimated 640,000 people who are homeless nightly, approximately two-thirds either stay in emergency shelters or in transitional housing. This leaves approximately 215,000 Americans who, on any given night, either sleep on the street, in their vehicles, in abandoned buildings, or stay illegally in other areas not meant for human habitation. Of course, many of these 215,000 individuals attempt to be admitted to emergency shelters, but are turned away, either due to the shelters being full, or because they were denied admission due to the fact they had been drinking or using drugs.

Even though I am blaming the homeless problem on our secondary cultural myth of "There is Not Enough", I have to admit, the actual situation is complicated. For instance, a large portion (39%) of the homeless population has some form of a mental health problem. For these individuals, it is often very difficult for them to take care of their responsibilities so that their rent can be paid on time. Many need more help than is often available to them. Also making a solution to the homeless problem difficult, 38% of the homeless population has alcohol abuse problems, and another 26% has other substance abuse problems.

Many of the homeless have serious health problems, and many are homeless because of the financial problems caused by their medical treatment. The myth of "There is Not Enough" still applies here, but the solution to homelessness is not as simple as building a few more homeless shelters. In keeping with the "There is Not Enough" cultural myth, however, I don't think anyone could refute that increasing the income of homeless people to a sufficient level so that their basic needs could be met would have a huge impact on homelessness. In fact, when you look at the research, all of the homeless advocates recognize that the two biggest reasons for people being homeless are insufficient income and unavailability of affordable housing.

When interviewed, reasons given by homeless people for their situation include a lack of affordable housing, home foreclosure, evictions from apartments or other rental properties, unemployment or low paying jobs, mental health problems, alcoholism and substance abuse problems, the need to flee an existing home due to domestic violence, recent release from prison, recent release from the armed forces, recent release from foster care (which happens on a child's eighteenth birthday), and the loss of housing through a natural disaster such as a fire, flood, hurricane, tornado, or earthquake.

Until recently, there had only been one piece of legislation signed into law which allocates direct funding to the problem of homelessness in the United States. This was the McKinney-Vento Homeless Assistance Act of 1987, and it helped to fund homeless shelters, soup kitchens, and other similar service providers. While this legislative act has helped considerably in dealing with the symptoms of homelessness, it has done little to help deal with the problem of homelessness itself.

During the past few years, however, we have seen some significant positive developments in regard to alleviating the problem of homelessness here in the United States. One non-profit organization that has had a significant impact is the National Alliance to End Homelessness. The Alliance was founded in 1987, and it remains a highly rated charitable organization today. In 2000, they released A Plan, Not a Dream: How to End Homelessness in Ten Years. Their twenty-four page Executive Summary is available for download on the Internet. Very significantly, there are now two hundred thirty-four plans filed by cities and/or counties setting out specific plans for their areas. One city that has filed its own Ten Year Plan and had very significant success in implementing it is Denver, Colorado. Denver filed its plan in 2005, and within two years they reported an 11 percent decline in overall homelessness, and a 36 percent decline in chronic homelessness. Clearly, Denver has made a major effort to address homelessness in their city that has been rewarded with tangible results.

Another major player in this arena that has been successful is the Interagency Council on the Homeless. This coalition of agencies was authorized in the McKinney-Vento Homeless Assistance Act of 1987, and re-authorized in the Homeless Assistance and Rapid Transition to Housing (HEARTH) Act of 2009, under its new name, the United States Interagency Council on Homelessness (USHIC). The HEARTH Act contained a mandate for the USHIC to create a national strategic plan to end homelessness, and provides that such plan be updated periodically.

The plan, called Opening Doors: Federal Strategic Plan to Prevent and End Homelessness, was presented to President Obama's staff and to members of Congress on June 22, 2010. I have read the plan and I can tell you I am very impressed with it. Here is a quote from the opening remarks of the USHIC chair, Shaun Donovan:

> This is the right time to align our collective resources toward eradicating homelessness. We have a legislative mandate from the HEARTH ACT of 2009 and bi-partisan support to adopt a collaborative approach. Most importantly, we now know how to address this important issue on a large scale. Over the past five years, the public and private sectors have made remarkable progress in reducing chronic homelessness. By developing the "technology" of combining permanent housing and a pipeline of support services, we've reduced the number of chronically ill, long-term homeless individuals by one-third in the last five years.
>
> I join my fellow Cabinet Secretaries and Council members to call for an alignment of federal resources toward four key goals: (1) Finish the job of ending chronic homelessness in five years; (2) Prevent and end homelessness among Veterans in five years; (3) Prevent and end homelessness for families, youth, and children in ten years; and (4) Set a path to ending all types of homelessness.

The USHIC has a staff of eleven people and an annual budget of $2,680,000. But the power behind this Council comes from the fact that the Council members are the heads of nineteen Departments and agencies. These are the U. S. Departments of Agriculture, Commerce, Defense, Education, Energy, Health and

Human Services, Homeland Security, Housing and Urban Development, Interior, Justice, Labor, Transportation, and Veterans Affairs, Corporation for National and Community Service, General Services Administration, Office of Management and Budget, Social Security Administration, United States Postal Service, and the White House Office of Faith-based and Community Initiatives. Shaun Donovan, whose "Preface from the Chair" I quoted from above, is the Secretary of the Department of Housing and Urban Development.

Here is the stated Vision of the USHIC from Opening Doors:

No one should experience homelessness-

No one should be without a safe, stable place to call home.

The four key goals from Opening Doors were already set out in Shaun Donovan's quote. Here are the Themes and Objectives:

INCREASE LEADERSHIP, COLLABORATION, AND CIVIC ENGAGEMENT

Objective 1:   Provide and promote collaborative leadership at all levels of government and across all sectors to inspire and energize Americans to commit to preventing and ending homelessness.

Objective 2:   Strengthen the capacity of public and private organizations by increasing knowledge about collaboration, homelessness, and successful interventions to prevent and end homelessness.

INCREASE ACCESS TO STABLE AND AFFORDABLE HOUSING

Objective 3: Provide affordable housing to people experiencing or most at risk of homelessness.

Objective 4: Provide permanent supportive housing to prevent and end chronic homelessness.

INCREASE ECONOMIC SECURITY

Objective 5: Increase meaningful and sustainable employment for people experiencing or most at risk of homelessness.

Objective 6: Improve access to mainstream programs and services to reduce people's financial vulnerability to homelessness.

IMPROVE HEALTH AND STABILITY

Objective 7: Integrate primary and behavioral health care services with homeless assistance programs and housing to reduce people's vulnerability to and the impacts to homelessness.

Objective 8: Advance health and housing stability for youth aging out of systems such as foster care and juvenile justice.

Objective 9: Advance health and housing satiability for people experiencing homelessness who have frequent contact with hospitals and criminal justice.

RETOOL THE HOMELESS CRISIS RESPONSE SYSTEM

Objective 10:	Transform homeless and housing stability for people to crisis response systems that prevent homelessness and rapidly return people who experience homelessness to stable housing.

This plan by the USHIC represents a major push by the federal government to deal with the problem of homelessness. And, this effort is having an impact, and it is definitely helping the homeless. Now, if only we would put the same energy and resources into the eradication of poverty itself.

LACK OF AFFORDABLE HEALTH CARE

The United States is the only industrialized nation on the planet that does not provide universal health care for all of its citizens. Just like all of the other modern, industrialized nations, the U. S. does have a single-payer, government-run healthcare system. But unfortunately, this system, which includes Medicare and Medicaid, only provides health care for 34% of our citizens. The other 66% of U. S. citizens are forced to find a way to obtain health insurance from one of the "for-profit" health insurance companies operating here. According to the Kaiser Family Foundation's website at KFF.org, in 2015, this 66% was comprised of 49% of citizens with employer-based coverage, 7% who purchased their own coverage, 2% who were covered by military based or veteran's-based coverage, and 9% who were uninsured.

For a researcher and a writer, writing about problems in the U. S. healthcare system is much like shooting ducks on a pond. There are just way too many examples showing how broken our system is in this country. For instance, in a recent study published by the Commonwealth Fund, it was reported that the United States government spends more dollars per capita on health care for its citizens, ($4,197) than Australia ($2,614), Canada ($3,074), Denmark ($3,841), France ($3,247), Germany ($3,677), Japan

($2,965), New Zealand ($2,656), Sweden ($4,126), Switzerland ($4,178), and the United Kingdom ($2,802). Of the thirteen countries studied, only the governments of the Netherlands ($4,495), and Norway ($4,981) spent more per capita for health care for its citizens. But, here is the thing.... For every country shown above, except for the United States, these per capita numbers for governmental health care spending represent what the government spends per capita on a universal health care system!

In contrast, the United States spends $4,197 per capita for each of its citizens, but only manages to provide health care for 34% of them. And the study also points out the governmental spending figure for the U. S. does not include the more than $250 billion dollars in tax breaks given to companies for providing employer-sponsored health insurance. If included, the per capita healthcare spending for the U. S. would be about $5,000. The study also goes on to compare relative spending on "out-of-pocket expenses" and "other" expenses. Only Switzerland spends more on out-of-pocket expenses. And, considering the "other" expenses include premiums paid for private insurance, it is certainly not surprising that the $3,442 the U. S. spends per capita dwarfs the $654 spent by Canada, the second highest spender in this category. The combined spending by the U. S. in all three categories comes to $9,086, which beats Switzerland's second place total of $6,325 by almost 50%.

I saw several articles on the Internet that commented on the Commonwealth Fund study. The headline for the Washington Post article was "Once again, U. S. has most expensive, least effective health care system in survey". The title for the CBS article was "US health-care spending is high. Results are... not so good". The Washington Post article made the point that there had been four previous Commonwealth Fund studies, and in each one, the U. S. was first in spending and last in health care outcomes of all of the countries studied. In the most recent study, the U. S. had the lowest life expectancy at birth, and the highest infant mortality rate, and the highest obesity rate.

The Commonwealth Fund study also reported that prescription drugs and other medical costs were significantly higher in the U. S. than in the other countries studied. A basket of in-patient pharmaceuticals was about 50% lower in Australia, Canada, and the United Kingdom than it was in the U. S. The average cost of heart bypass surgery was $75,345, which was more than $30,000 higher than the cost of the same bypass surgery in Australia, which had the second highest cost of all the countries studied. Not surprisingly, MRI and CT scans were also far more expensive in the U. S.

One of the most telling charts included in the Commonwealth study was one that showed both health care and social care as a percent of GDP. In terms of health care costs, the U. S., at 16% of GDP was by far the highest. And, in terms of social care costs, the U. S. was by far the lowest, at 9% of GDP. However, in terms of the combined percentage of both health care and social care, the U. S. was right in the middle, at 25% of GDP. Norway spends the same combined percentage of GDP on health care and social care, but the percentages are flipped. For 9% of GDP, Norway provides universal health care to 100% of its citizens. Plus, citizens of Norway live on average a full three years longer than U. S. citizens, and less than half as many Norwegian babies die during infancy. These efficiencies in their health care system enable Norway to spend almost double what we spend in the U. S. on social care, while spending the same percentage of GDP on the combined cost of both.

It seems obvious to me that twelve of the thirteen countries included in the Commonwealth Fund study recognize that health care is a basic need. Only one of the countries seems to think that health care is a commodity that should be purchased and paid for just like cars, boats, computers, cell phones, and television sets. Unfortunately, that one country that has things backwards is the richest, and most powerful country on the planet. And I happen to live there.

POLLUTION OF OUR AIR, LAND, AND WATER

By now, the direct link between an issue like pollution and our culture's basic cultural myth of "The world was made for man to conquer and rule" should be obvious to everyone. In the U. S. alone, more than 4 billion pounds of toxic chemicals are released by industrial polluters into the environment each year. Obviously, this wreaks havoc on our quality of life and negatively affects countless ecosystems. Do you think this situation could possibly exist within a culture that believed everything was connected and man was a part of the world and a part of the Community of Life?

Ten thousand years ago, when our culture was born, there was no place on this planet suffering from pollution. Remember, ten thousand years ago man had already existed for more than three million years, and our particular species of man had been around for more than two hundred fifty thousand years without polluting. And after the birth of our culture, the problem of pollution was slow to develop. Reasoning it out, we can guess the first signs of pollution that arose after our culture was born were the result of human waste affecting drinking water in some of the early settlements. The first air pollution significant enough to register occurred several thousand years after the birth of our culture, when some of our early civilizations began smelting iron. Evidence of this minor air pollution, which has been attributed to metal production by Greek, Roman, and Chinese civilizations, has been discovered by analyzing core samples taken from glaciers in Greenland. The air pollution associated with this activity, while significant enough to register in the glacier, was certainly not enough to disrupt a significant number of our planet's ecosystems.

But today, some three thousand years after the pollution from those ancient smelting fires settled into the ice as it was forming in that glacier in Greenland, there is no question that many of our world's ecosystems are in peril. And also without question, man made pollution of our air, land, and water stands out as one of the main causes. In order to thrive and live healthy lives, our species needs clean air to breath, clean water to drink, and uncontaminated soil to live on and to grow our food on. And not just humans, but all living creatures need these things.

It was the Industrial Revolution that brought about most of the pollution we are concerned about today. With the Industrial Revolution came big factories, and with them, pollution from their coal-fired furnaces and also pollution from the discharge of industrial chemicals. The Industrial Revolution began in Great Britain in the late 1700's, starting with the mechanization of the textile industry. Awareness of the immensity of the problem of pollution was slow to develop. Very little effort was made to contain pollution until events in the mid-to-late Twentieth Century related to pollution started opening people's eyes. One of the earlier of these was an event that occurred in London, which is known as the Killer Fog of 1952. Twelve thousand people died in this event when the smoke generated by coal-fired home heaters was trapped at ground level for four days by an inversion layer.

Other notable events which brought about awareness and eventually legislation to regulate pollution include the publication of Silent Spring, by Rachel Carson in 1962, the breaking of the news story of the cancer-causing chemical pollution at Love Canal in 1978, the grounding and breaking up of the Amoco Cadiz supertanker off the coast of France which also occurred in 1978, the disaster at the Union Carbide pesticide plant at Bhopal, India in 1984, and the lawsuit by the citizens of Hinckley, California against Pacific Gas & Electric in 1993. Actually, we probably would never have heard of the last event, but thankfully, the story was made into a movie in 2000, in which Julia Roberts won a best-acting Oscar for her role as the heroine, Erin Brockovich.

If you get an MBA degree, you will undoubtedly learn that another name for "pollute" is "externalize". The "externalizing of costs" in business basically means you get somebody else to pay for a portion of the production costs. So, in an effort to externalize their costs, the factory owners try to pollute as much as they can get away with simply because it costs more for them to pollute less. After all, these businesses are in business to make money. And the way this works in practice is that the "somebody else" who pays these costs is you and me, and the rest of the taxpayers. When these production costs are successfully externalized by the factory owners, we, the taxpayers, either pay for the eventual cleanup or suffer the effects of the pollution because it is never cleaned up.

Thankfully, as we will see in the Part Three, another name for "taxpayer" is "voter". This is significant because therein lies the answer to this outrageous situation.

LOSS OF OUR RAINFORESTS AND OTHER PRECIOUS TIMBERLANDS

I own and operate a one-man oil and gas exploration company called Stardust Energy, Inc. As I drive between my home in Austin and some of the projects Stardust has been involved in, I often try to imagine what the land I pass through must have looked like before our culture arrived and began transforming it. There is a road I sometimes travel called "OSR" which is short for "Old Spanish Road". Today, it is the address of some pretty nice horse farms and cattle ranches, many of which are dotted with oil and gas wells. But three hundred years ago, OSR was a trail between San Antonio and the Spanish outpost of Nacogdoches. At that time, Nacogdoches was located close to the border of French territory just across the Red River from a French outpost at Natchitoches. Driving that road is especially interesting because when I am on it, I am traveling down the same trail the Spanish and early Texas settlers were utilizing three hundred years ago. Three hundred years ago the ancient primeval forest was still present, disturbed only slightly by the existence of the lightly traveled road. Now, that ancient forest is completely gone.

Earlier, in Chapter Two, I made the point that ten thousand years was the blink of an eye when compared with the three-million-year history of man, or even compared to the two hundred fifty-thousand-year history of our particular species of man. On that basis, three hundred years is no time at all. In these terms, it was just yesterday that there was an entire region of undamaged primeval forest with a lightly traveled road traversing it in what is present-day East Texas. That ancient forest was the home of a rich and diverse ecosystem containing countless members of the Community of Life. Now it is completely gone.

As I drive the OSR and the other highways and secondary roads that traverse what was so very recently an ancient forest, it is often quite sad to see what our culture has seen fit to replace it with. Three hundred years ago the entire eastern half of what is now the United States was almost completely covered with an ancient, primeval forest. Now it is gone. For what? So our insane culture could continue growing without limit much like a cancerous cell would?

In 1998, oil was $10 per barrel and I had a consulting job for a client who had curtailed their operations because of the low prices. But they had a good team put together and they were reluctant to break it up. I was working for good friends and I realize also they were probably reluctant to let me go because they knew it would have been difficult for me to find other work when none of the other oil and gas companies were spending any money either. I had been coming into the office every day, and since we didn't have any actual work to do, several of us were spending our time playing the stock market. After a couple of months of this, I became a little bit uncomfortable taking money for nothing and I started thinking about what I could do to change the situation.

I had a little income from some oil and gas prospects I had invested in that had been successful. Also, I had just broken up with a girlfriend, so there were no relationships to keep me around. I had a pretty good start on a novel I had begun several years before, but had never made much progress on because I was always working. I started thinking that if I was in a Latin American country where the cost of living was lower, my oil income would probably be sufficient to sustain me for a few months while I worked on the novel. I researched the Latin American countries and Costa Rica popped out as the country with the most developed middle class and also the most active tourism trade. I decided I would drive down there and spend six months working on my novel, then return to the oil business when the price of oil and gas would presumably be higher.

But plans don't always work out as you think they will. Before coming home, I ended up meeting a native Costa Rican who was a musician and a high school music teacher, getting married and starting a family. And as a result, my six-month trip turned into me spending the better part of five years in Costa Rica. We had a beautiful little house in Costa Rica that my now ex-wife had built about three years before we met, which we fixed up together after we got married. The elevation there is about 3,500 feet above sea level. The temperature is a pretty constant 75 degrees year-round. You could see the ocean twenty miles away from the hills around our house. And from our front yard we had a view in the other direction of two eleven thousand plus foot volcanoes, the closest of which is about thirty-five miles away. The house had no air conditioner and no heater and no need for either.

Costa Rica has a reputation as being a big ecological haven. Indeed, it is a very beautiful country with some incredibly diverse tropical ecosystems. And Costa Rica deserves credit for protecting so much land in national parks. However, if you drive around looking at the country there in the same way I did during my travels here in Texas, you will see that the ancient forests outside of those protected areas are just as gone in Costa Rica as they are here in Texas. It's just that everything is so green in Costa Rica that it takes more of a trained eye to see it.

This issue of deforestation is a direct result of our most basic cultural myth.... **The world was made for man to conquer and rule.** I look now upon our remaining forests the same way I look upon our remaining tribal people... with a very deep sense of sadness. We are on the verge of losing both our last remaining tribal peoples and our last remaining ancient forests almost simultaneously. Unless a Critical Mass of people within our insane culture wake up very soon and decide to stop the destruction, then neither will be around for very much longer.

Certainly, a belief that everything is separate must be required for someone to be able to decide to destroy a diverse ecosystem like the one contained in any ancient forest. I don't think there is enough money in the world to motivate someone to destroy an ancient forest if that person understands that everything is connected and believes himself to be a part of the world and a part of the Community of Life.

I had a friend from college whose father made about one hundred million dollars in the oil business. One of the things he purchased with his millions was a 1,200-acre ranch in Colorado that had three and a half miles of a beautiful trout stream running through it. The property on both sides of the river was bounded by national forest land. The river was dammed up downstream and the big recreational Lake Vallecito reservoir bounded the ranch on the lower end. Upstream was another 2,000-acre ranch. And above that was a huge protected area called the Weminuche Wilderness.

My friend used to invite me to his family ranch twice a year. Most of the time, we would fly up there on his father's private jet. During the time when I was going up there, one of my favorite things in the world was to take the lookout hike. Starting out at the ranch at about 8,000 feet above sea level, I would hike about three and a half miles along a trail through the beautiful aspen, pine, and spruce forest, climbing about 2,000 feet in elevation to a destination on a 2,000-foot cliff with a view that included the river and lake below. The view upriver included several mountain peaks higher than 12,000 feet. It was an amazing and absolutely beautiful place to be able to spend some time every year. Over the years, I saw deer, elk, bears, eagles, bighorn sheep, and even one mountain goat on that hike.

Surrounded like it was on two sides by national forest and a third by a designated wilderness area, my friend and I both thought his property was pretty safe from encroachment. But that was before we understood that the Forest Service answered to the timber companies and not to the American people, or even to neighboring landowners. One year, my friend got notice that the Forest Service was about to open a new road into the undisturbed national forest above his ranch. Obviously, this was not something he was in favor of. Aside from providing easier access to the area for people in general, the new road would eventually lead to logging, which would potentially be devastating for the ranch and river below, not to mention the ancient forest itself.

After he engaged with the Forest Service and encountered stone wall after stone wall, we both came to understand that not only is the Forest Service not there to protect the national forests for we the people, their actual function was to subsidize the timber industry. Commercial logging activities in areas like these would never be profitable if the timber companies had to build their own roads. Building roads into remote, undisturbed ancient forests in order to provide access for timber companies turned out to be one of the most important tasks performed by our Forest Service.

But my friend had resources, and he was determined to do what he could to stop the road construction. He first tried the logical route of engaging the Forest Service bureaucracy on the specifics of their plans and attempting to debate them about why they shouldn't be carried out. At the time, neither he nor I understood the folly of utilizing this strategy. We didn't yet understand the Forest Service, and who they were composed of, who they answered to, and what their agenda was. When this tactic failed, my friend contacted another mutual friend from college who was making his living as a powerful lobbyist in Washington. His answer was simple. Make a strategic campaign contribution and handle the matter through the legislature.

Unfortunately, this battle became somewhat meaningless in 2002 when the Missionary Ridge Fire consumed more than 70,000 acres of forest, including much of the forest around this beautiful ranch. The drought conditions that year were the setting for thirty forest fires in the state of Colorado alone, as well as many others throughout the American West. Remarkably, the piece of forest I walked through on the lookout hike was spared, even though the fire touched it on two sides.

Here in the United States, a pitched battle has been fought for years between the timber companies who want to continue profiting and the "save our trees" activists who are becoming more and more sophisticated and effective. The activist's biggest asset in this David and Goliath battle is the fact that truth and justice are on their side. However, I think as long as the activists choose to fight about specific timber sales, they may win an occasional fight, but the overall war will continue to be won by the bad guys (the timber companies). I believe this battle needs to be fought at the most basic level we can fight it. For me, that means we fight it at the level of abolishing corporate personhood. We the people have allowed our government to be taken over by large corporations including these timber companies whose only reason for existence is to make a profit. The priorities of these huge corporations are very different from the priorities of the people of this country.

Up until now, the timber companies have been winning. And that is exactly why companies like Kimberly-Clark can continue making a profit by cutting down our last remaining ancient forests and turning them into toilet paper. The biggest advantage of the corporations in this battle is the fact that politicians everywhere are beholden to them because they have accepted their campaign contributions and would like to continue receiving them. Eventually, "we the people" are going to have to wake up to the fact that our senators and congressmen, and even our president, as well as many others in government, are beholden to these huge corporations. Therefore, these elected officials regularly put the welfare of those companies before the welfare of "we the people", or the welfare of these precious, ancient ecosystems. When enough of us understand the situation as it really is, then changes can be made. Until that time comes, the timber companies will continue consuming our last remaining ancient forests for profit.

And, the oil and gas companies will continue to make sure alternative energy sources are not developed, and alternatives to our dependence upon the automobile are not explored. And, defense contractors will continue to make sure someone somewhere is constantly fighting and using their war machines, and the bombs and bullets and missiles that go with them. And, pharmaceutical companies will continue to tell us that good health is dependent upon drugs and invasive surgery, while charging exorbitant prices for their drugs. And, coal companies will continue to talk about clean coal while continuing to burn the horrible stuff. And, chemical companies will continue dumping terrible poisons into our environment, because not doing so costs them more. And, manufacturers of all kinds of products will continue to pollute while claiming they don't.... And on and on and on... until "we the people" finally wake up and realize how insane it is to let all of these important decisions be made by corporations and by the politicians who are beholden to them.

OVERPOPULATION

As I was preparing to write this piece on overpopulation, I happened to see a small article on the second page of the Sunday paper here in Austin reporting that a Sumatran tiger had mauled two illegal loggers to death. The article also mentioned that three other people elsewhere had been killed within the past month by critically endangered cats. They reported that no effort would be made to kill the tiger in Sumatra, or to catch and relocate it, because it had not strayed from its protected habitat.

I've often said that being killed by a predator like a lion or a tiger or a bear or a shark would not be my preferred method of checking out from this lifetime. I'm sorry the illegal loggers had to die in this manner. I'm sure it was not pleasant for them. Most likely, they were just trying to make a living and provide for their families. However, at the same time, I must admit to a bit of a "Yahoo!" feeling in regard to the way that tiger protected his little piece of forest from those illegal loggers by making a meal out of them. The habitats for tigers and similar species are declining so rapidly and their situation appears so dire that I just feel compelled to appreciate and applaud this small victory on their behalf.

The issue of "overpopulation" is a big one. Many people around the globe are aware of this problem and are very concerned about it. To me, this little news piece regarding the tiger goes right to the heart of the most important of the effects of overpopulation. And that is that our species is taking up way too much space on this little planet. The result is that many, if not most, of the members of the rest of the Community of Life are suffering. Many of these species are disappearing altogether, which is another way of saying they are becoming extinct. If a reasonable person would take the time to look closely at the situation, they would see that tigers and other similar species are in very big trouble, and the obvious reason is there are way too many members of our species gobbling up the last remaining habitat, quickly destroying the last remaining ecosystems which could support species like the tiger's.

As we have previously discussed, overpopulation is a result of our culture having rejected our position as Responsible Members of the Community of Life and of our failure to adhere to the law of limited competition. Ten thousand years ago, before that particular tribe in ancient Mesopotamia began practicing totalitarian agriculture, there were only an estimated ten million humans living on this planet. And each of those ten million people were living sustainably on their own landbase as a member of a tribe whose way of living had evolved over millennia through an interaction between themselves and everything on that landbase. Today, ten thousand years later, the human population is almost 7.8 billion, and the only humans living sustainably are those few members of indigenous tribes who are still living on their ancestral lands in their ancient and proven ways.

In my meditations, I sometimes like to consider the vastness of the Universe, and to look at our little planet as the rare and incredibly beautiful little blue jewel that it is. If there are extra-terrestrial beings here on earth, then they have certainly traveled great distances to be here. Our astronomers have learned a lot about our neighboring planets and their solar systems here in our Milky Way Galaxy, and even a great deal about our more distant neighbors in other galaxies. From these explorations, one thing appears to be certain.... Planets like ours are rare. At the moment, finding another planet similar to earth, which is so full of diverse ecosystems, is a task beyond our capabilities. However, given the immenseness of our Universe... knowing there are billions of stars within billions of galaxies... I must come to the conclusion that it's likely there are other planets with ample water that also could have similar temperature and atmospheric conditions to ours, on which life could develop in a manner similar to the way life has developed here. But wherever we might someday find these planets... the life there as well as the planets themselves, would be just as impressive and just as precious as our own.

Accordingly, I feel a deep sense of responsibility to the Universe for the care of this beautiful planet... especially since it is the activities of my own insane culture which have placed these ecosystems in such peril. Our species has evolved here as one of millions of species who are all members of the Community of Life. Apparently, humans were the first of these species to become self-aware, although dolphins, whales, some apes and elephants appear to possess this capability as well. Who knows? Perhaps if we can restrain ourselves from destroying the rest of the planet's ecosystems, there may be other species who will eventually develop intellectual capabilities similar to ours. After all, it was a series of novels featuring an extremely intelligent and well-educated telepathic gorilla named Ishmael that opened my eyes to all of this in the first place.

Yes, human overpopulation is perhaps the biggest factor driving the terrible destruction of ecosystems, which is leading to such regrettable premature extinction of so many precious forms of life. The good news is that this situation is obvious to many of us who are very concerned about it. That fact is significant because in order for this problem of overpopulation to be solved in a conscious and thoughtful manner, a Critical Mass of us must understand the problem and desire to fix it.

It is on the root cause of overpopulation, that I find myself in the rare position of being in disagreement with Daniel Quinn. I know Quinn's assertion that overpopulation is attributable largely if not completely to an oversupply of food, was a controversial one for many of his readers. Certainly, our food production and distribution system is a contributing factor and it needs to be fixed for that reason, and for other reasons as well. But I submit my assertion that it is our basic cultural myth which is the main culprit here. Once we decide to drop the falsehood that the world was made for man to conquer and rule and realign ourselves with the true nature of the Universe... Everything is connected and we are a part of the world and a part of the Community of Life... then solutions to big questions like "overpopulation" will flow naturally out of that change.

I think a factor contributing to overpopulation that is much bigger than "too much food" is the continuing oppression of women in developing countries. (Survival of the Fittest Myth) Statistics back up this assertion. For instance, a study by the United Nations shows birth rates to be declining over the past fifty years, but unevenly. A close look at where the birth rates declined the most and where they declined the least supports this assertion. Also, take a look at the countries where most of the women wear burkas and compare their fertility rates to those of North America or Europe. One obvious fix for this is to educate women in developing countries and especially in the Moslem world. An educated woman is simply much harder to oppress and much less willing to submit to oppression. Ideally, the decision to bring more children into this world should be consciously made by two or more people who all desire to share in their care and upbringing. Failing that, educated and empowered women as a whole are certainly much more conscious about the potential for unwanted pregnancies resulting from unprotected sexual relations. Also they are much more proactive in the planning of their families than uneducated and oppressed women.

Another important side to this issue of overpopulation is the relative impact on the environment affected by an affluent person versus an impoverished one. After all, if we are concerned about overpopulation because of the negative effects of humans on the environment, then we need to compare the relative impact of an average person in a developed country versus the average person in an undeveloped country. When you do so, it becomes very apparent that the ecological destruction being caused by the 322 million citizens of the United States far exceeds that of the 1.25 billion inhabitants of India. Recently, a new measurement tool called the ecological footprint has been developed to deal with this issue. The computations set out in this ecological footprint formula currently result in the necessity of 1.6 earths to sustain our present worldwide rate of consumption with all of its ramifications. The obvious trend is for this situation to keep deteriorating.

Clearly, if we are going to avoid a serious crash, (a hard landing) something must be done... and soon. To me, the solution is an easy one. The key to solving this lies in the reality of our situation. The reality is that all but a very few of the 7.8 billion of us who are alive today will be dead within one hundred years' time. The key, then, is how many children those 7.8 billion of us bring into the world. If we all decide to voluntarily limit our reproduction to one child each, then since it takes a man and a woman to make one child, each succeeding generation will be half the size of the generation that precedes it. It is a simple matter, really. All it takes to solve it is a universal understanding of our problem, a realization of how simple it is to solve it, and a willingness to do so. According to my calculations, we could reduce our worldwide population by more than 50% in only 50 years! Once we get the population decreased down to a more reasonable carrying capacity… say… two billion or so…. We can adjust the birth rate upwards in order to sustain that population level. Again… the key is awareness, and then a willingness to address the situation. Simple. What good is self-awareness if we don't even use it?

Could we please get started with the fix on this one? We are in big trouble here. But as stated earlier, the rest of the Community of Life on this planet is in even worse trouble.

OZONE DEPLETION

This story of how we came to understand the problem of ozone depletion in our upper atmosphere… and then how we narrowly averted disaster by recognizing the danger early enough to actually do something about it, is a very interesting one. And especially interesting and significant but not widely understood, is the twist my research discovered: why we were able to react to this particular problem, when action seems so impossible regarding other issues we have previously addressed, like pollution and overpopulation, as well as global warming.

This interesting story, however, is somewhat shrouded in complexity. Chemical processes involving reactions between various molecules and sunlight are a big part of this story. And in order to follow it, one must understand these processes, at least to some degree. Another big part of the story is the process of scientific inquiry that allowed us to understand the existence of ozone in our upper atmosphere. And then there is the importance ozone plays in protecting us and other living things, like plants and plankton, from the harmful effects of UVB radiation by absorbing it in the upper atmosphere. Also significant to the story is the introduction of man-made chemical compounds into our atmosphere and how their presence in our upper atmosphere affects the ozone levels. In relating this story to you, I am going to attempt to simplify all of this complexity as much as possible so that the basic story itself can be more easily understood. The somewhat involved and complex details regarding all of this are readily available via Google Internet searches to anyone who is interested in learning about them.

Ozone is a naturally occurring substance and it is formed when three oxygen atoms bond together. Its presence in the stratosphere is crucial to our well-being, as well as the well-being of many other members of the Community of Life. This is because ozone in our stratosphere blocks harmful UVB sunrays from reaching the earth's surface. However, the same substance, when found in our near-earth atmosphere, is harmful to us and other forms of life. So, for humans and for other members of the Community of Life, ozone is good in the stratosphere and bad in the troposphere.

In the troposphere, meaning the near-earth part of our atmosphere, ozone is toxic to humans. Generally, ozone is formed at or near ground level by chemical reactions involving oxygen, sunlight, and pollutants from automobiles and factories. Around ten percent of the ozone that exists is located in the troposphere, and the ozone that is formed in this manner, generally does not travel to the stratosphere.

The other ninety percent of the ozone Is located higher up In the stratosphere, with most of it being located in a band about 75,000 to 80,000 feet above the earth's surface. In the stratosphere, ozone is formed by a chemical reaction that begins when sunlight strikes an oxygen molecule causing it to break up into two oxygen atoms.

Each of those oxygen atoms then bonds with another oxygen molecule forming two ozone molecules. Then, when the sunlight strikes the ozone molecule, it breaks up again into an oxygen atom and an oxygen molecule, which then recombine into another ozone molecule. Normally, this process is interrupted only when the free oxygen atom recombines with an ozone molecule rather than an oxygen molecule, resulting in the formation of two oxygen molecul

But it is the different length of the photons from the UV light, which react to break up the oxygen molecule as compared to the length of the photon which reacts with the ozone molecule that gives ozone its importance in the stratosphere. The UV light, which reacts with ozone, corresponds with the photons associated with the UVB radiation, and therefore, it is ozone which "absorbs" a large part of this harmful UVB radiation and prevents it from reaching the earth's surface.

All of these various chemical reactions result in a balance that determines the amount of ozone in the stratosphere at any given time. Many factors contribute to this balance, including the relative amounts of the various reacting gases, the amount of sunlight available, and the temperature, as well as other factors. This balance is interrupted when other free radicals, like chlorine or bromine or nitrogen oxides, are introduced into the mix.

Significant to this part of the story, research has shown that a widespread die-off of plankton that occurred approximately two million years ago corresponded with the occurrence of a nearby star going supernova. Researchers speculate that the plankton die-off was a result of the ozone layer being significantly affected when radiation from the supernova produced nitrogen oxides that affected this balance of chemical reactions in our stratosphere, resulting in significantly decreased levels of ozone. Without the presence of ozone in the stratosphere, the harmful UVB radiation reached the earth's surface unimpeded, and the plankton die-off, presumably together with nasty sunburns for some early humans, was the result.

Similarly, it was the introduction into our stratosphere of chlorofluorocarbons (CFC's) and other man-made ozone depleting substances that had our planet once again on the brink of a massive die-off. Freon is the trade name for a CFC invented by the chemical company DuPont, which is perhaps the most significant of these. CFC's were also in wide use as the propellant in aerosol sprays and as a cleaner for electrical components. When I began researching this issue of ozone depletion, I knew only that it was another scary problem much like overpopulation and global warming. But as I delved further into the research I was able to see that the dangers associated with ozone depletion have apparently been averted. How we were able to accomplish this great escape is quite a story and it involves smart scientists who were lucky enough to be working on the right problems at the right time. They figured it all out and were able to raise the red flag in time for a collective effort to be initiated, which actually saved us from this very real threat.

Three very deserving scientists were given the Nobel Prize in Chemistry in 1995 for demonstrating how sensitive the ozone layer is to the influence of emissions of certain compounds. The Nobel Academy cited the three for contributing to our salvation from a global environmental problem that could have had catastrophic consequences. These three scientists were F. Sherwood Roland, Mario Molina, and Paul Crutzen. Crutzen is Dutch and his work preceded Roland and Molina's who worked together at the University of California, Irvine. Crutzen first showed in 1970 that nitrogen oxides in our stratosphere react catalytically with ozone, resulting in a net loss of ozone. His work pointed out the dangers of microbe rich agricultural fertilizers and also of nitrogen oxide emissions from high altitude aircraft. In 1972, Roland and Molina began research regarding the effects of the release into the atmosphere of chlorofluorocarbons (CFC's). By 1974, the pair had figured out the connection between the release of CFC's and ozone depletion in the upper atmosphere. They sounded the alarm, and by the late 1970's the U. S., Canada, Norway, and Sweden had all agreed to ban the use of CFC's in aerosol sprays.

But in 1984, British scientists released their findings regarding the hole in the ozone layer that formed each Spring over Antarctica and everyone took notice. As a result of all the research, an agreement was reached in 1987 called the Montreal Protocol. The Montreal Protocol has now been signed by 150 countries, and it includes a complete ban on the production of CFC's. Scientists now estimate that if the basic research had not already been in place when the ozone hole was discovered, enabling the governmental authorities to take quick and decisive action, then global ozone depletion that measures about 4 percent today, would have been much higher now; probably around ten percent. Clearly, we narrowly averted disaster with this issue.

So.... How is it that we were able to act so quickly and decisively to avert disaster with this issue of ozone depletion when solutions to other global problems like overpopulation, pollution, global warming, and world hunger seem so out of reach? The answer, of course, is there was profit to be made in our salvation from ozone depletion. Solutions to those other problems would involve a reduction in the present level of profit as it concerns some rich and powerful corporations. And, as it turns out, it was just plain luck that the profit motive was available to motivate the chemical companies when quick action was necessary to avert disaster from ozone depletion. All you need to know about this connection is contained in the following quote from Dr. Mostafa Tolba, the former head of the UN Environment Program, which appeared in the June 30, 1990 edition of the New Scientist: " The chemical industry supported the Montreal Protocol in 1987 because it set up a worldwide schedule for phasing out CFC's which were no longer protected by patents. This provided companies with an equal opportunity to market new, more profitable compounds."

Once again, our most important decisions are being made by giant corporations based solely on profit considerations. Luckily for Planet Earth, this decision resulted in both profit and salvation. As we will continue to demonstrate, this situation does not happen often enough.

GLOBAL WARMING AND CLIMATE CHANGE

On the other hand, unluckily for Planet Earth, the issue of global warming and climate change provides a great example of an issue that has not received the proper attention simply because the fix will have devastating effects on the profits of some rich and powerful corporations. The main greenhouse gases that have raised the planet's temperature so dramatically are carbon dioxide from trucks, automobiles, airplanes, ships, factories and electrical generating plants and the fossil fuels that run them, along with methane from mining, natural gas, landfills, and livestock. Of course, the big corporations that manufacture stuff in these factories, as well as those who produce and refine the fossil fuels that run the cars and the factories and the power generating plants, don't want to make changes because the cost of making those changes would come right out of their bottom lines.

I can't think of a better indicator of how complete the takeover of our world by corporate interests is than this issue of global warming. Everyone is familiar with the recent debate, played out in the media for years now. Is global warming really happening? If so, is it really the result of human activities? What bullshit! So far, the fake debate has succeeded in delaying action in regard to this very real threat for more than thirty years since the first global efforts were made to address it. That's thirty years of continued profits for oil and gas companies and other corporations, and thirty years of deteriorating conditions with dire consequences for the world. And in reality, the global initiative to do something about this issue should have been begun much earlier than thirty years ago.

Al Gore made the point in *An Inconvenient Truth* that the battle of misinformation being put out in regard to global warming by pseudo-scientists paid by oil companies is very similar to the campaign of misinformation put out by the tobacco companies about the dangers of smoking. I certainly agree.

The issues involved with global warming and climate change are both simple and extremely complex. The simple part is that we have been pouring greenhouse gases into our atmosphere since the beginning of the Industrial Age, and the greenhouse effect from the addition of these gases to our stratosphere is having a direct and measurable and dramatic effect on planetary temperatures. As a result, our climate is changing. Our glaciers are melting. And our storms are getting stronger. There are countless reasons that we should be doing everything we can to avoid the consequences of our greenhouse gas emissions. But unfortunately, doing so would harm the bottom line of rich and powerful corporate interests, and therefore the problem continues.

The complex part is that there are so many interrelated causes and effects of all of the contributing factors that the powerful interests, who would prefer to keep the greenhouse gases flowing, are able to cast enough doubt upon what they term the question of global warming that nothing of consequence gets accomplished to stop it. The United Nations has been trying to do something. In 1988, they joined with the World Meteorological Association to form the Intergovernmental Panel on Climate Change (IPCC). Out of their work, came an IPCC assessment report of 1990, which drove the agenda for the United Nations Framework Convention on Climate Change, that was opened for signing at the Rio de Janeiro Summit in 1992 and entered into force in 1994. The second IPCC assessment, which came out in 1995, provided the policy framework for the Kyoto Protocol of 1997. The aim of the Kyoto Protocol, which has now been ratified by every developed country in the world except the United States, was to reduce greenhouse gas emissions by 5.2% as compared to the emissions from 1990. I don't know about you, but it sure appears to me that our culture's biggest effort over the past twenty years to do something about global warming has set its sights way too low.

By now, these greenhouse gas emissions have been spewed into our upper atmosphere for so long that even if we somehow stopped them completely today, our planet would still continue warming for many years to come. It certainly appears that we are going to have to deal with dire consequences coming from this issue no matter what we do now. Evidence today suggests that our polar ice caps may disappear completely no matter what we do to try to save them. At this point, I think it is safe to assert that global warming will have a dramatic effect on our climate, our sea levels, and our planetary ecosystems for the foreseeable future.

For those who would like to educate themselves a little more about this situation, I recommend starting with Al Gore's movie, *An Inconvenient Truth*. Gore was introduced to the issue of global warming way back in 1967 when he was a student at Harvard. One of his professors there, Roger Revel, was the first to suggest a connection between carbon dioxide emissions and global warming. Revel first began measuring carbon dioxide in the atmosphere in 1958. By the time Gore took Revel's class there was already a clear upward trend appearing in the data. The issue stayed with Gore, and when he was elected to Congress in 1976, he organized the first Congressional hearings on global warming. Gore's presentation of the issue of global warming and its effects is extremely effective. It's a shame he has not been able to accomplish more in his admirable crusade to save the planet from this peril.

Do you think the type of disconnect that is allowing global warming and climate change could be happening in a world where people believe themselves to be Responsible Members of the Community of Life and where everyone understands that everything is connected?

Consciously, or unconsciously, we have all acquiesced to this situation. I don't think there are too many individuals living today who would make a conscious decision to drive a car powered by an internal combustion engine if they truly understood the consequences and were provided with other reasonable options. But unfortunately, we live in a complex world where all of the big, important decisions are made for us by giant corporations... corporations whose sole basis for making any decision whatsoever is profit.

Fortunately, we can take our world back from these corporate interests who run things. They may have power and wealth, but in the end, they are just artificial creations made by we the people; and their continued existence will occur only with our continued consent. When the people of our culture wake up to the unnecessary destruction these artificial entities are causing, then some of our more pressing issues, like this issue of global warming and others like overpopulation and pollution, can finally be given the attention they deserve.

WAR

As I write this, Wikipedia reports there are fourteen wars being fought around the globe right now. The United Nations defines a conflict as a "war" if it results in the deaths of at least 1,000 people per year. The United States started two of these wars, although it could be argued that the war in Afghanistan was ongoing long before we sent our first troops there in 2001. Our soldiers have been dying and killing enemy combatants, along with innocent civilians, in Iraq and Afghanistan for thirteen and fifteen years, respectively. And in addition to the fourteen wars, there are twenty-seven other lesser conflicts ongoing today where people on one side are fighting and dying against people on the other side who are doing the same. That is a lot of fighting and conflict... Too much... I don't think anyone who really thinks about this can just shrug off fourteen wars and twenty-seven lesser conflicts all happening right now around the world as a natural and acceptable state of affairs.

Usually, we think of wars as armed conflicts featuring one nation against another nation. However, a check of the list of the fourteen wars and the twenty-seven lesser conflicts shows only three that fall into this category. These would be India/Pakistan, Russia/Ukraine, and Israel/Palestine. I'm sure some readers will object to calling the Israeli/Palestinian conflict a conflict between nations, but however you want to classify it... people are dying there on a regular basis, just as they have been for decades.

The conflict between India and Pakistan has been ongoing since 1947. There have only been a little over 200 deaths there during the past year and a half, but since 1947, there have been two all-out wars. Any war between these nuclear powers could easily prove to be problematic for the rest of us who would prefer not to have our planet plunged into a nuclear winter. Apparently, a disagreement over which country Kashmir should be a part of is causing the conflict. The majority of Kashmiris are Muslim, and although close to the border, Kashmir is located within India, which is mostly Hindu.

The last of the three interstate conflicts mentioned above is in Ukraine. I'm sure Russia would prefer to classify the conflict in Ukraine as a civil war, but it appears to me to be a thinly-veiled effort by Russia to take territory from the smaller, weaker country. Over 4,000 people died in this conflict during 2015.

A lot of these conflicts, especially some of the bigger ones with the highest number of casualties, can be classified as civil wars. Examples include the ongoing conflicts in Afghanistan, Syria, Iraq, Libya, Somalia, Yemen, and South Sudan. Of course, these are all Moslem-majority nations; so Islamic extremism is also present in each of these conflicts as well. Certainly, a part of the motivation for at least some of these civil wars is religious-based. At this point, I think it is safe to assert that the entire Muslim world is in turmoil due to the pervasive presence of the two main jihadist organizations, al Qaeda, and the Islamic State, who are competing with each other for Islamic supremacy. Each of them has various affiliates, and the situation is quite fluid.

Another major conflict is the drug war in Mexico, which is more of a criminal action where powerful drug dealers are fighting against each other while, at the same time, they are apparently attempting to break the will of Mexico's police and military by engaging them in gorilla type actions. The casualties of the Mexican drug war are significant... more than 8,000 in 2015, and more than 150,000 during the past ten years.

Then there are the ongoing ethnic conflicts like Darfur in the Sudan, India's Assam insurgency, and others. In Southeast Asia, Myanmar is embroiled in ethnic conflict between at least eight separate factions, each of which controls territory. The Hutu-Tutsi genocidal conflict that claimed more than 1 million lives in several Central African nations, is still simmering, as is the Kivu conflict. And, of course, don't forget the basic "My God is better than your God" wars. Several of the ongoing conflicts mentioned above have this element going on.

The reality is that we live in a very dangerous world. And it is our basic cultural myth of "The World Was Made For Man To Conquer and Rule" that fosters the sense of separation and makes our world so dangerous. During the past two and a half centuries, and especially during the past seventy-five years or so, this danger has been greatly magnified by new technology. Do you realize that more than 160 million people died in wars during the twentieth century? This includes 20 million in World War I and 55 million in World War II. The rest of the casualties occurred in more than one hundred other wars.

In the early days of our culture, before technology changed things, wars were very personal matters. In those days, all of the killing in battle was done by hand-to-hand combat. No matter how great a warrior you are, you can only kill one person at a time with your knife, or your sword, or your spear, or even with your bow and arrow. Now, with the aid of technology, one present-day person could push a button and send nuclear missiles flying to kill every inhabitant in several large cities. And he could do so from a safe location thousands of miles away. It seems like each new advancement in technology quickly turns into a new way to kill our enemies more anonymously. Many of the newest technological advancements involve robotics. Can war become any more impersonal than it is already? We are sending our robots out to kill people!

Is it pretty obvious to you that a sense of separateness is necessary for these wars to be happening?

Our culture's historic and present involvement in the activity called "war" is the most visible and tangible evidence of our failure to abide by the Peacekeeping Law. There are, of course, many other examples, most of which involve species like wolves or coyotes, or pesky insects like boll weevils or mosquitoes, or troublesome plants like dandelions or crab grass.

But 160 million members of our culture died in wars during the twentieth century. Although I was born nine years after the end of World War II, many millions of those millions of people who died in wars during the twentieth century did so during my lifetime. And many more are continuing to die today. For many of us, including myself, this is a very personal statistic. My uncle, who I was named after, was one of the people who died as a result of these wars. Is the fact that all of these wars are going on today, together with the fact that it is a certainty more will begin in the days to come, really okay with everybody? Is this something that we should just accept as a natural part of life? Or does anyone think we should consider taking a hard look at "war" and maybe decide to do something about it?

Certainly, one of the main factors leading directly to war and armed conflicts is military spending. And one of the main ingredients in this secondary issue of military spending is "profit". The world would be a much better place if we had been able to heed

Dwight Eisenhower's warning about the need to watch out for the "undue influence" from the military-industrial complex.

We should all keep in mind that every gun carried by every soldier anywhere on the planet, represents a piece of the bottom line for the corporation that manufactured and sold it. Likewise, every bullet fired from any of those guns, or any shell, or any missile, or any grenade, or any bomb used to kill and maim innocent civilians or enemy combatants in any of these fourteen ongoing wars, or these twenty-seven ongoing lesser conflicts... not to mention any of the tanks, ships, aircraft, or any of the other equipment utilized by any of the various armies around the world, somehow figure into another profit and loss statement for a corporation. There is no doubt... Eisenhower was right to warn us about "undue influence".

Ostensibly, the United States is a peaceful, modern democracy with no desires for conquest. Why, then, do we feel the need to maintain what is far and away the most powerful military on the planet? Here are some facts and figures I found online provided by The Center For Arms Control and Non-Proliferation. We are No. 1 in military spending. Our annual defense budget is bigger than the next 11 biggest national defense budgets combined... We are No. 2 in the number of soldiers, with more than 1,430,000 on active duty. (China is No. 1 with 2,285,000.) We have the third most number of tanks with 8,325. (Russia has the most with 15,000, and China has the second most with 9,150.) We have far more military aircraft and far more aircraft carriers than any other country. (Almost as many of each as all of the other countries combined.) And we are second to Russia in the number of nuclear weapons at our disposal. (7,506 to 8,504)

This issue of "war" was mentioned in Chapter Four under the heading of "Something Will Save Us". I said then that our cultural myth about war tells us the answer lies in preparedness. At least that is the myth that our culture tells those of us who live in the richest and most powerful nation on the planet. But the cultural myth about preparedness has definitely taken a beating during the past few years. The United States armed forces are certainly not as impressive and awe-inspiring after eight years with George W. Bush as their commander-in-chief.

A military action in Afghanistan that really should have been a police action looking for the criminal Osama Bin Laden was maybe somewhat justified (on one level, at least). However, the effort there lost its focus when the Bush administration lied us into an insane and ill-advised military action in Iraq which then dragged on and on as a war of occupation. Our men and women in uniform are tired of fighting unseen enemies and of dying in roadside bomb attacks and in other similar situations where there is no enemy lined up for them to fight. And consequently, we are much less prepared to meet new threats today than we were before these conflicts began.

But of course, the real answer to the problem of "war" does not lie in preparedness, as our insane culture would have us believe. That is just another of the many lies our culture tells us in order to perpetuate itself. The real solution to the problem of "war" lies in a return to an adherence to the Peacekeeping Law and to a rejection of the cultural myth that tells us the world was made for man to conquer and rule. Until we solve this one at the basic cultural level, there will continue to be classical wars involving nation against nation.... There will be civil wars involving a revolutionary force against an entrenched government.... There will be religious wars fought to determine whose God is the real God.... There will be racial wars fought over skin color or ethnic background.... And there will be economic wars of aggression fought over territory. And innocent people will continue to die... maybe even you or someone you love, or maybe even you and many someones you love.

It is also my contention that once the basic needs have been met for all people everywhere, then one of the most common, and one of the most basic reasons, for fighting and conflict will no longer exist.

TERRORISM

Several of the articles I read when researching this issue made the point that there is no widely agreed upon definition of terrorism. The reason cited is that, depending upon which side you are on, one person's terrorist is another person's freedom fighter. The best definition I found for terrorism was one proposed in 1992 by Alex P. Schmid, a Dutch scholar in terrorism studies, who was working for the Crime Branch of United Nations. His definition is "Act of Terrorism = Peacetime Equivalent of a War Crime".

Terrorism is a tactic designed to instill fear and insecurity within the general population. Acts of terror are almost always directed towards innocent civilians. Typically, it is the smaller, weaker side of a conflict that utilizes terrorism. The terrorists are almost always on the side not associated with an established government, and usually, but not always, the side not supported by a conventional military force. Examples of terrorist organizations that do have military forces are Hezbollah, Hamas, and ISIS. The implied threat of the terrorists is, "Give us what we want, or the next act of terror might be directed towards you or your family."

Common terrorism tactics include kidnapping, murder, car bombing, suicide bombing, other targeted IED bombings, and airline hijacking. According to a Wikipedia article, ISIS has claimed responsibility for more than 200 beheadings during the past two years and has posted videos of many of them. In their attack in Paris on November 13, 2015, ISIS employed a new tactic I call "suicide shooting". Another new tactic being utilized by terrorists is vehicular homicide where large trucks are driven into crowds of people.

The big worry faced by those of us who consider ourselves to be potential targets for terrorists is that the terrorists will acquire a dirty bomb, or even worse, a more sophisticated nuclear device. So far, thankfully, that hasn't occurred. I imagine it would be extremely difficult for a person possessed with a functioning moral compass to justify targeting innocent civilians, but apparently, there is a willingness by many of the underdog terrorist organizations and the people within them to do just that. If this issue of terrorism does not provide us with a strong indication that we live in a culture where people believe everything is separate, then I don't know what would.

I think it is pretty easy to see that if you live in a world where everything is separate, it is much more likely that your world is one where someone might blow I up on a crowded bus in order to kill one hundred of his or her supposed enemies, and to strike terror into the rest of us. Can you see this type of thing happening in a world where everyone understands that everything is connected, and where every individual knows himself or herself to be a part of the world and a part of the Community of Life? How about a world where nobody has to worry about their basic needs being met?

The U. S. State Department maintains a web page that lists foreign terrorist organizations. Currently, there are fifty-nine terrorist organizations on the list. Twelve others were formerly listed but have been removed. As I look through the list, it appears to me that all of the most active ones… being the ones I am most familiar with… are allied with Islamic extremism. Interestingly, when I researched domestic terrorism, many of the terrorist groups operating in the U. S, have fundamentalist Christian roots.

As discussed in the previous chapter, one big reason for terrorism is religious differences arising out of peoples' belief in a fairytale that tells them we will all answer to a judgmental God. By far, the biggest offenders here are the Muslims. The suicide bombers are all Muslims who believe they will be rewarded by Allah when they blow themselves up, along with as many infidels as possible, because they believe Allah wants desperately for the non-believers to die. This belief that a suicide bomber will be transported directly to heaven where he or she will enjoy many special privileges is widely held in the Muslim world. It arises by reading certain very explicit passages from the Quran. Another big reason for a person to

choose to be a suicide bomber is because, before they put on that
vest, they made arrangements with the terrorist group who planned
and enabled the attack, to provide for his or her family to be well
compensated for their sacrifice.

According to testimony before the House Subcommittee on
Counterterrorism and Intelligence given on April 29, 2015, by
Daniel L. Byman, the Research Director for the Center for Middle
East Policy for the Brookings Institute, the two most influential
terrorist groups at the present time are Al Qaeda, and ISIS. Of the
two, Al Qaeda has been around the longest. Osama Bin Laden
started Al Qaeda in the 1980's by capitalizing on the successful
jihad achieved by the Mujahedeen against the Soviet Union in
Afghanistan. By the mid-1990's, Al Qaeda had shifted its focus to
the United States, initiating numerous terrorist attacks against U. S.
targets with the stated goal of causing the U. S. to withdraw from the
Middle East. The attacks in the U. S. on September 11, 2001, were
Al Qaeda's biggest success, but they also resulted in intense
retaliation by U. S. forces. According to the aforementioned
testimony by Daniel L. Byman:

"... the U. S. counterterrorism response that followed
was devastating to both Al Qaeda and the broader
movement it purported to lead. Over the next decade, the
U. S. relentlessly pursued Al Qaeda, targeting its
leadership, disrupting its finances, destroying its training
camps, infiltrating its communications networks, and
ultimately crippling its ability to function. It remained a
symbol of the global jihadist movement, but its inability
to successfully launch another major attack against the
United States meant that symbol was becoming less
powerful. The death of the charismatic Bin Laden and
the ascension of the much less compelling Ayman al-

Zawahiri to the top leadership position further diminished the power of the Al Qaeda brand"

It is important to note that these successes by the U. S. against Al Qaeda as given in Byman's testimony, are for the most part not military successes. Almost all of the successful effort by the U. S. against Al Qaeda can be credited to efforts by U. S. Intelligence forces. I also think Byman's testimony points out a very important fact about the success of the counterterrorism effort. The successes he points to when he mentions "targeting its leadership, disrupting its finances, destroying its training camps, infiltrating its communications networks, and ultimately crippling its ability to function," are… to me… appropriate responses to the threat posed by Al Qaeda. On the other hand, the wars in Iraq and Afghanistan were not appropriate responses… far from it.

In his testimony, Byman pointed out that because the goal of both Al Qaeda and ISIS is to lead all Muslims everywhere, these two enemies of the U. S. are in competition with each other, a fact that serves to somewhat diminish their effectiveness. Byman also testified that Al Qaeda and ISIS have very different strategies. Al Qaeda has stated publicly on numerous occasions that the U. S. is its main enemy. Its main goal is to cause the U. S. to leave the Middle East, thereby leaving the many corrupt and apostate regimes vulnerable to being overthrown by Al Qaeda and replaced with "true" Islamic governments. ISIS, on the other hand, pursues a strategy based on controlling territory, and utilizing that territory as a base for further expansions. Here is another excerpt from Byrne's testimony in regard to ISIS:

"The Islamic State does not follow Al Qaeda's "far enemy" strategy, preferring instead the "near enemy" strategy, albeit on a regional level. As such, the primary target of the Islamic State has not been the United States, but rather "apostate" regimes around the Arab world—namely, the Asad regime in Syria and the Abadi regime in Iraq. Like his predecessors, Baghadi favors purifying the Islamic community first by attacking Shi'a and other religious minorities as well as rival jihadist groups. The Islamic State's long list of enemies includes the Iraqi Shi'a, the Lebanese Hezbollah, the Yazidis (a Kurdish ethno-religious minority located predominantly in Iraq), and rival opposition groups in Syria (including Jabhat al-Nusra, the official Al Qaeda affiliate in Syria)."

In June of 2014, in a move that shocked the world, ISIS military forces captured large parts of northern and western Iraq, including two major cities, and important infrastructure facilities. Afterwards, ISIS officially declared the establishment of a caliphate in the territory under its control and named their leader, Abu Kakr al-Baghdadi, the Caliph for all Muslims.

Unfortunately, as evidenced by major terrorist attacks in Paris (November 13, 2015) and Brussels (March 22, 2016), ISIS appears to have expanded their strategy to one including Al Qaeda's strategy of more far reaching attacks.

There is no doubt that Al Qaeda and ISIS represent a serious threat. But there is a reason they pose a threat to us.... They see the United States as an imperial power attempting to control the Middle East by power, influence, and a huge military presence. And their perception is correct. The United States has combat troops in Afghanistan and Iraq, and military bases in Kuwait, Bahrain, Qatar, the United Arab Emirates, and Oman. They have training facilities in Saudi Arabia and Jordan, and all of these nations plus Egypt have billions of dollars of the best fighter jets and military equipment that can be bought with their oil money. And don't forget the longtime beneficiary of U. S. defense aid... Israel. The terrorists want us gone. They want the Middle Eastern countries to govern themselves, without any Western influences.

Even though ISIS is garnering almost all of the media attention, we should keep in mind there are 58 other foreign terrorist organizations on that State Department list. And in addition to the foreign terrorist organizations, there are domestic terrorist organizations as well. Although I could not find a comprehensive list, I did find a "Top Ten" list of U. S. based terrorist organizations that included the Klu Klux Klan, the Sovereign Citizens, the Earth Liberation Front, the Jewish Defense League, and the Phineas Priesthood. In my lifetime, the world has seen dramatic acts of terrorism performed by the Weather Underground, the Black Panthers, the Palestinian Liberation Organization, the Irish Republican Army, and many others.

Of course, to many people around the world... the terrorists are us.

How do you think the people of Japan looked upon us after we dropped atomic bombs on Hiroshima and Nagasaki? How did the German people of Dresden feel about being fire bombed? How do you think the Vietnamese people felt about us after our soldiers burned their villages and after we carpet bombed their country with more than three times the total amount of explosives dropped by the U. S. and our allies in World War II? And that doesn't even count the estimated 8 million tons of napalm and 20 million gallons of Agent Orange we also dropped on them! In more recent times, how do you think the prisoners at Abu Graib, Guantanamo Bay, and the CIA black sites felt about being tortured?

Could we cite justifications for these actions? Sure, we could. But that doesn't make it right. And that certainly doesn't mean that innocent people in Germany, Japan, Vietnam, Iraq, Afghanistan, and elsewhere didn't suffer, and didn't blame the United States of America for their suffering.

I would like to close this examination of terrorism by considering our response to the attacks of 9/11. On May 2, 2011, almost ten years after 9/11, an elite force of U. S. Navy Seals, in an operation watched by President Obama and his National Security team on a live feed, Osama Bin Laden was made to pay the ultimate price for planning the 9/11 attacks. That is what I would call an appropriate response to the attacks of 9/11. As many have pointed out before me... terrorism is a tactic. And you can't wage a war against a tactic. Just like our "War on Drugs" is absurd, our "War on Terrorism" is absurd. Fortunately, as outlined in the Congressional testimony of Daniel L. Bynum, our intelligence agencies have been pursuing the correct course of action in regard to Al Qaeda. Unfortunately however, our military forces have been pursuing the wrong course of action.... The wars in Afghanistan and Iraq have only made the situation worse.

Did you know that the Taliban in Afghanistan did not refuse to turn over Osama Bin Laden? No.... They asked for proof of his guilt. But, instead of talking, and instead of providing evidence, the Bush administration called the request for evidence a "delaying tactic" and elected to engage our military in an illegal act of aggression. What did we gain by ignoring UN rules of engagement and starting an illegal war in Afghanistan? Fifteen years later, I don't see much of anything positive. On the other hand, the negative results are pretty apparent.

What would have been the harm in engaging the Taliban in a diplomatic discussion about turning over Osama Bin Laden? Could the problem with that option possibly lie in its potential for success? Did we need an excuse to send our troops and bombs that negotiation might have removed?

We in the United States of America hold ourselves out to the rest of the world as a superpower with principles. Yet, our response to a small, relatively insignificant, criminal organization, who managed to successfully pull off an act of terrorism that killed 3,000 of our citizens was to invade two countries in order to start two wars that have so far lasted seventeen and nineteen years, have resulted in the loss of hundreds of thousands of lives and have destabilized an entire region of the globe. Certainly, if we really were a principled superpower, then we could have created a more principled (and successful) response.

When the planes hit on 9/11, the innocent victims and our shocked nation had the sympathy of the whole world. Candlelight vigils were held in Tehran, and in Beijing, tens of thousands of people left flowers, cards, funeral wreaths, and notes of condolences on the sidewalk in front of the U. S. Embassy. Too bad for us, and too bad for the world, that we didn't have any leadership here in the United States of America that were capable of calming our fears and taking the proper action in regard to the small band of criminals who had attacked us.

THREAT OF NUCLEAR WAR

To the surprise of many of us, we somehow survived the Cold War. I'm sure there were times when our survival seemed problematic to the Russian and U. S. leaders who had their fingers hovering over the launch button. Without question, the Cuban Missile Crisis was a close call. Apparently, the thing that saw us through the Cold War was the concept of "Mutually Assured Destruction". The Russian leaders knew as well as we did, that if one of us pushed the button, then the other would do the same.

Today, there are nine countries that have nuclear arsenals at their disposal. Together, these nine nuclear powers have the capability of destroying this planet one hundred times over. So far, the United States is the only country that has used these terrible weapons against another country. Harry Truman holds the responsibility for making that terrible decision. He shouldn't have done it.

Up to now, the world has survived this very real threat because the people with the authority to launch nuclear weapons within those countries are aware of the terrible consequences and have shown the proper restraint. But, Pakistan is a country with Muslim majority and an unstable government. They have a large nuclear arsenal. What happens to those nuclear weapons in the event of a governmental coup by Islamic extremists?

And don't forget the other nuclear power that is run by the most oppressive dictator on the planet, North Korea. Kim Jong-un has been in the news lately because he has been developing his missile capability. He wants the ability to launch his nuclear bombs on long-range missiles, just as the United States, Russia, and the other nuclear powers can. Clearly, the rest of the world cannot stand by and let this obviously deluded maniac have the ability to launch a nuclear attack with long-range missiles. Our new president, Donald Trump seems to think brinkmanship is the answer. We shall see.

At some point… hopefully soon… our world leaders are going to have to realize it is not healthy for any of these nuclear weapons to exist anywhere. In a world where everyone knows that everything is connected, and man behaves as a responsible member of the Community of Life, what purpose would nuclear weapons serve? We have to disarm, before something terrible happens.

RAMPANT CRIME

Most people, especially people living in any city in the world, think about protecting themselves from criminal activity every day. For instance, do you lock your door when you leave your house or your car? Do you avoid certain areas where you might otherwise go because of a concern for your safety? What does this say to you?

Everyone understands that criminals are everywhere. Anywhere we go on this planet, we all understand there are people somewhere in the vicinity who will steal our possessions if we don't secure them. And worse, there are people all over the planet who would forcibly take our cash or other valuables from us if they thought they could do so and get away with it. Home-invasion robberies are common. You read about them all the time. And car-jackings are common as well. Every day in every city on the planet, people are forcibly robbed when they thought they were safe just walking, or even driving down the street. We all know this goes on. I think each of us just prays it doesn't happen to us or to someone close to us.

Every nation has laws in place prohibiting theft, murder, assault, and forcible rape. And, most countries have laws prohibiting counterfeiting, forgery, tax evasion, money laundering, fraud, bribery, embezzlement, arson, blackmail, extortion, and trading in stolen property. Certainly, the laws regarding the sale, use, and possession of illicit drugs vary somewhat among nations, as do laws regarding gambling and prostitution. If you commit a crime, then you have performed an illegal act that can be punished by government. If you are charged with the commission of a criminal act in the United States, then you are "presumed innocent until proven guilty". If you are charged with a crime in a country with a more authoritarian government, this may not be the case.

What motivates people to steal things? It depends upon which things you are asking about. If you are talking about somebody shoplifting diapers from the corner store, the motivation is probably economic stress either brought on or magnified by the responsibilities of parenthood. If you are talking about the motivation for armed robbers, or burglars, or jewel thieves, the answer is almost always that they do it because they are completely and totally devoted to a lifestyle of crime.

The extent that a person considers himself or herself to be a criminal is a yardstick by which we can measure the extent of that person's rejection of our culture, and that person's participation in the counterculture of criminality. This fact is significant because it is important for us to recognize that there are millions, of people living all around the world who have already rejected our culture. Unfortunately, though, the rejection of our culture by criminals is not the sort of rejection we are advocating in this book.

Some examples of powerful criminal organizations are the American Mafia, the Irish Mob, the Russian Mafia, the Japanese Yakuza, the Chinese Triad, the Medellin Cartel, the Cali Cartel, the various Mexican Cartels, including the Zetas, Sinolas, and the Gulf and the Tijuana Cartels, and the Sicilian Mafia, otherwise known as the Cosa Nostra. Some of the organizations set out above are either no longer in operation, or their power has been greatly diminished. The defeated crime syndicates include the Medellin and Cali Cartels of Columbia. And the American Mafia and the Irish Mob, while still in operation, may not be as powerful as they once were, at least relative to the other criminal organizations.

It also should be noted that although Al-Qaeda, the Taliban, and ISIS have mostly religious and political goals, they also have many similarities to organized crime syndicates. For instance, it has been widely reported in the news recently that ISIS has a daily income of more than one million dollars. I assure you... The bulk of this income is not derived from legitimate means.

Although organized crime or the criminal counterculture, in the form of pirates, highwaymen, and bandits, has been around for millennia, the formal criminal organizations of today represent a much more powerful and structured organization than seen previously. The reason for their increased power is that these modern crime syndicates have branched out from the historical model of piracy and general banditry into the businesses of providing people with illegal goods and services. Among the new, more profitable practices are gambling, prostitution, and the sale of illegal drugs. Of course, one of the biggest events to jumpstart the existence of modern-day organized crime was the prohibition of alcohol in the United States, which was accomplished by Constitutional Amendment, and was in effect between 1920 and 1933. I think it is safe to say that if it had not been for Prohibition, we would never have heard of Al Capone. While it is obvious to most progressive thinkers that a totally analogous situation is transpiring today with the criminal organizations involved in the sale and distribution of illegal drugs, it appears that our lawmakers do not make that same connection.

Most of the large, organized crime syndicates of today operate internationally. A big part of their operations involves money laundering, and the process is accomplished with the help of many crooked banks and governments. It is estimated that over $750 billion is laundered from illicit gains to quasi-legitimate businesses annually, with $300 billion of that total going through the United States.

A rung down on the level of organized crime is the gang level. Gangs, which are also known as youth gangs or criminal street gangs, are comprised of three or more individuals, usually between the ages of 12 and 24. In order to meet the recognized definition of a gang, these young individuals must consider themselves to be members of a gang, and also be involved as a gang in organized criminal activities. Gangs can be found in most of the high-crime, disadvantaged neighborhoods located in every large city in the U. S. Two of the larger and more famous gangs are the Crips and the Bloods from South Los Angeles.

Did crime exist in the tribal societies we eradicated? Maybe a little, but certainly not to the extent it exists in our culture. Remember, in a typical tribe nobody was cold or hungry unless everyone in the tribe was cold or hungry. Crime in tribal societies was unusual for sure. But if a member of a tribe ever stole a possession that didn't belong to him or her, it was an aberration that was dealt with in accordance with ancient and proven tribal customs. The main reason it was unusual was because tribal people were born into a world where people knew themselves to be a part of the Community of Life. Everyone knew that everything was connected. Besides, the food was not locked up for the tribal people like it is for us. When everyone's basic needs of food, shelter, water, health care, and sanitary living conditions have been met, there is much less of a motivation for anyone to steal anything.

It is my contention that all crimes and all criminal activity of today can be traced to this first criminal act from ten thousand years ago, of somebody locking up the food. That is why people devote themselves to a lifestyle of crime.... They have been born into an insane culture based upon the false premise that everything is separate.

Of course this is a huge subject... and a controversial one, as well. Certainly, one of the more popular and widely accepted theories about the reasons people resort to crime is that criminals are just too lazy to work, and they also lack the moral character that keeps a normal person from becoming a criminal. My point is this... Civilization could have been established without locking up the food. Although, if it had been done that way, there would be no need for me to be writing this book. Our world could have transitioned from one populated by tribes of hunter-gatherers to an agricultural-based, civilized society without the inequality and strife and depravity that characterizes our culture of today. So, given the obvious wrongness of the act of locking up the food... How can you blame a person from that world of ten thousand years ago for stealing the food that should never have been locked up in the first place? And, by extension.... How can you blame a person in our present-day world for resorting to theft after they are born into an insane culture that tells them there is not enough resources for them to be able to have food or shelter, or sanitary living conditions, or medical care, simply because they do not have enough money to pay for it? Especially when the actual reality is that those resources are indeed available. And most especially, how can you blame desperate and poor people for resorting to crime when they can look around themselves and see all of the unpunished financial crimes involving zillions of dollars that are being committed by the Wall Street firms, and other big corporations, and by the wealthy and the privileged?

Why do you think the story of Robin Hood is so popular? Or how about the story of Pancho Villa? Or, Butch and Sundance? Bonnie and Clyde? Or, how about the present-day story of Coltin Harris-Moore, the Barefoot Bandit?

I do not want to give the impression that I consider every person who commits a crime to be a heroic figure, I certainly do not think that is the case. I do, however, want to make the case as strongly as possible that the inherent injustice that exists in our insane culture is directly responsible for a large portion of our criminal activity. Hopefully, I have accomplished that.

I also would like to point out... When the Critical Mass of people who understand how we came to be where we are as a culture has been achieved, and we stand ready to re-build a new culture based upon the truths that everything is connected, and humans need to take their place as Responsible Members of the Community of Life, then we will need to include as many people as possible from this criminal counterculture. In fact, it will be imperative that we strive to include every person who is willing. Those who are not, will need to be dealt with in another manner. Hopefully, we will be able to ignore them until they either decide to join us, or until their organizations wither and die from attrition. If not, then our elected leaders will need to make some important decisions.

OVERCROWDED PRISONS

Yes, people in our culture steal things. And they sell illegal drugs. And they possess and use illegal drugs. And they fight amongst themselves. And sometimes people assault or kill each other. And sexual deviants and sexual predators molest others whenever they find an opportunity to do so. And unless you happen to be a privileged member of the upper class, if you commit one of these crimes, then you could very well go to prison.

Prisons, along with capital punishment are our culture's answer to crime. We all know there are lots of bad people out there who will steal our stuff if we are not careful. And worse, there are many who are prone to violence that we need to be protected from. And don't forget the sexual predators who might forcibly rape us or someone we love, or even sexually molest our children if given the opportunity. Prison, or the threat of capital punishment, is here to act as a deterrent. Prison is there so each of these bad people can think twice before committing a criminal act. Bad people need to realize that if they make a bad decision and commit a crime there is a high likelihood they will be caught and punished. And if the deterrent doesn't work, then catching these dangerous people and executing them or putting them behind bars keeps the rest of us safe from them by preventing them from committing more crimes.

Let's take a look at this "lock 'em up" strategy in terms of how it is working here in the U. S. The United States has 2.3 million of its inhabitants behind bars, and another 5 million of our citizens are either on probation or out of jail on parole. In terms of the number of people incarcerated, that is way more than any other country in the world. China, despite the fact that it has a population of more than four times the population of the United States, comes in a distant second in this category with 1.6 million of their inhabitants in jail. In terms of the percentage of the population in jail, the U. S. is also first, although Russia is not too far behind. In the United States, approximately 751 out of every 100,000 people in the country are in prison. In Russia the number is 627 out of every 100,000. No other county in the world even comes close to Russia and the United States in regard to this statistic.

Accordingly, if the strategy is to put all the bad guys behind bars, then the U. S. should be a good test of that strategy. So.... How's it working for us? As we said in the beginning of our earlier discussion about crime, we do not feel safe. Accordingly, there must still be a few more people out there who need to be locked up for us to feel safe. What if we built enough prisons so that we could put the five million of us who are either on probation or parole in prison? If we did so, then one out of every 32 adults would be behind bars. Do you think that would be enough? Or do you think we better build even more prisons. How many more people do you think we need to lock up in order for us to feel safe from crime? Two million? Ten million? More?

Where does this "lock 'em up" strategy end? How many of us have to go to prison so the rest of us can be safe? Is crime going to be over when we have thirty out of every one hundred adults in prison?

I submit to you that a much better strategy would be to walk away from this flawed and doomed culture, which is based on separation, and to establish a new culture based upon the true nature of our universe… Everything is connected.

Except for a very few people born with certain genetic flaws, these so-called bad people are not actually born with a predisposition to do bad things. Many of them are just made desperate by the fact that they are born into a world where everyone is separate, the food is locked up, and only the strongest (or richest) survive. Most are born into dysfunctional families, with parents who were, themselves, born into dysfunctional families. And, most of them are born into the lower class and grew up in a world where they had to struggle just to meet their basic needs of food, water, shelter, clothing, etc. Not only that, but they have had to watch many of us move around them every day in our fancy cars and nice clothes, knowing that our level of affluence was something completely out of their reach.

In 1997, 3,500 people came together in Berkley for a three-day conference in which a nationwide organization called Critical Resistance was formed. The stated purpose of Critical Resistance wants to abolish the prison industrial complex. Here is the mission statement for Critical Resistance as set out on their website.

> Critical Resistance seeks to build an international movement to end the Prison Industrial Complex by challenging the belief that caging and controlling people makes us safe. We believe that basic necessities such as food, shelter, and freedom are what really make our

communities secure. As such, our work is part of global struggles against inequality and powerlessness. The success of the movement requires that it reflect communities most affected by the PIC. Because we seek to abolish the PIC, we cannot support any work that extends its life or scope.

Like the members of Critical Resistance, I also believe that providing basic necessities such as food, shelter, and freedom to all people can make our communities secure. According to the Equal Justice Initiative website, we spend $182 billion on mass incarceration annually. They make the point, as I did earlier in this piece, that even with all of these people being incarcerated, we still do not feel safe. I contend that the $182 billion we spend each year on mass incarceration could be much better spent by providing food, shelter, medical services, and other social services for underprivileged people. If we spent the money on basic needs instead of on incarceration, we would feel much safer, as well as much more connected and responsible.

POLICE BRUTALITY

In 1963, the Los Angeles Police department was the first to adopt the motto, "To Protect and Serve". Since then, many other police departments across the country, including our municipal police department here in Austin, have adopted that same slogan. After researching this issue of police brutality, it appears to me that maybe these police departments should consider adopting different mottos. Some suggestions I have are "To Scare and Intimidate". Or how about "To Murder and Incarcerate". Or maybe, "To Protect and Serve Ourselves and the Wealthy Elite".

There is no question that our police departments around the country are full of police officers who joined their local police forces for good, altruistic reasons, including ones that would be compatible with a "To Protect and Serve" slogan. Once there, though, almost all of them found themselves to be a part of a twisted and sick organization that was full of violence and systemic racism, whose abuses were concealed behind the "blue code of silence". Because fellow officers never snitch on each other, transgressions by policemen that run the entire spectrum of wrongs, from the trivial all the way up to and including murder, are routinely swept under the rug. After all, the police are an integral part of the justice system. Considering the relationship of the police with the prosecutors and the court system, not to mention their supposed position as our protectors, together with the extremely powerful blue code of silence, it is not too surprising that the police around the country could escape culpability for a lot of wrongdoing.

When you look into their history, police departments in this country have never, ever come close to living up to their "To Protect and Serve" motto. Here in the US, our modern police departments were born during colonial days as slave patrols. As you can imagine, there were not a lot of regulations in place in those early days of our country that were meant to keep the slave patrol personnel from using excessive force and intimidation against slaves. The first two cities to establish their own municipal police departments were Boston in 1838 and New York in 1845. By 1890, all of the major US cities had police departments, and corruption and brutality were common within all of them.

These days, with all of us carrying around easily accessible video recording devices as a part of our smart phones, we have all seen numerous videos of police brutality and murder that in earlier times would never have been recorded. Without the video evidence, the officers would typically deny any excessive force or wrongdoing, and their fellow officers would either adhere to the blue code of silence or corroborate the offending officer's false account of the incident. Typically, before the age of widespread video, the prosecutors and the court system always sided with the officers and enabled them to either escape culpability totally, or to accept a slap on the wrist such as a minor suspension or reprimand. Now, with all of this video evidence, we may be on the verge of seeing some real accountability for many of these cases of brutality, excessive force, and murder.

On March 3, 1991 in Los Angeles, before the advent of smart phones, a bystander used a camera to videotape Rodney King's brutal beating by eight police officers. It happened after a protracted high-speed chase when King refused to stop his car after officers attempted to pull him over for speeding. King and his two friends who were in the car with him had been drinking and watching a basketball game, and King later admitted that he was attempting to outrun the officers because a DUI conviction would have violated the terms of his parole and returned him to prison.

The video of the beating was provided to local news, and it subsequently went viral before "going viral" was even a thing. Because of the undeniably brutal beating by these peace officers, four of the them were charged with assault and excessive force. On April 29, 1992, when a jury acquitted all four of them, riots broke out in Los Angeles and in several other cities as well. During the six nights of riots in LA, 63 people died, 2,383 were injured, and almost $1 billion of property was damaged.

Due to the strong public sentiment, a second trial was immediately undertaken in federal court, and in that trial, two of the officers were found guilty of violating Rodney King's civil rights. Both of the convicted officers were sentenced to 30 months in prison and the two other officers were acquitted. King also won a civil lawsuit against the city of Los Angeles and was awarded $3.8 million. Because of the video and all of the hoopla that came with it, King never faced any charges for speeding or attempting to evade arrest.

The past several years have provided numerous high profile police killings of mostly black citizens in condemnable circumstances, and each of these killings has caused mass protests and calls for justice and reform. Among them were the killing of Eric Garner whose suffocation while a police officer held him in a chokehold on Staten Island was captured on video by a bystander; Tamir Rice, a 12-year-old playing with a toy gun at a local park in Cleveland, whose shooting was captured by a surveillance camera; Walter Scott, who was shot in the back while running from an officer after a traffic stop for a broken tail light in North Charleston, and whose murder was captured on video by a bystander's cellphone; Freddie Gray, who died in police custody after being arrested in Baltimore when he tried to run away for no other reason except that he was scared when he saw two policemen on bicycles in his vicinity; Michael Brown, who was shot six times by an officer attempting to arrest him in Ferguson, MO; Terence Crutcher, who was shot by the police officer who was called to investigate why Crutcher's SUV was stopped in the middle of a Tulsa street with the engine running; and Philando Castile, who was shot five times at close range while in his car after a traffic stop in a suburb of St. Paul.

We have had way too many killings of black men by the police right here in Austin, including our most recent one that took place on April 24, 2020, when Michael Ramos, a 42-year-old black man who attended the same high school as my son twenty-two years earlier, was shot while trying to drive away from an unnecessarily out of control police confrontation in front of his apartment. The entire incident was caught on video by a bystander and was also widely viewed. The APD officer who shot Michael Ramos was also one of two officers who shot and killed a man experiencing a mental health crisis in downtown Austin in July of 2019.

On May 25, 2020, the killing of George Floyd, whose suffocation death by a Minneapolis police officer was captured on video, has caused nationwide and even worldwide protests that lasted more than a month after Floyd's killing. The large crowds of demonstrators took to the streets protesting all of these killings along with the more recent killing of Breonna Taylor and Rayshard

Brooks. Breonna Taylor was a 26-year-old, totally innocent EMT who was shot eight times and died in a hallway of her apartment on March 13, 2020, after Louisville Police executed a no-knock raid wearing plain clothes. They entered her apartment by breaking down her door in the middle of the night. No drugs were found. Rayshard Brooks was another unarmed black man killed by a police officer. His shooting that took place on June 12, 2020, in the parking lot of a Wendy's in Atlanta was videotaped, widely viewed, and served to increase the fervor and participation in the nationwide protests that were still ongoing after George Floyd's killing.

And the protests are having an impact. George Floyd was killed by Minneapolis police officer Derek Chauvin who knelt on Floyd's neck for almost nine minutes while Floyd laid face down on the pavement, handcuffed and repeatedly saying "I can't breathe". During this time, two other Minneapolis police officers also helped to restrain Floyd, and a third prevented bystanders from intervening. Floyd was motionless and had no pulse during the final three minutes that Chauvin knelt on his neck.

All four of these officers have been fired from the Minneapolis police department, and all four have been arrested and charged with crimes in connection to George Floyd's death. Chauvin was initially charged with third-degree murder and second-degree manslaughter, but after reactions by protesters, a charge of second-degree murder was added. The other three officers have been charged with aiding and abetting a person who committed second-degree murder. Chauvin and one other officer are still in jail pending trial. Two other officers have posted bail of $1 million and are free pending their trials. It certainly appears that all four officers are in very big trouble, and rightfully so.

Garrett Rolfe, the Atlanta police officer who shot Rayshard Brooks twice in the back as he was running away, has been fired. He also has been charged with eleven crimes including felony murder. He has been denied bond and is being held in an Atlanta jail pending his trial. Devin Brosnan, the other officer involved in the attempted arrest of Rayshard Brooks has been placed on administrative leave and has also been charged with four crimes including aggravated assault. Brosnan is free on bail.

Unfortunately, since Breonna Taylor was killed during a no-knock raid on her apartment pursuant to a legally acquired warrant, her family is probably not going to receive a lot of justice for her death, though it is likely they will ultimately receive a sizable settlement from the city of Louisville. Of the three Louisville police officers who fired their weapons in Breonna Taylor's apartment, one has been fired and the other two have been placed on administrative reassignment. The fired officer, Brett Hankison has also been accused of sexual assault by multiple women in recent weeks who say the assaults happened after he offered them rides home from bars, where they had become too intoxicated to drive themselves. Considering that Hankison will probably escape punishment for his role in the death of Breonna Taylor, I imagine he is probably in a lot of trouble for the sexual assault allegations, which of course, he should be anyway.

But it is definitely a positive development that the families of George Floyd and Rayshard Brooks are so likely to see justice done in regard to the officers responsible for their deaths. The police officers who killed Eric Garner, Tamir Rice, Freddie Gray, Michael Brown, Terence Crutcher, and Philando Castile, have all avoided prison sentences. The district attorney here in Austin is recommending charges against Christopher Taylor, the officer who shot Michael Ramos, but due to the COVID-19 epidemic, there is currently no grand jury to consider the matter.

After watching that video, I am guessing that once justice takes its course, Taylor will serve some significant prison time for killing Ramos. To date, out of all of the police officers I reported on above who killed all of these black citizens, only one officer is serving time in prison. That officer is Michael Slager, the former North Charleston police officer who shot Walter Scott in the back after stopping him for a non-functioning brake light. Slager is currently serving a 20-year term in federal prison for second-degree murder.

In addition to justice for the families of these victims of police brutality, we are also finally seeing a lot of reforms to police departments, as well as a lot of proposals for reform, and a lot of discussions about further reform that is needed. One of the most promising proposals is the mandatory use of body cameras by police. On the face of it, the requirement to wear body cameras while on duty seems like a sure thing for deterring police brutality and for holding officers accountable when they cross over the line representing excessive force. In reality though, body cameras have been in use for several years now, and they have not proven to be that much of a help, either as a deterrent or as an aid in achieving accountability.

In addition to the fact that many of these cameras seem to have a tendency to "malfunction" at critical times, the main reason for the inefficiency of body cameras in holding police accountable is that the police departments themselves own the videos. And since the police departments own them, they control whether or not the videos from these devices are shared with either the public, or the media, or with the victim/accused/defendant. As you can imagine, the police departments have been choosing not to share with anyone, except for maybe when those videos are helpful to the police department's side of things.

Despite this hurdle, body cameras, as well as dash-mounted cameras, hold great promise in the arena of police accountability for excessive force. The key that can make body cameras and dashboard cameras serve to hold the police accountable lies in who owns the videos and who controls how the videos are shared. If this ownership and control were to be transferred to an independent police accountability agency, then real reform through the proper use of these videos could be greatly enhanced.

Another subject that is getting a lot of attention in regard to its potential to reduce police brutality is the banning of chokeholds. In the short time since George Floyd's untimely passing through the use of a chokehold, a lot of jurisdictions have been quick to ban their use by their own police forces. Also widely discussed is the problem frequently encountered in holding police accountable: interference in the process by the police unions. Another is a lack of reporting requirements for police brutality cases and for excessive force and lethal force actions taken by officers, as well as instances of terminations and complaints, including complaints for things like falsifying a police report.

A national registry of police conduct has been proposed to handle this. And there has been a lot of talk about expanding the role of civilian review boards so that police are held accountable to a powerful organization outside of themselves that has the power to hire and fire, and to discipline officers for wrongdoing. There has also been a lot of talk about the need for removing qualified immunity, or at the very least passing legislation that will preclude the legal concept that allows so many officers to escape punishment for egregious actions because of a technicality. Another idea that is getting lots of attention is the idea of deducting settlement amounts for police wrongdoing from the offending police officer's pension fund.

Another much-discussed topic in these post George Floyd days is no-knock raids. Our police departments in this country are conducting an estimated 20,000 no-knock raids per year, which averages out to a little more than 54 such raids every day. No-knock raids have harmed a lot of innocent people, so from that standpoint, it is a good thing that the Breonna Taylor killing has served to shine a light on them. Typically, these no-knock raids are carried out by local SWAT teams after obtaining a no-knock warrant. Almost all of the search warrants are issued in regard to drug cases, and the no-knock, or the surprise aspect, supposedly gives the police a chance to capture the drugs that are within the house before the suspects can have a chance to flush them down the toilet.

In reality, these no-knock warrants are way too easy to obtain, and because of the serious lack of accountability in regard to their issuance, as well as the reckless way in which they are carried out, way too many innocent people have suffered the trauma of experiencing them. Numerous no-knock raids on mistaken addresses, as well as on innocent people who are not involved in the illicit drug trade, have caused injury and death in some cases, and property damage in all of them. When they have been woken up in the middle of the night by armed intruders who have forced their way in by breaking down their doors, most people think a home invasion crime is taking place. This is just what happened in the Breonna Taylor case. Thinking they were being robbed by violent, armed criminals, Breonna's boyfriend shot one of the officers in the leg as he was coming through the door. The boyfriend fired only the one round in the encounter. The three policemen fired an estimated 25 rounds in return, eight of which struck the well-regarded emergency medical technician, resulting in her death.

Although there is not a lot of agreement as to what it means, a lot of the protestors have called for defunding the police. Camden, New Jersey, a formerly thriving manufacturing center that is now an economically challenged town of 77,000 residents, located just across the river from Philadelphia, is often cited as a positive example for defunding the police. Due to budget cuts by the state in 2010, around half of the police force of 360 officers were laid off. Things were bad in Camden before, but after the layoffs, things got even worse. In 2012, there were 67 homicides and 172 shooting victims, ranking Camden with the highest per capita murder rate in the country.

Then, in 2013, the Camden police force was disbanded, and a new, county-based force was established that was outside of the purview of the all-union city police force's union. The new force was larger, but lower paid, and the chief of police, Scott Thomson, who had been the city-based police chief since 2008, implemented progressive changes focused on community policing. The new police force developed a body camera policy and adopted an 18-page document recognized as one of the nation's most comprehensive use-of-force policies. There is some controversy surrounding who deserves the credit, but for whatever reasons, the Camden police force has made substantial improvements since starting over from scratch seven years ago. In the wake of the George Floyd killing, it appears that Minneapolis will attempt to do something similar to what was done in Camden.

Defunding the police can also refer to the act of diverting funds formerly allocated to police departments in order to fund social services such as education, food subsidies, services for the homeless, housing subsidies, health care, and youth services. During the George Floyd protests, candidates for city council in New York City have called for reducing the NYPD budget by $1 billion over four years. And the mayor of Los Angeles has said that instead of the increase of $120 million he was planning to ask for, he is now proposing to cut the LAPD budget by $150 million, and he proposes to divert those funds to community initiatives. Similar redirections of funding away from police budgets and towards community services have been proposed in San Francisco, Chicago, Milwaukee, and Nashville, as well as many other cities.

Any examination of potential reforms to policing in this country must recognize that our policemen have been asked to perform a lot of tasks and duties they have not been properly trained to handle. The organization that is frequently cited when pointing to success in this arena is located in Eugene, Oregon, and goes by the name of CAHOOTS, which is an acronym for Crisis Assistance Helping Out On the Streets. Since 1989, the 911 personnel in Eugene have been trained to determine whether calls for help should be directed to CAHOOTS, or to the police, and calls related to addiction, disorientation, homelessness, or mental health crises are always given to CAHOOTS. In 2018, CAHOOTS was asked to respond to 20% of all 911 calls in Eugene.

CAHOOTS teams are two person teams consisting of an EMT and a mental health professional, and both team members have also undergone extensive training in crisis management and de-escalation. Without a doubt, this model can and should be duplicated everywhere as a means of responding more humanely, non-violently, appropriately, and effectively to many of the emergency calls for help by citizens. Plus, as an added bonus, the use of CAHOOTS is a much more cost-effective way of handling the emergency calls that are appropriate for them. CAHOOTS is currently working with the cities of Olympia, Denver, Oakland, New York, Indianapolis, Portland, Austin, and Chicago to help them to implement similar programs.

Another topic that comes up regularly in all of the post George Floyd talk show discussions about police reforms is the need to demilitarize our police departments. Michael Bloomberg once bragged that, as mayor of New York City, he commanded the seventh largest army in the world. Our policemen in this country dress like soldiers. They have many of the same military style ranks as soldiers, and like our soldiers, they are armed with an array of deadly weapons. And that does not even begin to describe our policemen that comprise the SWAT (Special Weapons and Tactics) teams that are embedded within almost every police force in this country.

Typical SWAT teams consist of at least one trained sniper armed with a sniping rifle, and the other "armed to the teeth" team members have access to submachine guns, assault weapons, riot shotguns, concussion grenades, tear gas grenades, and even armored vehicles, many of which are armed with high-caliber automatic weapons. All of the SWAT team members are protected by the latest state of the art body armor and they all wear the latest standard US military helmets. Then, with all of this military gear in place in literally every community in this country, the problem becomes, "What good is all of this equipment and all of this gear if we don't use it?"

Way too much of our policing efforts in this country are directed towards the sale and use of illegal drugs. That paragon of virtue, Richard Nixon, started it. He called it the War on Drugs. His motivation for starting the War on Drugs was to use it to fight his two biggest enemies, the hippie war protestors who smoked marijuana, and the post-civil-rights black population who was organizing and resisting, and occasionally rioting. They didn't use drugs any more than any other group, but used enough of them so that drug arrests could be used as a weapon in the war against them. For more than fifty years now, the main target of all of this raw police power has been the drug users, and to a lesser extent, the drug dealers.

And, as difficult as it is for all of us to admit, the secondary, somewhat hidden target of all of this police power, has been our poor, mostly black, urban citizens who are disproportionately represented in our prison populations. Our police suit up every day in their body armor, strap on their guns, tasers, and batons, grab their pepper spray and their tear gas, and get into their state-of-the-art vehicles, and head out to fight the war on drugs. On a good day, an officer of the law who is a part of a police force whose motto is "To Protect and Serve" will arrest a couple of our citizens who have taken part in a consensual, non-threatening act of purchasing, or selling, or possessing an illegal drug, and begin the process of bringing them into our burgeoning prison population.

Rather than fielding an armed police force with the goal of locking up as many of our poor, mostly black citizens as our prisons can hold, I submit that a better strategy would be to legalize all drugs and free all of our prisoners who are in prison on drug charges. This would reduce our prison population by 400,000 and prevent the arrest of 1 million of our citizens annually. At the same time as we end this insane and unwinnable war on drugs, we can begin providing basic needs to all people everywhere. Then, after we have given our desperate poor population a little time to heal, we can disband and disarm our police departments to the extent warranted by how much crime has been reduced. Since the basic needs of poor people will no longer be a concern to them, and our police forces will no longer fighting an unwinnable war on drugs, I am guessing this will be by a very significant amount.

After this, since our police forces will be greatly reduced, we can significantly raise our educational requirements and our other requirements for hiring policemen. Making it a requirement to have a four-year college degree in order to become a policeman would go a long way towards having a more community-oriented police force, staffed by officers capable of understanding the concepts of racism and civil rights from all sides. All of these highly significant reform measures will actually cause cultural shifts that will result in an increase in the number of us who know ourselves to be **Responsible Members of the Community of Life**, and that in itself will create another huge cultural shift.

Then, we need to close as many of our prisons as we possibly can and turn the few remaining prisons into facilities whose goal is rehabilitation, education, raising consciousness and conscientiousness, and the preparation of the prison inmates to rejoin our communities as Responsible Members of the Community of Life. Much like our new smaller police forces, these new smaller prisons will be staffed with professional, well-educated guards and other mental health professionals and educators.

GOVERNMENTAL CORRUPTION

A study by The Economist ranks the 167 countries of the world from most democratic to least democratic according to an index compiled through an assessment of the answers to sixty questions. Coming in as the most democratic county on the 2015 list is Norway, and the least democratic nation on earth is North Korea.

According to the study, 116 countries are considered democratic and the other 51 are considered authoritarian. Of the 116 countries deemed to be democratic, 20 are considered fully democratic, the next 59 are deemed to be flawed democracies, and the governments of the remaining 37 democratic countries are classified as hybrid democracies meaning they have components of democracy and also authoritarianism. Because of our problems with police brutality and voter suppression, the United States has been sliding slowly downward in the years I have been following this index. We are now number 25, between Japan and Malta, and into the "Flawed Democracy" territory.

For the simple reason that it is easier to accomplish and easier to get away with, more governmental corruption will be found in a corrupt dictatorship than a democracy. Therefore, you would expect to see more corruption on the bottom of the Economist's list than at the top. Over the years, people who have been in powerful governmental positions, whose actions are not transparent or subject to oversight, have often chosen to capitalize on the situation, either by profiting or by exploiting their positions for other sometimes very sinister purposes.

Sarah Chayes authored a recently published book on this subject titled *Thieves of State, Why Corruption Threatens Global Security*, in which she writes about present-day kleptocratic governments in Afghanistan, Egypt, Nigeria, Uzbekistan, and Tunisia, as well as historical kleptocracies in the Catholic church and medieval Florence, Persia, and elsewhere. Clearly, the U. S. war in Afghanistan would have gone much better, had we been able to address governmental corruption there. A population that is being exploited so terribly by their own government is certainly going to be looking for alternatives. As seen in Afghanistan, they will even consider ones provided by religious zealots with all of the baggage that comes with them.

But sadly, governmental corruption is not limited to authoritarian governments. You will find governmental corruption in democracies as well as dictatorships. A good example of governmental corruption in a democracy can be found right here in the U. S. in the recent George W. Bush administration. Those "wink, wink" tax incentives, and those "wink, wink" relaxations of governmental oversights were nothing more than an eight-year giveaway of enormous resources to big business and the wealthy. In the aftermath of that disaster, the economy teetered on the brink of collapse, and the remedy utilized by the Obama administration and the Congress involved another 800-billion-dollar giveaway to big businesses called the Stimulus Package.

There are many forms of political and governmental corruption including bribery, graft, embezzlement, cronyism, etc. Power corrupts, or at least, power often provides many temptations. But I would rather steer this discussion of governmental corruption in a slightly different direction. I would like to take a look at the purpose of government and then examine how governments often fail to meet that purpose. Therefore, for this discussion, let's just say that governmental corruption is any action taken by a government, or by any authority within a government that is not made with the intent of adhering to the spirit of responsibly administering a country's common resources for the benefit of the country's people. That is why people of our culture need governments. As an example of what I'm talking about, let's review the preamble to the U. S. Constitution.

> We the people of the United States, in Order to form a more perfect Union, establish Justice, ensure domestic Tranquility, provide for the common defence, promote the general Welfare, and secure the Blessings of Liberty to ourselves and our Posterity, do ordain and establish this Constitution for the United States of America.

These reasons for having a government are well stated, even if the 200 plus year-old language is a bit antiquated. Our country's founding fathers did some very good work in laying the foundation for our government. But considering the state of our union today, it is pretty obvious they didn't go quite far enough. My take on the U. S. government is that we all owe a huge debt of gratitude to our founding fathers. The U. S. Constitution and the Bill of Rights are far from perfect, but I think the hearts of the founders were in the right place. They tried very hard to design something that would serve the people and endure.

Two hundred plus years later, I see two ways our founders failed us in that regard. First, they failed by not foreseeing the problems that would arise if a two-party system developed within the framework of the government they designed. As a result, we are saddled today with two parties who run things, both of which answer only to big business. Our country's two parties are known as the Republicans and the Republican Lights, although the Republican Lights are sometimes also referred to as the Democratic Party. I like to say that Bill Clinton, the President who kept us safe while marshaling through legislation covering NAFTA, GATT, and the WTO, is the best Republican President this country has had since Dwight D. Eisenhower. And I also like to say that Barak Obama was the best Republican President since Bill Clinton.

The United States was the first modern democratic nation. According to the Economist, it is considered fully democratic and is ranked as the twentieth most democratic country in the world. The U. S. Constitution was finalized in 1787, and the U. S. government and the original thirteen states began operating under that constitution in 1789. Other democracies that were founded after ours have fixed this "only two parties running things" problem. There are two methods, which have been devised by democratic countries formed after the United States, which assure that all power is not vested in only two parties. The first of these methods is coalition governments. This method is probably familiar to most everyone in the U. S. through news pieces regarding the workings of the Israeli government. Other countries who use this process include all of the Nordic countries, plus Germany, Ireland, Japan, New Zealand, Pakistan, and India. These countries elect candidates to their parliaments from multiple parties who then must form coalitions in order to pass legislation and govern. Additionally, the cabinet members are appointed by their Parliaments rather than by their head executive and this also results in coalitions.

The other way of avoiding two-party domination, which works very well, is by a process called instant runoff voting. In an election where three or more people are vying to win a single position, voters rank the candidates from first to last. If enough first votes are made so that one of the candidates has 50% or more of the total votes, then that candidate is declared the winner. However, in the event that no candidate receives a plurality of first votes, then the last place candidate is eliminated from consideration and the second-place votes for all of the voters who selected that last place candidate as their first choice are then allocated to the candidate indicated on those ballots as the second choice. If there are three candidates vying for the position, then this process will decide the election after eliminating the candidate coming in third. However, if there are more than three candidates, this process can continue in the same manner until one of the candidates has more than 50% of the votes.

Here in the U. S., where we do not have instant runoff voting in our Presidential election, if a third-party candidate runs for President, then he or she has maybe a snowball's chance in Hell of winning. Plus, the unfortunate result of having the third candidate in the race is that he or she will serve to take votes away from whichever candidate of the two major parties with which he or she is most closely aligned. Recently, we saw how Ross Perot helped elect Bill Clinton by taking votes away from the elder George Bush. Then, we saw the same thing happen when Ralph Nader helped elect George W. Bush the two times he ran when he took votes away from first Al Gore, and then John Kerry. If we had utilized instant runoff voting in those elections, it is likely that George H. W. Bush would have defeated Clinton, and Al Gore would have defeated George W. Bush. In that event, Gore would have been the incumbent in 2004 and John Kerry would not have run been running for President in that election.

Examples of instant runoff voting include Australia who utilizes the method for electing members to their House of Representatives. Also, the president of the Republic of Ireland is elected by a process that includes instant runoff voting. Other places use it as well, including even some places within the U. S. like the city of San Francisco. Personally, I think it would be a great fix for our two-party problem if used nationwide in this country.

And the other way in which our founders failed us in their attempt to design a government that would work well for the people and would endure is that they failed to adequately protect us from our government being taken over by big business. Today, I can state unequivocally that big business owns and operates the government of the United States, as well as many other supposedly democratic governments around the world. Of course, the only reason this outrageous situation is allowed to continue is because the people of our country don't understand it. Once they do, then fortunately we still have a government that operates within a framework of elections by "we the people" and checks and balances, etc., and the problem can be fixed fairly easily. Until that time, big business will continue to run things, and all of our major decisions will be made by large corporations and based upon profit considerations.

Thom Hartmann wrote a great book about this situation called *Unequal Protection*. Hartmann explains in the book exactly how the government of the United States has been stolen from the people. It all started with a lawsuit styled *Southern Pacific Railroad versus Santa Clara County*, which reached the U. S. Supreme Court in 1886. The case was about property taxes, and Southern Pacific's arguments included an assertion that corporations are artificial persons and therefore entitled to the protections and rights of people under the Constitution and the Bill of Rights. The court decided in favor of the railroad, but specifically did not address the railroad's assertion of corporate personhood. However, the clerk of the Supreme Court was a former railroad executive, and he wrote in the head notes of the case that the court had accepted the argument for corporate personhood. Although untrue, the assertion was subsequently relied upon and now it is so entrenched in other case law, that it is, in fact, the current accepted legal position.

As I stated earlier, there is an easy fix for this outrageous situation, which requires only that a sufficient number of voters understand it, and to demand that it be fixed. We will dig much deeper into this subject in the next chapter.

Here in the United States and in most other democratic nations as well, all of the big political battles are fought over conservative versus liberal ideals. And invariably, the arguments all revolve around the definition of the commons. To me, this conservative versus liberal debate strikes very closely to the "separate versus connected" theme we have been pursuing in this book. For the conservatives, the commons need to be as small as possible. For them, everything is separate and they believe in the survival of the fittest (richest). They want to be able to profit from the world's natural resources without restriction. They think the national forests and the wilderness areas should all be opened up to logging. The North Slope in Alaska and the Federal waters off Florida need to be available for oil and gas development. Health care should be all about profit. Government should stay away from business in regard to pollution, etc. After all, business needs to make money. They seem to think that if you are an individual who makes a lot of money, it is because you are smart and industrious and you deserve to be rewarded. The degree to which these people are willing to close their eyes and ears to the devastation and destruction their profit-making activities are causing to the world sometimes seems incredibly surreal… Until I remember these people are operating within the framework of our basic cultural myths which foster separation.

The liberals in this country are still members of this insane culture, but their viewpoint is much closer to the "connected" viewpoint of the tribal people. To them, our air, water, and natural resources are precious and should be protected from profit-crazed companies and individuals. Liberals believe the neediest individuals among us should be protected and cared for and provided with opportunities for advancement. They think the government has a responsibility to the country's working-class people. They believe we should act to prevent our jobs from being exported to developing countries where desperate starving masses can supply labor forces, which can be exploited for incredibly low wages. Actually, here in the United States, we used to protect our workers from this. We did it through protective tariffs and they no longer exist.

I'd like to make a final point regarding corruption in the U. S. government. My point is that although the government of the United States of America was founded on very high ideals… ideals about breaking away from the tyranny of the British rule in order to form a government of the people, by the people, for the people…. The U. S. government has never in its history operated within a framework whereby those high ideals were not being contradicted in extremely tangible ways by its actions. For instance, our founding fathers had to deal with the issue of slavery, which was already in place during colonial times. There were those among the founders who opposed slavery on moral grounds, and there continued to be many who argued against it after the country was formed. However, the other founders who were profiting from the practice, and the rich and powerful slave owners who came after them were able to keep the institution in place for an additional eighty-two years after the government began operations. The issue continued to dog the young republic until 1861, when Abraham Lincoln issued the Emancipation Proclamation during our American Civil War.

Then, after slavery was finally abolished, the problem of racial discrimination rose to the forefront. It took the government just over one hundred years from the time of the Emancipation Proclamation until 1965 for meaningful legislation to finally be enacted. And the problem didn't just disappear because Civil Rights legislation was finally passed. Before, during and after that time, there were issues dealt with poorly by our government regarding sexual discrimination, as well as issues regarding gay rights and other issues involving minority rights.

There are, of course, many other issues where actions or inactions on behalf of the government served to diminish our government's ability to take the high moral ground. Due to national security clearances, I'm quite sure there are many other travesties we don't even know about. But far and away the biggest of the ones we do know about involves the theft of the lands on which our country is built from the tribal peoples who were peacefully occupying those lands when we arrived. As we have discussed herein, this theft from the Native Americans was a continuation of the process that began when our culture was born ten thousand years ago in Mesopotamia.

I know of no great debates in our Congress or our newspapers or our state assembly halls or our town halls whereby it was ever argued that taking this land was wrong. They must have occurred, but for some reason, no great champion arose from within our culture to defend the Native Americans. No.... Apparently there was too great of a need for this land and too much profit waiting to be taken. Manifest Destiny was the rallying cry behind this despicable situation.

Yes. The United States of America was the first of the modern democracies and it was founded upon high ideals.... And yes; our country has grown into the richest and most powerful nation on earth.... And yes; it was largely due to our late entrance into World War II that the world was saved from the Nazi and Japanese aggressors.... And yes; we won the Cold War over world domination with the Soviets.... And yes; we put a man on the moon. Those of us who live in this country are often fond of asserting our claim to high morals and of hyping our historic significance to the modern world.

But here in the U. S., we also have much to answer for. And until we reject the basic cultural myth that the world was made for man to conquer and rule, and decide to become Responsible Members of the world, and of the Community of Life, we are not going to be able to make a lot of progress in answering for our shortcomings and our mistakes.

ALCOHOLISM AND DRUG ADDICTION

By far, the most used drug is alcohol. According to statistics provided by the National Institute of Health, approximately 67 percent of Americans had at least one drink last year. If you are 21 years old, then you can legally purchase alcohol in the United States. And despite the illegality, consumption of alcohol by minors is very common. Beer is the world's most widely consumed alcoholic beverage. And, it is also the third most popular drink of any kind overall. Only water and tea are consumed more often. In the U.S., it is estimated that about 12% of adults have had an alcohol dependence problem at some point in their lives. Here are some other facts about alcohol:

- ❖ Alcohol is the third largest cause of death in the United States, behind only heart disease and cancer.
- ❖ Alcohol is the leading cause of death for people between the ages of 15 and 24.
- ❖ Alcohol and other drugs contribute to over 50 percent of all suicides and over 50 percent of all violent crimes.
- ❖ Over 50 percent of all admissions to emergency rooms are either directly or indirectly due to drug or alcohol usage.

❖ Over 50 percent of all traffic accidents involve the use of drugs or alcohol.

Most people drink alcohol in order to achieve a pleasant, mild state of inebriation. In this relaxed state, people enjoy a decreased feeling of anxiety and a loss of inhibitions. Literally, zillions of sexual encounters have occurred during this state that never would have happened otherwise. This, of course, is a huge selling point for beer, wine, and liquor retailers, as well as club and bar owners.

Drinking beyond a certain threshold, however, can quickly become problematic. After progressing past a mild state of inebriation, people experience a loss of coordination, poor balance, slowed reaction times, slurred speech, and dizziness. And, each of these debilitating conditions will become worse as more alcohol is consumed. Additionally, many people experience negative mood swings towards anger and aggression. Extreme consumption will cause memory loss, and a complete loss of coordination. Alcohol poisoning can even result in death.

Probably the biggest problem with alcohol consumption is the tendency of people to think it is okay for them to drive when they are intoxicated. This is a problem that has received a lot of attention during the last thirty or forty years. According to the National Institute of Health, alcohol was a factor in over 60 percent of traffic fatalities during the mid 1970's. After forty years of increased attention, and scrutiny, and harsher penalties for people who were driving while intoxicated, the National Highway Traffic Safety Administration reports that there were 16,885 alcohol related traffic fatalities in the United States in 2005, representing a reduction to 39 percent of all traffic fatalities. Nice progress, but I'm sure the families of these 16,885 lost souls would tell us there is still more work to be done on this problem.

Marijuana is the next most utilized drug. Around half of the U. S. adult population has tried marijuana at some point in their lifetime. It is estimated that 12.3 percent of adults in the U. S. smoke marijuana.

Reasons people use marijuana include a desire to experience relaxation and to alleviate stress, something smoking marijuana definitely provides. Many people also smoke or ingest pot in order to enjoy an increased sense of awareness, especially in regard to taste and smell. Abstract thinking can be enhanced while under the influence of marijuana, often leading to deeper thoughts and a better understanding of philosophical thinking. Ideas can flow more easily for people who are stoned on marijuana. Appreciation of music is often enhanced when people are high. Appetite is often stimulated. (A condition often referred to by stoners as "the munchies".)

The negative effects of using marijuana include the potential for impaired coordination, skewed sensory and time perception, difficulty with clear thinking, difficulty with concentration, difficulty with problem solving, a shortened attention span, and a potential for a negative effect on motivation. Other than the potential of being arrested and put in jail for marijuana possession, probably the worst of the potential negative effects of using marijuana is the possibility of becoming psychologically addicted to being stoned, which happens to approximately one in ten people who use the drug regularly.

Marijuana is not legal… at least not at the federal level, where it is classified as a Schedule 1 controlled substance, the same as heroine. Technically, according to this Federal classification, marijuana is more dangerous than cocaine, amphetamines, and opium, which are all classified as Schedule II drugs. If you get caught selling or growing marijuana, you could go to jail for a very long time. You could even get a life sentence. And even getting caught with a small amount can get you a jail sentence… Especially if you have dark skin. The National Organization for the Reform of Marijuana Laws, known as NORML, reports that although only 11% of marijuana users are African American, 75% of those arrested for marijuana possession or sale are Black. The ACLU reports that more than 7 million people were busted for having pot between the years 2001 and 2010. The Drug Policy Alliance reports that almost 750,000 people were arrested for marijuana law violations in 2012, and 88 percent of these arrests were for possession only, with the other 12 percent being for either intent to sell or cultivation.

Nobody dies from the effects of smoking marijuana, but eighty-five thousand people die annually from drinking alcohol. Ten percent of people who smoke pot regularly end up addicted, versus fifteen percent for alcohol. People who smoke marijuana never become physically addicted, while many alcoholics who stop drinking go through a physical detoxification process. Heavy, long-term drinkers incur damage to their livers, kidneys, and other organs, while no such damage occurs to marijuana users. Though neither a stoned person nor a drunk person should be operating a motor vehicle, a stoned person has been shown to be much more capable of doing so.

Yet, it is alcohol that is legal and marijuana that is illegal… at least at the Federal level.

Thankfully, the legality of possessing and selling marijuana is undergoing some changes. Beginning with California in 1996, twenty-nine states plus the District of Columbia have legalized marijuana for medical uses. Plus, eight of those states, plus the District of Columbia permit the recreational use of marijuana. From purely a fairness standpoint in regard to having legitimate reasons for incarcerating people, this is a trend that needs to continue.

Here is some usage data regarding drugs and alcohol posted by DrugWarFacts.org:

Estimated Past-Month Substance Use in US by those aged 12 and Older for 2015 (Numbers in Thousands)

Alcohol	138,322
Heavy alcohol use	17,326
Marijuana and Hashish	27,080
Cocaine	1,876

Crack	394
Heroin	329
Methamphetamine	897
Ecstasy	557

As shown above, by far the most utilized drug is alcohol. Marijuana is next, followed by cocaine, which comes in a distant third. Then, there is another big drop-off in the number of users before we get to crack, heroin, methamphetamine, and ecstasy. These last four drugs are fairly close to each other in their usage rates, all falling between 897,000 and 329,000 users in any recent one-month period.

From a physiological perspective, heroin is by far the most addictive of any of these drugs. Physical dependence on this drug can come very quickly, especially if the user utilizes the intravenous method of delivery. Risk of death by overdose or of contracting the AIDS virus through the sharing of needles are very real for people who shoot up with heroin. Heroin is a depressant that affects the central nervous system. People who overdose on heroin inject such a large amount that their breathing becomes suppressed to the point of death.

Heroin users experience a feeling of total relaxation and intense euphoria, which is the condition they seek to repeat on subsequent uses of the drug. One of the reasons the drug is so dangerous is because over time, heroin users develop a tolerance for the drug, meaning larger doses are needed in order to experience the same high. But the main reason the drug is so dangerous is the potential for physical addiction. There is no precise timetable, but at some point, after repeated use, the body becomes dependent on the drug. Physical addiction to heroin will usually occur within three to six weeks of daily use. This is a purely physical condition and it has absolutely nothing to do with the strength of will of the user. Heroin addicts can begin experiencing withdrawal symptoms, which include muscle and bone pain, diarrhea, and vomiting, within only a few hours after their last use of the drug. It is estimated that almost one-fourth of the people who experiment with heroin become addicted to using it. For some, it takes only a few weeks, especially if they use it every day. Others safely chip away as casual users for years before becoming addicts.

I think it is important to make a distinction here at this point of the discussion between psychological addiction and physical addiction. Psychological addiction is a complicated issue, with many intricacies involving mental health and emotional problems, which are different for each individual. At its root, though, the very basis for any psychological addiction is compulsive behavior. It can be said however, that physical addiction is not really an addiction, but a physical condition that occurs when the body has undergone changes due to the drug use to the point where the body requires the drug in order to continue functioning in a semi-normal fashion. (That is, without the muscle and bone pain, and the diarrhea and vomiting.) When a person is physically addicted, it no longer matters whether or not they are psychologically addicted. They need the drug in a very real and tangible way. At this point, compulsive behavior no longer has anything to do with it. Many heroin addicts are addicted physically, but not psychologically.

Cocaine is almost as addictive as heroin from a psychological perspective, but much less so from a physiological one. Cocaine is by far the most expensive of any of these drugs, so people who develop a psychological dependence on cocaine can quickly burn through a lot of cash, potentially wreaking devastation with their personal finances. Even casual use of this drug can prove very expensive. Often, the expense of using cocaine versus the relative affordability of using heroin drives people to switch to using heroin, a much more dangerous drug. Another problem with cocaine use is that the buzz enables people to drink far more alcohol than they could normally handle, causing alcohol dependence to occur much more rapidly than it otherwise would.

While heroin is a depressant, cocaine is a stimulant. Nevertheless, users of both cocaine and heroin report a sense of euphoria when using these drugs. When high on cocaine, instead of feeling completely relaxed, people feel energetic and powerful. Only a small percentage of people who try cocaine go on to become heavy users. It is estimated that around twenty percent of heavy users go on to become addicted to cocaine.

My research indicates that contrary to what most people believe, there is no real difference between cocaine and crack cocaine. Crack is also cocaine and both affect the mind and body in the same manner. Cocaine is a powder that can be snorted or injected, or even smoked, if it is converted to its freebase form. Most people who use cocaine snort it. Crack is a rock or crystal form of cocaine that can only be smoked. Crack first became widely used in the mid 1980's, and during that time there was a lot of fear and misinformation about crack, mostly due to the fact that crack was popular within inner city inhabitants, where there was already a lot of crime and violent crime. As a result of this fear and misinformation, Congress passed some legislation about mandatory sentencing for crack possession requiring jail sentences of five years for possession of as little as five grams of crack. Meanwhile, the Wall Streeters, and the other, more affluent people who preferred the powdered form, were not subject to a five-year mandatory sentence unless they were caught holding 500 grams or more, (More than one pound!) of the powdered form of coke.

Methamphetamine is another illegal drug that ruins many lives through addiction. Meth is the only one of these illicit drugs that actually has a pharmaceutical counterpart licensed by the FDA. The drug is sold under the brand name Desoxyn, and doctors may prescribe it for attention deficit hyperactivity disorder, obesity, or narcolepsy. The street drug, crystal meth, used to be made mostly in labs run by drug traffickers in Mexico and California. But since the mid 1990's, smaller, independent meth labs have sprung up everywhere, and they have taken a significant percentage of this business. Mostly, these small labs make the drug by chemically altering over the counter drugs made to treat colds and allergies. These small labs are dangerous for their proprietors and also for their innocent neighbors. Many suffer fires and explosions that expose the public to hazardous chemicals that are used and generated in the process.

Like cocaine, meth comes in both a powder form that can be snorted, smoked, swallowed, or injected, and a rock form that can be smoked or injected. Both cocaine and meth are stimulants, but methamphetamine produces a stronger and a longer lasting high than cocaine.

Meth is used in order to improve concentration and increase energy and alertness. Students use it to study all night for tests. Truckers use it so they can stay awake to drive all night. Clubbers use it to help them keep their shit together while partying and drinking alcohol all night. Fat people use it in order to lose weight. Addicts just use it. If you become addicted to meth, you are in for a very rough time. The National Institute on Drug Abuse reports that chronic, long-term methamphetamine abuse significantly changes how the brain functions, adversely affecting emotion, memory, and cognitive abilities.

Like all of these illegal drugs, it's hard to come up with a reliable percentage for people who use the drug versus those who become addicted. As with the others, many people who try the drug don't end up becoming regular users. All of the addicts come out of the pool of people who are regular users. I've seen several conflicting numbers in regard to addiction percentages, so I'll just report that the online Wiki Answers posting I read seemed reasonable when it reported that approximately 30% of regular users become addicts. Additionally, the Wiki Answers piece called meth the second most addicting substance known to man. Meth is physically addictive. However, the withdrawal symptoms are not so severe as those for heroin, so the physical addiction is more easily overcome.

Ecstasy is a club drug that is part stimulant, part hallucinogen. It was invented by the pharmaceutical company, Merck, in 1912, and patented as MDMA, short for its technical, chemical name, in 1914. Initially, Merck hoped it might be effective in controlling bleeding. When that didn't work out, not much happened with the drug until a chemist named Alexander Shulgin synthesized it in his personal laboratory sometime around 1975.

Shulgin, who has a Ph.D. in biochemistry from U. C. Berkley, was working for Dow Chemical when he had his first psychedelic experience after ingesting mescaline in 1960. The experience motivated him to use his expertise in chemistry to experiment and test other mind-altering compounds. Noting how a small dose of MDMA felt very much like an early alcohol buzz, Shulgin called it his "no calorie martini". He was so impressed with MDMA that he gave some to a psychologist friend, thinking its ability to induce friendliness and empathy might help in therapy. The friend, Dr. Leo Zoff, not only used the drug extensively in his own practice, but his use and endorsement of the technique caused thousands of other licensed practitioners to use MDMA in their practices also. Many of these therapists reported the use of the drug had been instrumental in inducing the sort of counseling breakthroughs for their patients that usually required many months of therapy.

One therapist who reported using MDMA as a therapeutic aid for 80 of his patients was Dr. George Greer, a psychiatrist. Dr. Greer was quoted in a New York Times article I found online as saying, "Without exception, every therapist who I talked to or even heard of, every therapist who gave MDMA to a patient, was highly impressed by the results."

During this time, the drug was not illegal. Dr. Greer reported that by lowering the patients' defenses, the drug allows them to face troubling, even repressed memories. Another psychiatry professor from UCLA, Dr. Charles Grob, was quoted in the same New York

Times article as praising MDMA for its ability to help patients achieve an empathetic rapport.

But by 1985, MDMA had gotten so popular, and its recreational use and availability had become so prevalent, that the DEA placed it into their most restrictive class of drugs, being Schedule 1.

From my research, it appears that MDMA, otherwise known as ecstasy, is not a particularly dangerous drug, especially when compared to cocaine, heroin, meth, or even alcohol. Actually, of all of the drugs discussed in this section, ecstasy comes the closest to representing the real-world equivalent of Aldous Huxley's fictional drug, soma. The biggest problems with ecstasy probably stem from impurities used in its un-licensed un-supervised, un-regulated, and illegal manufacture, and also from people taking way too much of it. After all, ecstasy does not come in a pretty package with recommended doses and warning labels. At higher doses, the drug can trigger increases in muscle tension, heart rate and blood pressure. One of the characteristics of the drug that helps prevent people from becoming addicted is that with repeated use, people become tolerant, and more is needed to achieve the same pleasurable high. Yet with the increased dose, people get the same high plus increased negative side effects, making it unattractive to most everyone for regular use.

Do you think there would be 140 million alcoholics and 27 million drug addicts in our world if everyone understood that we are all a part of the Community of Life and everything was connected?

I contend there would be exactly zero alcoholics and zero drug addicts if everyone understood that all-important truth. What would anyone have to escape from in such a world? In a world where everyone understood that we are all a part of the Community of Life and everything is connected, we would take care of each other. There would not be one soul on this whole planet who lacked food, or shelter, or medical care, or who didn't have clean water and sanitary living conditions. And furthermore, the rest of the

Community of Life would not be suffering because of our presence as they are now. In such a world, we would not be cutting down our last remaining ancient forests, and polluting our air, and our land, and our rivers and streams, and our oceans.

But our world of today is much different. Remember that list of problems we are examining in this chapter? Well... that is our world.... We live in a world full of big problems, and there are not very many of us who escape unscathed. Many of us end up with problems of our own. Even if we are not facing hunger, or starvation, or poverty, or homelessness, then perhaps we are only a couple of missed paychecks away from one or more of those conditions. And, even if we are okay financially, then we still live in a world where nine wars and seventeen lesser conflicts are ongoing at this moment. And, if that is not enough, then we all have to wonder how global warming and overpopulation will affect us all in the near future. As I have mentioned at least a couple of times before... our culture is insane. A lot of us drink or take drugs in order to get some temporary relief from the anxiety that naturally comes from living in such a world. And many of us find that temporary relief a slippery slope indeed.

Most of us though, don't end up addicted to drugs or alcohol, even after a period of regular use. Those of us who do end up addicted are the ones who cannot control our compulsive behavior. Some of us experience a pleasant high, or an escape from our worries, pains, or anxieties, and we are compulsively drawn to repeat the experience, regardless of the negative consequences. Most of us who are unable to control this compulsion have mental problems. And most of these mental problems are caused by childhood traumas resulting from being born into dysfunctional families in this insane world. Other mental problems causing compulsive behavior that can lead us to addiction may have arisen from a severe trauma or loss that happened after our childhood years.

The consequences of becoming addicted to drugs or alcohol are terrible, both for the addicted party and for his or her family and loved ones. And there is a huge cost to society for these addictions as well. Although the risk of addiction may not be that great for trying one of these drugs, should you become addicted, you will definitely wish that you resisted the urge to ever try it. From this standpoint, there is no question that you are taking a huge risk if you decide to experiment with drugs, especially if you decide to dabble with heroin, cocaine, or meth. People who are addicted to these drugs suffer terribly. Definitely, we should do what we can to prevent people from becoming addicted to alcohol or to any other drug. And also, we should do everything we can to help those who become addicted despite our best efforts to prevent them from doing so.

Locking these addicted people up in prison, however, is not the answer. Our prisons of today are far too full of people whose only crime was possession of one of these illegal drugs. Obviously, there is going to be a supply of these drugs available for as long as there is a demand for them. No War On Drugs will ever change that situation. There is just too much money to be made, and there are just too many people ready to profit, no matter what the risk of incarceration might be for them. We need to declare ourselves the losers of the War On Drugs and legalize them all. Just as ending Prohibition put an immediate stop to the profitable illegal alcohol business, the legalization of drugs can put an end to the extremely violent and profitable illegal drug trade. Basically, we win the War On Drugs with the stroke of a pen when the President signs the legislation. Then, all of these currently illegal drugs can be produced and sold legally, and the taxes on their production and sale can be earmarked for helping cure people with addictions. After we legalize these drugs, addicts will no longer need to seek out criminal dealers in order to make their purchases. Instead, they will make their drug purchases in a public place, which could be a liquor store or a similar licensed and regulated retail establishment. The emphasis will be on identifying addicts and finding a way to help them defeat their addictions.

RACISM

Here, in the United States, our racism has a history that often goes unacknowledged. As a result, our racism persists. That history of racism includes the racism of the white people in the 17th, 18th and 19th centuries who considered it okay to buy and sell dark-skinned people from Africa as if they were property and force them to toil in the fields as slaves. After slavery was abolished, that history of racism included the racism of all of the white people who considered these dark-skinned former slaves and their descendants to be genetically inferior and not worthy of the same rights, protections, and benefits as white people.

The history of racism in our country includes the racism of the Senators, Congressmen, and state legislators who passed the Jim Crow laws mandating the segregation of public schools, public transportation, public restrooms, public drinking fountains, and other public places. The history of racism in our country includes the racism of all of the white people responsible for the extra-legal lynchings of hundreds if not thousands of black people. The history of racism in our country includes the racism of all of the white people who dressed up in white robes and rode out with their fellow Ku Klux Klan members to murder, scare, and intimidate black people in an effort to keep them from asserting their rights and privileges as citizens of this country. The history of racism in this country includes the racism of all of the white people who prevented the black veterans returning from WWII to receive the educational and low-cost mortgage benefits afforded to returning veterans in the G. I. Bill.

And despite the repeal of the Jim Crow laws, and despite the court cases that have determined segregation to be illegal, and despite the passage of the Civil Rights Act, and despite the passage of the Voting Rights Act, and despite the fact that so many of our citizens have transcended the racist beliefs and tendencies of our parents and grandparents and those that came before them, that racism continues today. In fact, the continuing problem of racism in our country includes the racism of the current President of the United States, Donald J. Trump. And the continuing problem of racism in our country includes the racism of Donald Trump's ardent supporters who support him and vote for him specifically because he is a racist.

Racism is based upon the mistaken belief that one "race" of people possesses greater intelligence, or other superior genetic traits, when compared to other races of people. The history of our culture is full of terrible examples of racism, almost all of which involve the white race imposing their economic, technological, and military superiority over other races. Obvious examples include the white versus black racism of the United States, which has been here since our country's founding, and continues today; the terrible racism of the Nazis and their plans for world domination by the Aryan race; and the Apartheid system of racial segregation imposed by the white supremacists upon the native black population of South Africa.

Among modern anthropologists, the concept of race, and whether or not there is any validity to classifying humans into racial sub-groups, has become a controversial one. The controversy arises because modern anthropologists and geneticists all agree there is no one gene, characteristic, trait, or group of genes, characteristics, or traits that can be utilized to define a person according to race. Since this fact makes it impossible to definitively classify people according to race, anthropologists are pretty much evenly divided as to whether it is appropriate to even attempt to do so.

To me, the main point that needs to be made about racism is the same point that Jared Diamond made in his Pulitzer Prize winning book, *Guns, Germs, and Steel.* As Diamond explained it, the book was the result of a conversation Diamond had in 1972 with a black native of New Guinea named Yali. During their talk, Yali asked Diamond, "Why is it that you white people developed so much cargo and brought it to New Guinea, but we black people had little cargo of our own?" *Guns, Germs, and Steel,* which describes the rise and the spread of civilization, is Diamond's attempt to answer Yali's question.

Diamond never actually says it in *Guns, Germs and Steel,* but the book does provide a refutation of the concept of racism. It turns out that Diamond's answer to Yali, which took him 25 years to formulate, is that the reason the white man has so much cargo, and the black man so little, is the result of pure luck. White people populated ancient Mesopotamia. If instead, it had been populated by black people, then they would have been the ones to cultivate the wheat and barley and domesticate the animals and develop class societies with division of labor that led to technological inventiveness. In this scenario, it could have been black people who flew their airplanes full of cargo to New Guinea and brought metal tools for the white people who lived there to use in place of their stone ones.

Although the Nazis were defeated, Apartheid abolished, civil rights legislation was passed, and more and more babies continue to be born every year to non-racist parents, the terrible problem of racism continues to plague our society. Racism is just one very tangible indication that our culture is based upon a myth that fosters separation. In reality, millennial-long isolation of geographically diverse groups of human beings has resulted in certain physical characteristics, such as skin color, eye color, hair color, hair texture, etc., that serve to provide the basis for racial discrimination. In reality, every person on this planet has common ancestors who lived in Africa.

I contend that every person who connects the dots from "How things came to be this way," to "We are a part of the Community of Life," to "Everything is connected," to "We need to resume our former roles as Responsible Members of the Community of Life," will have transcended any tendency towards racism. In the meantime, racist thoughts and racist tendencies provide a barrier to many people in regard to their own ability to connect these dots. If you happen to be born into a family with one or more parents who are racist, or if your role models happen to be racist, then you will need to utilize your education, your capacity for self-reflection, and your intellectual capabilities in order to escape from this terrible affliction.

SEXISM

According to Merriam-Webster, "sexism" is "prejudice or discrimination based on sex, especially against women". Much like the previous issue of racism, I contend that once a person has connected the dots from "How things came to be this way", to "We are a part of the Community of Life", to "Everything is connected", to "We need to resume our former roles as Responsible Members of the Community of Life", that person will have transcended most of their tendencies towards sexism.

You may notice that I said "most" instead of "all" as I did in the previous issue of racism. This is because to me, the issue of whether or not there is any validity whatsoever to racism is more black and white (pun intended), and the issue of whether or not there is any validity to sexism is more nuanced. I am not saying it is correct to discriminate against women. In fact, I will argue strongly to the contrary. I am only saying that in contrast to racial discrimination, which has no basis whatsoever in physical reality, there are definite, real, and tangible differences between the sexes.

As discussed above in the piece on racism, modern anthropologists are in agreement that it is impossible to definitively classify people according to race. And even if it were possible, there is no validity whatsoever to the contention that one "race" of people could be said to be superior to another race of people, intellectually or otherwise. We are all Africans. Some of us have more recent ancestors in Western Europe. Some of us have more recent ancestors in the Far East. Some of us have more recent ancestors in the Western Hemisphere. Some of us have more recent ancestors in the South Pacific. Some of us have ancestors who never left Africa. And, most of us have ancestors from more than one of these places. Very likely, these more recent ancestors will have passed along physical traits and characteristics to each of us such as skin color, eye color, hair color, hair texture, bone structure, etc., that will make us identifiable to others as having a certain heritage. Discriminating against those of us whose more recent ancestors came from someplace other than Western Europe is just wrong. It has no basis in reality whatsoever.

On the other hand, there is absolutely no question that men and women are different. They think differently, they relate to their feelings differently, and because of their different roles in the reproductive process, they have different bodies. Generally speaking, men are bigger and stronger than women. Hence, generally speaking, men are more capable of asserting their dominance over women by force. This dominance over women by force has been going on for ten thousand years now. It started when the food was first locked up in that first settlement in ancient Mesopotamia. And, it continues today.

In that original agricultural settlement in ancient Mesopotamia, the locking up of the food was, undoubtedly accomplished by a man who was aided by other men. I guess I could be wrong with this assertion, but it is certainly hard to imagine why a woman would do such a thing, or even why a woman would participate in such an endeavor. And ever since that original event when somebody first locked up the food, our culture has been a culture that can be characterized as a male dominated, patriarchal culture. For ten thousand years, the culture (ours) that began with food surpluses resulting from the cultivation of wheat and barley, and the domestication of animals, has been conquering and ruling the world as our basic cultural myth demands.

Sexism, feminism, male chauvinism, patriarchy, gender bias.... These are the terms we are all familiar with today. I think most of us here in the United States think of these words in terms of "women's rights" and have a sense that we can relax about this issue due to everything that has been accomplished in our recent history. For instance, after being denied the right to vote for 144 years, the 19th Amendment to the U. S. Constitution, ratified and put into effect in 1920, finally granted women the right to vote. Our current 535 member U. S. Congress has 20 women Senators and 84 women members of the House of Representatives, comprising 19.4% of the total Congressional membership. Hilary Clinton recently made history as the first woman nominated for President by one of the major parties. Unfortunately, though, she lost in the general election to Donald Trump, a racist and a misogynist.

But there is a lot more to this issue than voting rights and the male-female ratio of elected officials. Lurking at the very center of this issue, like a piece of fruit that is rotting from the inside out, is patriarchy. According to Merriam-Webster, "patriarchy" is a family, group, or government controlled by a man or a group of men. I contend that this pernicious system of worldwide male dominance called patriarchy has been in place ever since the birth of our culture. And, much like our culture itself, people have been accepting it as the "natural way" for so long, that it hardly ever gets questioned anymore. Our culture is insane. And one of the big reasons our culture is insane, is because of its patriarchal basis. Patriarchy is just wrong. Everything is connected, and any system that is based upon domination is operating outside of that basic reality. I also contend that even though we are making real progress with this issue of sexism, we are never going to fix it completely until we replace this flawed and doomed culture of separation with a new culture based upon the reality of connectedness.

In a world where everything is connected, and every person understands themselves to be a part of the world and a part of the Community of Life, sexism would not exist. But in a world where every person does not understand this fundamentally important truth, this long-standing tradition of patriarchy, and these physical differences, along with these more subtle, cognitive differences, provide a basis for sexism. Sexism has it roots in our basic cultural myth that tells us, "The world was made for **man** to conquer and rule". And sexism is reinforced by one of our culture's most pervasive secondary cultural myths that tells us that success in this world depends upon the **survival of the fittest (strongest or most powerful).** I contend that once we have succeeded in providing basic needs for all people everywhere, stopped cutting down our forests, and begun the process of ceasing to pollute, then this issue of sexism will magically disappear.

PHYSICAL, SEXUAL, AND EMOTIONAL ABUSE

As I have asserted a time or two in the preceding pages, our culture is insane. And, this particular issue of physical, sexual, and emotional abuse, which undoubtedly affects more of us than we realize, provides a strong argument in support of my assertion. After all, the vast majority of the victims of physical, sexual, and emotional abuse are children. And, not only that, but the vast majority of the perpetrators of physical, sexual, and emotional abuse are family members, family friends, and other trusted caregivers. How can things be any more insane than that? Through no fault of their own, countless numbers of our children are born into a situation where instead of receiving the nurturing and care they need in order to grow and develop physically, mentally, and emotionally, they become victims of abuse. Many of them never heal from the emotional trauma of having been subjected to the abuse. And many grow up to be adults with severe emotional and mental problems who then have their own children and become abusers themselves.

Physical abuse often starts out as punishment or correction, and then progresses from there to something very dark, and very traumatizing. Sexual abuse is all about the sexual gratification of the perpetrator. Emotional abuse can occur by itself, or it can accompany one of the other forms of abuse, which it often does. Many of these abusive situations are never known to anyone except the victim and the perpetrator. And even worse, since children have no knowledge of the wider world, many of the victims never realize there is anything wrong. And often, if they do know there is something wrong, these innocent victims wrongly believe the fault must be their own.

One action that can be taken to help reduce abusive behavior is the implementation of classes and programs in our schools teaching emotional intelligence. As stated earlier, because many of these abused children never successfully process the emotions and feelings that result from the abuse, many grow up to be abusers themselves. Admittedly, just learning about emotional intelligence in a classroom may not be sufficient for many of these victims to take the information and process the trauma on their own. However, as the classes work through the curriculum, it will be obvious to the teachers of those classes which students need additional help which can then be provided for them. When we help these children to process the trauma associated with being victims of abuse, then they will no longer be doomed to live their life under the shadow of the abuse and will be free to develop and grow emotionally, intellectually, and conscientiously.

If somebody abuses another person, whether it be physically, sexually, or emotionally, then that person is someone who does not understand the basic truth of reality.... Everything is connected. I contend that if you are born into a world where everyone understands that everything is connected, and nobody has to worry about their basic needs being met, and one where everyone knows their neighbors to be Responsible Members of the Community of Life, then the prevalence of these types of abusive behaviors will drop dramatically.

SUICIDE

According to the World In Data website, 54 million people died worldwide in 2017, and almost 794,000 of those deaths, or 1.5% of them, were by suicide. The numbers in the US for that year were proportionately similar. For 2017, there were 2,813,503 registered deaths and 47,173 of those, or about 1.7% were by suicide.

Whether you focus on the worldwide numbers, or just the numbers for the US, this is a lot of people who choose to end their own lives. Everyone who commits suicide has their own reason for doing so. Some of the people who kill themselves leave a note, but most do not, leaving the rest of us with the task of ascertaining their reason for taking this significant and dramatic action. Many people who choose to end their own lives are depressed, and the causes of that depression vary widely.

Some reasons for suicide include the loss of a personal relationship such as a divorce or a breakup with a romantic partner, the death of a loved one, financial trouble, being the victim of abuse or bullying, or being the victim of a violent crime such as a rape or a physical assault. The source of depression for a lot of people has been shown to be unresolved childhood trauma. Depression can also be brought on through chronic physical pain. A feeling of hopelessness and helplessness because of the seeming insurmountability of alcoholism or drug addiction is a contributing factor in many suicides. Trepidation about something that may happen such as a criminal prosecution or a pending incarceration can also trigger suicidal thoughts. Fear of exposure for wrongdoings like embezzlement or sexual predation and the resulting shame, humiliation, and punishment that goes along with it has caused many to end their own lives. A medical diagnosis of a fatal illness that is certain to cause great physical hardship and suffering prior to a certain death has led many people to commit suicide. In fact, having received such a diagnosis is a part of the process required for euthanasia, or assisted suicide, which is legal in nine states plus the District of Columbia and in certain other countries as well.

In a post-soft landing world where everyone knows that everything is connected, where basic needs have been provided to all people everywhere, where our precious forests are no longer being cut down, and where we are no longer polluting our air, land and water, and where everyone knows themselves and all of their family members, neighbors, and friends to be Responsible Members of the Community of Life, depression will not be nearly as prevalent as it is today. And neither will violent crime or abusive behavior. Consequently, the number of people who contemplate suicide in our post-soft landing world will be greatly reduced. However, I would imagine that euthanasia, or rational, assisted suicide as an option for people with a terminal diagnosis will become far more accepted than it is today.

DEPRESSION

One definition of depression is a persistent low mood accompanied by an aversion to activity. People suffering from depression can be either mildly, moderately, or severely depressed. Many severely depressed people become so depressed and averse to activity that they literally cannot bring themselves to get out of bed. According to an annual survey by RTI International called the National Survey on Drug Use and Health, 17.3 million adults in the United States experienced a major depressive episode in 2017.

In this country, if you are feeling depressed, and you decide to turn to a trained professional for help, then it is highly likely that you will be prescribed antidepressant drugs. According to psychiatry, depression is caused by a chemical imbalance in the brain which can and should be treated with drugs. Accordingly, if you choose to consult with a psychiatrist or another MD about this issue, they are almost certainly going to tell you that your relief lies in a pill. A study released in 2011 by the National Center for Health Statistics (NCHS) reports that one of every 10 people in this country are taking an antidepressant drug. This means more than 30 million US citizens are taking antidepressants. Physicians regularly prescribe these drugs citing their ability to correct a deficiency of serotonin in the brain. In reality, there is not a single peer-reviewed article that directly supports this claim of serotonin deficiency in the brain, nor is there a peer-reviewed article showing that a chemical imbalance is the cause of depression. There are, however, numerous peer-reviewed articles that present evidence to the contrary for both of these assertions.

Typically, the other avenue besides medication that is available for a depressed person lies in psychotherapy. Although psychiatrists are trained in psychotherapy and are, of course, licensed to provide it, there are very few psychiatrists who are interested in providing psychotherapy for their patients. Because of this, patients who chooses psychotherapy are usually guided by a licensed professional psychotherapist who is not a psychiatrist. In psychotherapy the patient undergoes an exploration of their personal life looking for the root cause of the depression. Sometimes through the process of psychotherapy, the cause of depression is identified as something in the patient's recent past that is obvious to both the patient and the psychotherapist, in which case coping mechanisms are explored. But other times the cause is hidden in suppressed memories from early childhood. Often, these explorations of early childhood uncover painful childhood memories of a psychological trauma that has been suppressed from their conscious memories. Very often these traumas occurred because the patient was the victim of some sort of abuse. After bringing these suppressed and buried memories out into the open, relief can be provided by showing the patient that they were not to blame for being the victim of abuse.

Another frequently utilized and often effective psychotherapeutic tool for the treatment of depression is Cognitive Behavioral Therapy. CBT is a type of psychotherapeutic treatment that helps people learn how to identify and change destructive or disturbing thought patterns that have a negative influence on behavior and emotions. The treatment can be undertaken with the help of a therapist, or it may be self-guided with the help of books or online courses. Other practices that have been widely shown to provide lasting relief for people suffering from depression include changing their eating habits to a healthier diet free of sugar and junk food, getting regular exercise, and undertaking a regular meditation practice.

Any guesses about what I am going to say about depression? Of course I am going to tell you when we have successfully transformed our insane culture to a sane one that is based upon the truth that everything is connected, depression will largely disappear. When we all know ourselves and all of our neighbors to be Responsible Members of the Community of Life we will all feel a lot better about things. When we have succeeded in providing basic needs to all people everywhere, when we have stopped cutting down our precious forests, and when we have ceased polluting our air, land, and water, there will be significantly fewer situations that could cause us to be depressed.

Johann Hari wrote a wonderful book on this subject wherein he asserted that the root cause of depression is definitely not because of a chemical imbalance in the brain but instead it is societal and cultural. In fact, his main theme is that depression and anxiety are caused by widespread disconnection at a cultural level. The book is called *Lost Connections: Why You're Depressed and How to Find Hope*. There are chapters on disconnection from meaningful work, disconnection from other people, disconnection from meaningful values, disconnection from childhood trauma, disconnection from status and respect, disconnection from the natural world, and disconnection from a secure future. His solution is for us to culturally achieve a reconnection with all of these things. He advocates for the providing of a universal basic income as a first step.

Here is a quote from his concluding chapter:

> Once we understand that depression is to a significant degree a collective problem caused by something that has gone wrong in our culture, it becomes obvious that the solutions have to be to a significant degree collective too. We have to change our culture so that more people are freed up to change their lives.

It is gratifying to see a book that echoes so many of the things I have been asserting herein to be so well received both by the critics and the public. Everything is connected!

GUN VIOLENCE

When you look at the countries that have a lot of guns in private ownership and compare them to countries where their citizens don't own so many guns, you find just what you would expect to find. The countries who have more guns have more gun violence. They have more people who are shot by guns. They have more gun-related homicides, and they have more suicides by guns.

Much like the problems of overcrowded prisons and the high cost of health care we have examined earlier in this chapter, if you want to look at the extreme end of the issue, then take a look at the United States. Even though the US population represents only 4% of worldwide population, private citizens within the US own 48% of the 875 million guns owned by private citizens worldwide. An estimated 34% of these guns are handguns. If you do the math, this means we have around 143 million handguns in this country.

According to the FBI, approximately 68% of the almost 13,000 firearm-related homicides that occur annually are accomplished with handguns. Suicides by firearm outnumber gun-related homicides 2 to 1, and almost all of those suicides are accomplished with a handgun.

Here is what the rock group Lynyrd Skynyrd has to say about handguns in their hit song, "Saturday Night Special".

Handguns are made for killin'
They ain't good for nothin' else
And if you like to drink your whiskey
You might even shoot yourself
So why don't we dump 'em people
To the bottom of the sea
Before some ol' fool comes around here
Wanna shoot either you or me

That song came out in 1975. Apparently, they were listening in our nation's capital, because in 1976, Washington D.C. passed a law banning handguns. Unfortunately, only one other major US city followed suit, and that city was Chicago who passed their own ordinance banning handguns in 1982. Handguns remained illegal in D.C. for 32 years until the handgun ban there was deemed to be unconstitutional in a 2008 Supreme Court decision styled *District of Columbia v. Heller*. Then, two years later in 2010, the ban in Chicago was struck down in another Supreme Court decision. As you would expect, these handgun bans, situated as they were in areas where purchasing, selling and owning handguns remained legal all around them, had a somewhat limited result. All during the times when these bans were in effect there were still plenty of illegal handguns in both of these cities.

Probably the main reason the US has so many more guns in private ownership than other developed nations is because of the Second Amendment which reads in its entirety as follows:

Second Amendment. A well regulated Militia, being necessary to the security of a free State, the right of the people to keep and bear Arms, shall not be infringed.

Throughout our country's history, there has been a lot of debate about what the framers had in mind when they wrote the Second Amendment, and especially what they had in mind when they mentioned the Militia. The 2008 Supreme Court decision in District of Columbia v. Heller has settled this question, at least for the moment. According to *District of Columbia v. Heller*, the right to bear arms is an individual right independent of service in a state militia. However, Justice Scalia wrote in the majority opinion that the right is not unlimited, and it does not preclude certain long-standing prohibitions, such as those forbidding possession of firearms by felons and the mentally ill. And it does not preclude restrictions on the carrying of dangerous and unusual weapons. I would assert that handguns and assault rifles would qualify as "dangerous and unusual", but for now at least, that is not the accepted legal view in this country.

Unlike other modern, developed nations who look at the facts and then decide to impose common-sense restrictions on gun ownership, in this country we cannot even establish a requirement for universal background checks before a citizen is permitted to purchase a firearm. Other countries have looked at handguns and assault weapons and correctly ascertained that their only purpose is to kill other human beings, and therefore have either banned the ownership of these lethal weapons by private citizens, or regulated and restricted their sale, use and possession. We actually did have a nationwide ban on ownership of assault weapons in this country. But unfortunately, the ban only ran between 1994 and 2004, and it is no longer in effect.

The US has the 11th highest per capita rate of gun violence in the world, surpassed only by Honduras, Venezuela, Swaziland,

Guatemala, Jamaica, El Salvador, Colombia, Brazil, Panama, and Uruguay. But when you look at the per capita statistics for gun violence within high-income countries, the US stands out like a sore thumb. Compared to an average for other high-income nations, the United States has a gun homicide rate that is 25 times higher. Certainly, one big reason for this is that we have so many more guns in private hands in this country than do citizens in the other developed nations.

But I propose another factor that I believe is even more relevant than the "too many guns" reason for the high rate of gun violence in the US. And that is the high level of economic stress and deprivation in our cities. We just don't take care of our poor citizens as well as the other developed nations do. When people are packed together in small spaces, and everyone is struggling to provide their basic needs, then life is not near as precious for the general population as it is for other people who do not struggle so much. Our 25 largest cities contain only 10 percent of the US population, but 20% of the homicides by firearm take place within them. When you are constantly struggling to provide your basic needs, then killing, or being killed or injured by gunfire, does not seem so outlandish as it does to a person who is looking forward to attending the opera.

I have every confidence that radically reducing our level of gun violence in this country will be one of the many immediate, positive benefits we will receive when we decide to provide basic needs for all people everywhere.

MASS SHOOTINGS

I remember looking incredulously at the huge headlines in the newspaper when it reported on the University of Texas clock tower shooting. It was 1966, and I was 12 years old. "How could this be?" I wondered. "What would cause a man to kill all of those innocent people like that? This is crazy!"

I also remember the 1991 massacre in Killeen. It was a huge story, and it happened only a short drive from Austin, where I had been living for almost two years. A 35 year-old guy had driven his pickup into a Luby's cafeteria and opened fire with two 9mm semi-automatic pistols, killing 24 people and injuring another 20 before killing himself.

And I remember other mass shootings. There was the disgruntled post office worker in Edmond, Oklahoma who killed 15 people in 1986. The 1984 mass killing in the McDonald's in San Diego was another big one. That guy killed 22 people and wounded another 19. And there were other mass killings during those earlier years. But during that time there seemed to be some space between incidents. Mass shootings during those times were unusual enough to be really shocking when the big ones took place. But then came the shooting by two killers at the Columbine High School in Littleton, Colorado, and the pace of the mass killings seemed to speed up. Some of them happened in the workplace. Some happened at church. Others at stores, or restaurants or shopping malls. There was another really big one at a movie theatre in Aurora, Colorado. They were all terrible tragedies.

But the really terrible ones happened at schools where the innocent, young children were taken from us all before they had a chance to make something of their lives. 13 were killed and 24 more were injured at Columbine. The total was 32 dead and 23 injured at Virginia Tech. 20 elementary school students were killed along with 6 teachers at Sandy Hook Elementary School. 10 high school students were killed at Santa Fe High School near Houston. 17 more high school students killed in Parkland, Florida. And there were other terrible, tragic shootings as well. The two most prolific mass shootings in history have taken place during the past four years. These are the Orlando night club massacre in which 49 people died, and the Las Vegas Strip massacre in which 58 people were killed and another 546 people were injured. The shooter in Las Vegas targeted concertgoers from the 32nd floor of a hotel using semiautomatic rifles modified with bump stocks to make them operate like automatic weapons.

There have been a lot of different studies done on mass shootings utilizing somewhat varying criteria. *The Washington Post* found there to be 163 such instances in the US between 1967 and June of 2019. In their piece, the Post specified that mass shootings were an act of public firearm violence in which four or more people are killed not including the shooter. For the purposes of their report, gang killings, domestic violence and terrorist acts were excluded. *Mother Jones* has an online database showing the details of 118 similarly defined mass shootings that took place in the US between 1982 and 2020. The information on the *Mother Jones* site includes the location, the date, a summary of the shooting including the name of the shooter, the number of people killed and injured, whether it took place at a school, religious setting, military base, workplace, or other public place, the age of the shooter and the shooter's race and gender, whether the shooter had prior mental health issues, and the weapons used, including where they were obtained, and whether or not they were obtained legally.

There have also been a lot of different studies done on the mental states of the shooters, as well as a lot of studies done on how the shooters obtained their weapons and whether or not stricter gun laws might have prevented the shooters from obtaining them. Typically, the gun-rights advocates want to blame these killings on the insanity of the shooters, and the gun-control advocates want to blame them on the easy access to guns, as well as the easy availability of high capacity clips, bump stocks, and assault rifles. There have been so many of these mass shootings that each side on this argument has been able to point to certain incidents that seem to support their positions.

To me, the formula in every one of these incidents was for somebody to decide they are going to commit suicide and their life is over. But for one reason or another, they decide they want to make some news and take some innocent people out along with them. While, in many cases, a desire to end one's own life can be understood on a rational basis, a desire to take innocent lives at the same time is much harder to understand and rationalize. The only motivation I can see that even remotely makes sense is that the act of indiscriminately murdering others in a very public way is done as revenge against our culture in general for the fact that the shooter feels their own life is not worth living.

One of the studies I read about in my research into this issue was funded by the National Institute of Justice. I found an op-ed in the *LA Times* that said the study had included building a database going back to 1966 of every shooter who killed four or more people in a public place, and of every shooting incident that took place in a school, workplace, or place of worship since 1999. One of the main findings of the study was that the vast majority of the shooters had experienced early childhood trauma and exposure to violence at a young age. If this is actually correct, and these shooters are motivated by revenge for the fact that their own lives are not worth living, then the solution available to our collective society is to help these potential shooters to work through the issues from their childhood that are causing them to think/feel that their lives are not worth living. I believe this is actually doable, but it needs to be done earlier in the shooter's life, before the unresolved trauma reaches a crisis point. And the way to accomplish it is via emotional intelligence classes and programs in our schools.

Very few of us come from two parents who are both highly functional emotionally. And even if both of our parents are highly functional emotionally, it is still possible for us to experience emotional trauma when we are little through other causes. Accordingly, since we are not trained or learned in emotional intelligence, the emotional dysfunction that we are exposed to throughout our childhoods is often carried with us resulting in our own dysfunctional behavior that becomes a part of our own parental practices when we have children of our own. High quality programs and classes teaching emotional intelligence in our schools will teach our children how to properly process the traumas that they experience as children so that the emotional blockages resulting from these traumas are not carried forward and become debilitating to them and potentially dangerous to others. At the same time, children who have experienced traumas that they are unable to process can be identified, and these children may be given the additional help they need in order to work through and properly process their traumas at an early age.

Please understand, I don't believe the implementation of these emotional intelligence classes would magically solve our mass shooter problem in its entirety. I do believe, however, that such a program would be highly impactful on reducing the number of potential mass shooters. But even more importantly, over time it would have a profoundly positive impact on our collective consciousness.

And of course, when our children are born into a world where everyone understands that everything is connected, and where basic needs have been provided for all people everywhere, and where our forests are no longer being cut down, and where we have ceased polluting, and where everyone knows themselves and all of their neighbors to be Responsible Members of the Community of Life, then I contend these potential mass shooters will not feel so motivated towards revenge against our culture in general.

FINAL THOUGHTS ON THE WORLD'S BIGGEST PROBLEMS

In closing, let me ask.... In the absence of the achieving of a cultural shift along the lines advocated herein, do you foresee a time when wars are not being fought in multiple locations around the globe? Do you foresee a time when all of the nuclear-capable countries have voluntarily relinquished their nuclear arsenals? Do you foresee a time when you don't have to worry about crime or terrorism? Do you foresee a time when millions of people around the world are no longer starving and nobody is struggling to provide themselves and their families with their basic needs? Do you foresee a time when racism and misogyny are problems of the past? Do you foresee a time when millions of our citizens are not zonked out on drugs and alcohol in a futile effort to escape the insanity of living in a world with so many insurmountable problems?

My answer is, "No... I cannot foresee such a time."

However, in a world where basic needs have been provided for all people everywhere, where our precious forests are no longer being cut down, and where we are no longer polluting our air, land and water, I can definitely foresee such a time.

This is what I was so excited about when I first read *Ishmael*. There is a way out of this mess! The fix is at the foundational level of our culture! We can do it! All it requires is the creation of a Critical Mass of people who understand the need for change and who stand ready to remake our present insane, separation-based culture into our new, sane culture that is grounded upon the reality of connectedness.

We can do it!

We can resume our roles as **Responsible Members** of the Community of Life!

We can save the world!

If we are going to achieve this world-saving cultural shift, then we need to understand that one of the biggest barriers to bringing this flawed and doomed culture in for a successful soft landing is the fact that so much of what goes on in this insane world is the result of big corporations manipulating legislation and regulation (or lack thereof) in order to enhance their growth and increase their profits. This is something that needs to be rectified as soon as possible. As we shall see in the next chapter, action to rectify this does require a Critical Mass, but not the same Critical Mass we have been talking about in regard to cultural shifts.

7

Our Corporate Rulers

If anyone reading this is still looking for proof that our culture is insane, please consider this.... Do you think that in a sane world, corporations would make all of the biggest, most important decisions regarding how our world should be ordered? (With corporate profits being the main decision-making criteria.) Do you understand that this is what has been happening in our world for a very long time? For instance, did insurance companies have our collective wellbeing in mind when they poured millions of dollars into our United States Congress in order to prevent health care legislation that would render them useless? Did the financial sector have our financial wellbeing in mind when they influenced that same Congress to repeal the legislation that was put in place after the Great Depression in order to prevent another great depression? Do you think the main goal of the pharmaceutical companies is for each of us to enjoy total and complete health? Do the military-industrial companies want a world free of conflict and war? Do you think the oil companies want us to make the transition to electric cars and renewable energy? Do the auto manufacturing companies want us to have cheap and reliable mass transit systems, and communities planned with bicycles and walking in mind?

The answer to each of these questions is.... "Of course not." Despite what the public relations departments of these huge corporate entities might say, these corporations are interested only in their own bottom lines. They want to increase their profits and they want to get even bigger than they already are. Sustainability, environmental consciousness, and our collective wellbeing are simply not important considerations for any of them. And they have gotten so big and powerful that, with our very government itself working at their beck and call, they have taken over the decision-making process that pertains to all of the biggest issues facing our world of today.

Once we achieve a Critical Mass of people who understand that our present culture is insane and we make a collective decision to return to a culture based upon the reality that everything is connected, then of course, we will realize immediately that we must take our world back from the huge and powerful corporations that have stolen it from us. And fortunately, once enough of us understand the necessity of doing this, taking the power back is something that is within our grasp to be accomplished. All we have to do is to wake up enough of our fellow citizens to the fact that our government has been stolen, and then we can simply take it back. Here in the United States, the corporate powers are calling all of the shots. But they will continue to do so only for so long as "we, the people" allow them to. Once "we, the people" demand that our government be returned to us, then through our votes and the legislative process that has been in place since 1789, it will be.

Just like the larger issue of replacing our entire culture with one based upon the reality that everything is connected, this issue of taking the power back from corporate interests will be accomplished by achieving a Critical Mass of people who understand how things came to be this way and stand ready to make a positive change for the better.

Today, there are millions of people who are looking for answers because they can see that our glaciers are melting, our sea levels are rising, and our storms are getting stronger. Likewise, there are many millions of us who have seen the insanity of allowing these huge corporate interests to have so much influence in our government and our legislative process. Recently, we went through a huge financial crisis. To many of us, it was obvious that the crisis was caused by deregulation and the lack of governmental oversight and enforcement of safeguards that had been in place to prevent these types of abuses. And immediately after experiencing the financial crisis, we all watched as the legislative battle for a health care bill waged. Anybody who didn't notice the influence exerted on the legislative process by the insurance industry and the pharmaceutical companies simply wasn't paying proper attention.

Just as technology, by itself, is not evil or wrong, corporations, by themselves, are not evil or wrong. There are good reasons for allowing corporations to exist. Basically, corporations are one of a handful of vehicles people can utilize to conduct business in lieu of sole proprietorships or partnerships. The limitation of stockholder liability, which is afforded to corporations, allows individuals to invest in a corporation with the knowledge and understanding that their losses will be limited to the amount of money they choose to invest in purchasing the stock. Without this limitation of liability, it would be very difficult to get people to invest in an enterprise where they have so little personal control of the business itself. Also known as the corporate shield, this aspect of corporations allows stockholders to conduct business through their corporate vehicles with the assurance that any liability incurred will be limited to the assets of the corporation and cannot be transferred to them, personally. Again, without this shield, it would be much more difficult to attract investors.

There is nothing wrong with the basic concept of corporations. The problem is that we have allowed corporations to become too powerful. Little by little, over time, corporations have used their wealth to amass power. We should not have allowed it, but we did. And now, the time has come to rectify the situation.

Those of us who have already studied this issue understand that the fix is easy. Since we are currently prohibited from discriminating against corporations because of a legal concept called "corporate personhood", all we need to do is to get rid of that insane concept... by abolishing corporate personhood. For those not familiar with this, abolishing corporate personhood means rescinding the case law we have in place telling us that these artificial entities called corporations should enjoy the same rights and privileges as individual, living and breathing people. The term "corporate personhood" refers to the legal fiction that the rights set out in the Bill of Rights and the Fourteenth Amendment to the Constitution apply not only to individual citizens, but also to corporations, which are called "artificial persons". Once it again becomes clear to a majority of the voters in this country that the Bill of Rights and the Fourteenth Amendment were written with real people in mind, we will be able to abolish corporate personhood and resume the sane practice of discriminating against these artificial entities... something that we are currently prevented from doing.

Abolishing corporate personhood is something that doesn't have to wait. Although this is a huge issue, it is a smaller, simpler problem than replacing our insane culture, and it can be dealt with now. All that is needed is the collective will of a majority of voters. Even within the framework of our present insane culture, it is easy to see that allowing huge corporations to make all of the most important decisions about how our world operates needs to be fixed. The corporations who make these decisions don't care about human suffering. They don't need breathable air or drinkable water. They don't need health care because they can't get sick, and they have no physical body to be injured or even incarcerated if they break the law. Consequently, corporations and living, breathing, people have different sets of criteria to analyze when making decisions.

When deciding whether or not to cut down an ancient forest or to pollute or not to pollute a body of water or our atmosphere, a corporation simply looks at how much risk is involved and how much it will cost versus how much profit they will receive. And since these artificial entities don't care about our environment or drinkable water or breathable air, they usually decide to cut down the forest and to pollute as much as they can get away with. As previously mentioned, the term the MBA students learn in business school is the "externalizing of costs". The corporations dump the pollutants because it costs them less, and the cost of cleaning up the mess is "externalized" by passing it along to the taxpayers.

If actual people were making these decisions based upon considerations other than profit, then of course, we would decide not to pollute. Why? Because the pollution harms our environment and it is difficult and very expensive to clean it up. Dirty air and foul water make us sick. And it also makes life tough for our fellow members of the Community of Life on this planet. Besides, the pollution eventually has to be cleaned up and it simply costs much less not to pollute in the first place than it does to clean it up. Foremost in our decision, of course, would be the fact that those of us who are not stockholders in a corporation which is deciding whether to pollute or not to pollute or even how much to pollute, don't care whether the corporation makes a profit or not. We just want them to stop fouling our air and water and expecting the rest of us to either live with it or pay to clean it up.

Let's take a look at how things came to be this way. Until the Declaration of Independence was signed in 1776, the thirteen colonies were subject to British rule. All serious students of early American history understand that, in a large part, our American Revolution was fought because of unfair taxes imposed on the colonists by England, as well as other issues. One of those issues was tea. American colonists were not only unhappy with the tax on tea imposed by the Townsend Acts, but by the high cost resulting from other laws concerning its importation from India through England, that also served to raise the price. In response, a thriving smuggling business of Danish tea had been established.

The stockholders of the British East India Tea Company were the King of England and other members of the royal family, together with other members of the British aristocracy, as well as many members of the British Parliament. In other words, the stockholders of the British East India Tea Company were men of considerable power and wealth who had no qualms about passing legislation designed to exploit the colonists in order to increase their corporate profits. The Tea Act, passed in 1773, was an effort by the British Parliament to undercut the smugglers and save the financially troubled British East India Tea Company. The bill eliminated the requirement that Indian tea be sold first in England, thereby cutting out the additional cost of the middleman, and it also eliminated the export tax that had previously been imposed. The very objectionable tax on tea, however, remained in force.

By 1776, the colonists had had enough of the exploitation and 56 brave men laid their lives and their fortunes on the line when they signed the Declaration of Independence. The rest... as they say... is history.

Here, in the United States, we have much to be thankful for in terms of our heritage and the legacy left to us by our founding fathers. Between the signing of the Declaration of Independence in 1776 and the ratifying of the Constitution in 1789, our founding fathers worked out a framework for the world's first, modern democracy. Included in the Constitution was a brilliant system of checks and balances designed to ensure that none of the three branches of our government could usurp too much power without being thwarted by the other two branches.

In his book *Unequal Protection: How Corporations Became "People" and How You Can Fight Back*, Thom Hartmann reported it can be seen in the Federalist Papers that Jefferson and Hamilton argued and debated between themselves as to whether or not there were sufficient safeguards included within the Constitution regarding corporate abuses of power. In the end, Hamilton prevailed and the additional safeguards Jefferson wanted were not included. Part of the problem Jefferson faced in debating Hamilton about the necessity for additional safeguards from corporate abuses of power was that in the early days of our nation, corporate charters were granted for very limited purposes, and also for limited time periods. After all, the American Revolution had just been fought in part as a result of unfair trade advantages enjoyed by the British East Indian Tea Company. And consequently, everyone in the fledgling nation was very aware of the dangers of unchecked corporate power.

Accordingly, very few corporate charters were granted in the early days of our nation. And those that were granted were for very specific purposes and for limited times as well. As a part of their process in receiving a charter, they had to demonstrate a benefit to society for their very existence. In the event one of these corporations, after having received their charter, began acting outside of their original, stated purpose to the perceived detriment of the society at large, then the corporate charter was forfeited and the corporation was dissolved. Also, the granting of corporate charters has always been a function of state governments, and this is another reason the safeguards were not addressed in the Federal Constitution. Furthermore, corporations were prohibited from participating in political elections, and the fines and jail terms for any corporations who made campaign contributions were extremely harsh. It was understood by everyone that corporations had no business engaging in politics in any manner whatsoever.

But today, corporations are under no such mandate to demonstrate any benefit to society. On the contrary, eBay prevailed in a Delaware court in 2010 when they asserted that craigslist, Inc., was obligated to its shareholders to pursue corporate profits over community service. (*eBay Domestic Holdings, Inc. versus Craig Newmark, James Buckmaster, and craigslist, Inc. Delaware Court of Chancery Cause No. 3705-CC)* In the future, when the politicians call on the corporations to be more socially responsible, it is our individual responsibility to recognize that plan for what it truly is....

Complete bullshit. It might be appropriate for a politician to call for corporations to be more law abiding, but corporations actually have a legal duty to their shareholders to pursue profit over community service.

Not only can these immortal, artificial entities amass unlimited wealth by pooling the resources of thousands of investors, but also, because of the lobbying process and changes in campaign finance laws, these huge corporations have basically taken ownership of our government itself. The 2010 U. S. Supreme Court decision in *Citizens United versus the Federal Election Commission,* which asserted that corporations have a First Amendment right to spend money in elections, was without a doubt, one of the worst developments in our country's entire history in terms of how it has undermined the ability of our government to represent "we the people". Today, I think it is safe to say that no law gets passed in Washington, D. C. that the corporate interests do not approve.

During the 1800's the big corporate powers were the banks, along with the manufacturing, mining, and railroad companies. All of these sectors grew tremendously as a result of increased government spending during the Civil War. And as they grew, these big corporations began to whittle away at the safeguards set up to keep them in check. I guess it is only natural that a big, powerful corporate entity, like these railroad companies, would endeavor to test the established boundaries like the constitution and the various statutes that were in place in order to keep these corporations from becoming too powerful. (And that is why Jefferson was correct when he argued with Hamilton over the need for additional safeguards.) In *Unequal Protection,* Hartmann showed how these railroad companies figured out that if corporations could be considered as "artificial people" in regard to the Constitution and the Bill of Rights, then many of the restrictions placed upon them in order to keep them in check could be circumvented.

After the Civil War, the Thirteenth, Fourteenth, and Fifteenth Amendments to the Constitution were passed in order to protect the rights of former slaves. The Fourteenth Amendment was especially attractive to the railroads… It prohibited discrimination.

Ironically, after the Amendments were passed in order to help integrate freed slaves into our culture, the railroad companies saw the broad language used to prevent discrimination and began asserting that the amendments were designed to protect them as well. Their strategy was to win a United States Supreme Court case asserting their rights as "persons" to be protected from discrimination under the Fourteenth Amendment. So, beginning with *Paul versus Virginia* in 1868, they began pushing cases all the way to the United States Supreme Court at every opportunity, asserting that corporate personhood should extend the protection of the Fourteenth Amendment to these artificial entities.

Many times, the cases themselves were not that important to them. But they knew, if they kept trying, there was an excellent chance that eventually, they would succeed with their assertion of corporate personhood. Time after time, they either lost the case or the case was decided in their favor but the decision was based upon other arguments. Then, in 1886, a case titled *Santa Clara County versus Southern Pacific Railroad* made it to the Supreme Court.

In the grand scheme of things, it was just another unimportant case concerning property taxes. But, as part of their arguments, Southern Pacific asserted the rights of corporations to "personhood" and the protection afforded to people under the Fourteenth Amendment to the Constitution and the Bill of Rights. The court ruled in favor of Southern Pacific, but specifically did not address the railroad's assertion of corporate personhood. However, the clerk of the Supreme Court was an ex-railroad company executive, and he incorrectly (fraudulently?) put in the header for the case that the court had decided on the issue of corporate personhood and declared corporations to be artificial persons.

Despite the inaccuracy of this assertion, the case was relied upon subsequently, and corporations have used their "personhood" in order to assert their rights as people under the Constitution and the Bill of Rights ever since then. And, due to the many cases having been decided since that time which were based upon this incorrect or possibly fraudulent assertion, the concept of "corporate personhood" is so entrenched in case law, it has become a basic part of the law here in the United States.

Do you think the founding fathers had corporations in mind when they wrote the Constitution and the Bill of Rights? Maybe even more importantly... Did Abraham Lincoln pass the Fourteenth Amendment in order to help corporations? Do you think these artificial entities called corporations, which are designed to pool the wealth and resources of thousands of people, can live forever, do not require clean air to breathe, don't care about clean water to drink, and make all of their decisions based solely upon considerations of profit and growth, should actually be afforded the same rights as people? What possible benefit to society could there be in giving these protections to corporations?

Clearly, Thomas Jefferson would not be happy to see the present state of our nation or, for that matter, the world... That is, of course, unless he enjoyed being right more than he enjoyed seeing his concept for a new nation manifested. Our situation of today is exactly what Jefferson feared... Corporate rule. For more than two hundred years now, corporations have been chipping away at the safeguards set up to protect "we the people" from the terrible power the founders knew they could wield if left unchecked. The key battle took place in the United States Supreme Court and was won by the corporations when they claimed "corporate personhood" and protection from discrimination under the Fourteenth Amendment. Little can be done to rectify this situation until "we the people" regain the ability to "discriminate" against these giants. Once we abolish the legal fiction of "corporate personhood" and again regain the ability to treat these artificial entities like artificial entities, then something can be done.

Until that time comes, we will all live in an insane world where not only is the culture itself insane, but that insane culture is ruled by corporate entities whose sole reasons for existence are to grow and to profit. If you think I am overstating the situation, then please consider this.... There is a series of annual studies ranking the top economic entities from largest to smallest utilizing revenue for corporations and GDP for countries. According to the study, the economy of the United States is far and away the largest economic entity in the world. However, a 2011 study has the European Union, slightly ahead of the U. S. Of course, the EU is comprised of 28 countries, so that is not a fair comparison. But, more pertinent to our discussion of corporations, in the year 2000, according to a study conducted by the Institute for Policy Studies, only 49 of the world's 100 largest economic entities were still countries.

In that study, the top 22 entities were countries, but coming in just behind Turkey at number 23, was General Motors. Four of the next five spots were held by corporate entities, namely Wal-Mart, ExxonMobil, Ford, and Daimler/Chrysler, resulting in five corporate entities occupying the top 28 spots. Since then, several groups have updated this list including Forbes Magazine who reported that 95 of the world's 150 largest economic entities were corporations in the year 2005. That list had three of the world's largest oil companies plus Wal-Mart in the top 25 and ranked above such countries as Indonesia, Saudi Arabia, Norway, Denmark, Poland, South Africa, and Greece.

The 2011 study by *Fortune Magazine* has the top three corporate entities coming in at 26th through 28th, right behind Norway. Corporations held 43 of the top 100 spots in 2011. My research wasn't able to turn up any follow up studies after 2011, until Global Justice Now, a charity focusing on alleviating poverty, started putting out new rankings in 2014. However, rather than using GDP figures for countries, the Global Justice Now rankings utilized government revenue figures taken from the CIA World Factbook, and revenue figures for corporations came from *Fortune Magazine's* Global 500 list. This change resulted in a large increase in the inclusion of corporations. The 2015 study included 69 corporations in the top 100, and a total of 153 corporations in the top 200 of the world's largest economic entities.

If corporations are to be afforded the rights and protections of people under the Constitution of the United States of America, then how in the world are we supposed to protect ourselves from abuses by these huge artificial entities? Of course, most of the wealthy corporations on these lists, as well as thousands more, are operating here in the United States. Now that they have claimed the rights and protections of people under the Bill of Rights and the Fourteenth Amendment, how much influence on the workings of our federal, state, and local governments do you think these rich and powerful corporations have in relation to "we the people" and our measly votes?

But perhaps the biggest question we should be asking ourselves is, "What benefit to society does the existence of these humongous corporations represent?" And remember, these giants are artificial entities whose right to exist is predicated on our permission. Let's look at the corporations on these lists in terms of the sectors of the economy that each of them represents and examine whether that sector benefits our society, or whether the business sector represented by these behemoths causes problems attributable to the influence wielded by their wealth and power.

CAR COMPANIES

Since GM was listed as the world's largest corporate entity in the study from 2000, let's begin with the automobile manufacturers. Nine of the 51 corporations from the Institute for Policy Studies list were car companies. Cars are nice, especially if you can afford to buy a more expensive luxury or high-performance model. But do we really want to live in a world where everyone needs to own a dependable personal automobile in order to meet our daily obligations of traveling back and forth to work, school, and the grocery store? Clearly, if actual people had been in charge of deciding how to organize our modern society, then these car companies would not be enjoying the benefits coming from our actual situation where every person living in the United States and in many other developed nations are dependent upon their personal automobiles to the extent that we are today.

Here in the U. S., the dad needs one car, the mom needs another, and any kids who are old enough to drive, need their own auto as well. Organizing our urban areas so that people could walk or ride bicycles from their homes to shopping areas, and also setting up a dependable and cheap mass transit system in our cities and even our smaller towns, would have been a very easy thing to do. Now, it is not going to be so easy to accomplish.

This was not an oversight. The car companies and the other big businesses that benefits from this insane situation... the oil companies... made sure to assert their influence so that mass transit systems were not developed. These companies wanted us all to be dependent on the automobile. This is actually a very well-known and much studied situation known as the General Motors Conspiracy Theory. I don't need to get into the details here. I'll just ask you to consider.... What has happened? And, who benefited? And, to remember the old adage that warns us, "Where there's smoke, there's fire".

Something must be done about reducing the extent to which our population in developed countries, and especially in the U. S., is dependent upon personal automobiles.

Of course, another very significant side to this question regarding our dependency upon personal automobiles, and to whether it benefits or hinders our society, is in regard to how much the use of personal automobiles is contributing to global warming. According to the pre-Trump EPA website, Transportation represents

27% of total U. S. greenhouse gas emissions. A study by Ames Laboratory, a U. S. Department of Energy contractor located on the campus of Iowa State University, states that light trucks and personal automobiles represent almost 60% of the total carbon dioxide emissions attributable to transportation.

It has been obvious to me for a very long time that we are all way too dependent upon personal automobiles. And furthermore, why aren't the personal automobiles that we do drive electric cars powered by solar panels located on the rooftops of our homes? If it were not for Elon Musk and his Tesla Motors, very little progress towards this achievable goal would have been made. Tesla has caused quite a stir with their Model S and its "Ludicrous Mode", which enables the car to go from 0-60 mph in only 2.3 seconds. In addition to increased performance, this tiny corporation has also made great strides in improving batteries. These Teslas with their 200 to 300-mile range, are finally making electric cars practical. Now they have the less expensive Model 3 in production, further cementing their practicality. Thanks to Elon Musk and Tesla, electric cars are no longer equated solely with golf carts.

It should be noted that Tesla is nowhere on any of the Institute for Policy Study or Fortune or Forbes lists regarding the world's largest economic entities. It appears the existence of this tiny corporation has pushed some of these enormous car manufacturers to concentrate more on reducing carbon emissions through electric motors, hydrogen fuel cell powered motors, and compressed natural gas (CNG) and propane (LPG) powered vehicles. If these giants had a conscience, something it seems to me an artificial person should definitely have, then they would have recognized the need for reducing carbon emissions decades ago, and this issue would already have been addressed.

WAL-MART

Wal-Mart is not actually a sector, but what about Wal-Mart? Is our society being well served by this huge corporation? Who benefits by the existence of Wal-Mart? Do Wal-Mart customers actually save enough money shopping there to compensate for all the pain and suffering caused by the Wal-Mart way of doing business? Do I actually need to go into details about the complaints that have been made about Wal-Mart? Is this possibly an area where it would be good for society to be able to discriminate against a corporation? Are you aware of all the communities who fought unsuccessfully to keep Wal-Mart from opening stores in their areas? Clearly, Wal-Mart knows how to play the anti-discrimination card.

OIL COMPANIES

The oil companies on these annual lists of the world's largest governments and corporations are all "integrated" oil companies, meaning they are involved in oil and gas exploration and production, and in the refining and marketing of oil. Most of the natural gas they produce is put into sales lines that are connected to the well after it is completed. These integrated oil companies, therefore, produce three main products... oil, natural gas, and refined petroleum products, the most important of which, by far, is gasoline.

In the U. S., about 68% of our oil is refined into gasoline and diesel fuel and used in cars and trucks for moving passengers and freight. Personal autos, including personal SUV's and personal trucks, use by far the largest part of this. The two other major uses for refined petroleum are heating oil and jet fuel. There are a myriad of other uses for the other by-products that come out of the refining process, and many of them, such as plastics, asphalt, and lubricants, are essential to our daily lives, but none of them represents a significant percentage of the total output from a barrel of oil.

So... as we have established, the primary use of oil is to provide fuel for vehicles with internal combustion engines. We often look at oil in terms of its relative contribution to our energy needs. And, it is often cited that oil represents a little over 35% of the total energy consumed in the United States. Although this is a true statement, there really is no need to make it. The fact is, we are dependent upon oil for transportation... period. Since oil has a different end use than the other forms of energy, there really is no need to lump it in with coal, natural gas, nuclear, and the renewable energies, all of which we are dependent upon for other uses. Oil is all about cars and trucks, and to a lesser degree, airplanes, trains, tractors, and industrial uses. If we didn't have so many internal combustion engines moving vehicles up and down our roads and highways, then we wouldn't need so much oil.

Oil companies do explore for and produce natural gas, which has very limited but growing use for transportation (less than 1% of total natural gas consumption goes for this), but a very significant part in electricity generation (27.4%). Natural gas is also used for heating homes and businesses, and for cooking much of our food and heating much of our hot water. It also has significant contributions to energy needs in the industrial sector. However, as noted earlier, oil companies typically sell their natural gas at the wellhead, and have no part in its transportation or its ultimate sale to the end users.

Obviously, the largest corporate entities in the world wield a lot of power. But what if they didn't wield so much power? What if ExxonMobil and their fellow giant oil companies, like Royal Dutch/Shell, BP Amoco, Chevron, and Conoco-Phillips, didn't have the ability to dictate which form of energy we would choose to utilize in order to transport ourselves and our freight from Point A to Point B? Let's consider, just for a moment, what our world might be like if we were not so dependent upon oil.

For one thing our communities would be organized so that people could walk or ride their bicycles, between their homes, their places of employment, their schools, and the shops, and grocery stores, at least to a much greater extent than they can today. Just this ability of the general population to be able to choose to walk or ride a bicycle would cut oil consumption dramatically, as well as provide lots of presently sedentary people with opportunities for much needed exercise. Then, dependable mass transit systems could be put into place in all of our cities.

Establishing dependable light rail, train and bus travel routes, both within and between cities and towns, could also save a lot of gasoline currently being used for travel in personal automobiles. Wouldn't you like to at least have the option of conserving this precious resource, while saving some money, polluting less, and cutting down on greenhouse gas emissions by walking or riding your bicycle, or taking a form of mass transit instead of driving yourself? Wouldn't it be nice if a family could get by with one car instead of three?

Cars are wonderful inventions. But I think that in a world where important decisions like "How much should individuals depend upon personal automobiles for basic travel?" are answered by "we the people" instead of giant corporations, whose sole criteria for making decisions are profit and growth, that "we the people" would look at the following facts and decide it is time to minimize our dependence upon cars.

❖ Exploration and production of oil and gas is a major contributor to pollution of our rivers and streams and our oceans, as well as increasingly to our groundwater sources of drinking water. Many of the biggest environmental disasters our world has known, as well as many thousands of others we don't hear about, have come about because of oil exploration, production, or transportation.

❖ Oil refineries are major polluters of our atmosphere and the land and waters near their locations.

❖ CO_2 emissions from personal automobiles are one of the biggest sources of the greenhouse gases that are driving global warming and climate change.

❖ Exhaust emissions from cars and trucks are the main source of atmospheric pollution in our cities.

❖ If not for the lobbying efforts of oil companies, we would be much farther along with mandates regarding fuel-efficient cars, as well as with the transition to electric cars.

❖ Automobiles powered by electric batteries operate with zero emissions of pollution or greenhouse gases.

And, in addition to reducing our dependence upon personal automobiles, we would definitely dictate that the cars and trucks we do drive should be more fuel-efficient. Ideally, we should all be driving fully electric cars powered by solar panels located on the rooftops of our homes. Realistically, we should recognize that personal automobiles are using up a precious and finite resource very rapidly, and the pollution and the greenhouse gases generated from using this fuel are having an extremely detrimental effect on our cities and on our planet. There is no doubt that we should be trying harder to transition off our dependence on oil. Definitely, if the oil companies and the car companies were not dictating to "we, the people" how our world should operate, then we would be making some very different choices.

Our present, worldwide daily consumption of oil has risen to around 96 million barrels per day; an amount that can be translated to more than 1,000 barrels per second. Imagine that next time you are stuck in traffic! The people on this planet are consuming 1,000 barrels of this stuff every second of every day! Do you think the oil companies are concerned about what is going to happen to our world full of people, whom they have made dependent upon this finite resource, when we run out of it? Of course not! Quite to the contrary.... They are looking forward to the increased prices they will receive as the demand begins to seriously exceed the supply. Just like every other company on these lists of the world's largest, their motivations are completely self-centered, and revolve around their own growth and profit... which puts them at odds with "We, the People" and our desires regarding a pollution-free planet with ice caps intact, for the benefit of ourselves, our children, future generations, and for the rest of the members of the Community of Life.

DEFENSE CONTRACTORS

Here is a sector of our economy that is literally tearing our world apart. Please consider again a question I asked earlier.... Do you think the arms industry and the defense contractors want us to live in a world free of conflict and war? Of course they don't. How would these giant corporations make any money selling tanks, warships, airplanes, missiles, guns, and bullets in a world like that? And considering that this is the reality, we must ask another question.... Do you think it might be possible for the giant corporations involved in the business of war to exert any influence as to whether the various nations of our world are at peace or at war with each other? Of course they can. And they do.

In January of 1961, Dwight Eisenhower famously warned us in his farewell speech of our need to "guard against the acquisition of unwarranted influence, whether sought or unsought, by the military-industrial complex."

Where is that peace dividend everyone was talking about after the Berlin Wall came crashing down in September of 1989? Stolen, I guess, by nineteen Muslims on September 11, 2001. No... scratch that.... It was stolen by the military-industrial complex that Dwight Eisenhower warned us about!

A quick Internet search indicates the wars in Iraq and Afghanistan have cost us more than one trillion dollars, and probably more than 3 trillion when all pertinent costs are included. I think enough time has passed now so that we can safely say that the war in Iraq was either a mistake caused by faulty intelligence... or sending our men and women to fight and die was a choice made by George W. Bush and accomplished by lies and fudged intelligence. Seventeen years later, Saddam is gone, but is Iraq any better off? Is the region any better after all of the lives have been sacrificed and the trillions spent? And how about Afghanistan? By what rationale did we ever send troops there in the first place? Wouldn't it have been more appropriate to treat the capture of Osama Bin Laden and his Al Qaeda associates as a police action rather than a military one? Who made the decision that Afghanistan was ready for democracy? And who decided it was up to our country to make it happen with a military invasion?

Have you ever tried to imagine how much money a trillion dollars is? Whether we realize it or not, "we the people" are making a choice to spend this money on wars of occupation, when we could choose instead to spend the money on education, health care, infrastructure, and social programs, all of which are in dire need of funding right now. How is this choice to spend the money made? I'll tell you. It is made by the defense contractors and the arms manufacturers because "we the people" allow them to do so. These for-profit corporations make it happen by pouring millions of dollars into Washington in order to influence the decision makers.

According to the International Institute for Strategic Studies, the United States spent more than $597 billion on defense in 2015. According to the same source, the country with the next highest defense expenditure was China, with $146 billion. Next was Saudi Arabia with $82 billion, and then the UK with $56 billion.

Do you think it is okay that the country that is famous for implementing the world's first modern democracy should be outspending the next eleven countries with the highest defense spending numbers combined? Yes.... This is true. The United States spends more on defense in a given year than China, Saudi Arabia, the United Kingdom, Russia, India, France, Japan, Germany, South Korea, Italy, Brazil, and Australia, combined! Does this fact indicate to you that the focus of the United States might be more offensive than defensive? Or, alternatively, could the reason for this travesty possibly lie in the profit motive for large corporations engaging in the business of providing arms and weapons and soliciting lucrative contracts from the Department of Defense?

And, of course, the most important point that needs to be made about the business of war has absolutely nothing to do with money. But it does have to do with everything being connected. War is going to be a part of our lives for as long as we continue to live in an insane culture where the people believe the world was made for our species to conquer and rule it, and where the food continues to be locked up. Once we make the transition to a world where each of us know ourselves to be Responsible Members of the Community of Life, and where each of us is secure in the knowledge that basic needs for all people everywhere have been provided for, and where each of us knows that we have finally stopped the destruction of our precious forests, and the pollution of our air and water, then all of these wars we are experiencing all over the globe today, will quickly disappear.

Until that time comes, however, we can help ourselves tremendously by recognizing the situation we are in today, where for-profit corporations operating in the business of war are exerting their considerable influence as to whether or not our world is at peace or at war. Let's cut our defense budget in half as a prelude to cutting the remaining half by 90%. I guarantee you; the military, the arms manufacturers, and the defense contractors will be the only ones who complain.

Transforming our culture is a huge undertaking. The only way it can ever be done is by achieving that all-important Critical Mass of people who understand that it must be done. But between now and then, we can help ourselves and improve our world considerably by taking a clear-eyed look at our situation and then by taking reasonable steps to improve what we see. For instance, we need to recognize that there is an inherent conflict between what is best for "we the people" and what is best for the huge corporations operating within the defense industry. Basically, "we, the people" want peace. And the defense contractors and arms manufacturers want to profit and grow larger... something that is hard for them to do in the absence of armed conflicts. So, these corporations sell arms and weapons to unstable and undemocratic nations with authoritarian regimes, and, largely because of the instability they cause by arming our enemies, they influence our own government to spend more money on defense than the next eleven top spenders combined. If we would simply recognize this situation for what it really is, then we could take steps to mitigate the influence that these huge for-profit corporations are exerting on our world.

If it were up to me, I would bring all of our military personnel from all over the world, home tomorrow, cut our defense budget to the very bone, and begin cashing in on the peace dividend. The trick in doing this would be in finding a way to do this when the extremely powerful defense contractors, and arms and weapons providers, will not give up their profits and their desire to grow larger, without a fight. And you must understand that the defense contractors and arms manufacturers have the ability to fight. After all... Fighting is their business.

This issue of war, and the role that the huge corporations representing the defense contractors, and arms and weapons manufacturers play in it, is not only one of our toughest problems, it is one of our most insidious. For when you look deeply enough... When you look behind the veil of the corporations... and see into the eyes of the individuals back there pulling the strings and levers... you see people who believe themselves to be completely hidden. And, you realize these are people who want to profit by war and all of the pain and suffering that it represents. Like every one of the wars our country has been involved in since the end of World War II, all of which were completely unnecessary.

PHARMACEUTICAL COMPANIES

Here is another question I asked earlier.... Do you think the main goal of the pharmaceutical companies is for each of us to enjoy total and complete health?

No. The main goals of the pharmaceutical companies are to profit and grow larger. Just like the defense contractors don't want peace, the pharmaceutical companies don't want us to be healthy. For where is the profit in that?

This being the case, don't you think we need to protect ourselves from these huge corporations who want to profit from our un-wellness? Or maybe even more to the point.... Do you think we need to protect ourselves from these for-profit companies who want to profit and grow larger by selling us dangerous drugs with dubious effectiveness for ailments that in most cases could probably be better addressed by improved diets, more exercise, and by reasonably priced natural remedies that in most cases cost a fraction of these outrageously expensive drugs with their dangerous side effects?

Here is the situation.... Pharmaceutical companies are corporations. And as we have learned, corporations hold themselves out to be artificial people. According to the current case law of this country, these huge, multi-national corporations are entitled to the same protections granted to "we the people" under the Constitution, the Bill of Rights, and the Fourteenth Amendment. Our courts have determined that these corporations are entitled to free speech just like we are.... But wait! Corporations can't talk. And recognizing this, the courts have agreed with the assertions of the corporate lawyers that corporations talk with their money. And therefore, these giant, artificial entities, many of which have more cash at their disposal than most of the countries on this planet, must be allowed to spend their money contributing to political campaigns, and by hiring attorneys to lobby our elected officials in order to influence legislation and oversight. Never mind if "we the people" don't have the money to send our own lobbyist to Washington to compete with them. After all, didn't we elect those same congressmen based upon their campaign promises to work for "we the people?" Where, in their campaign promises did these senators and congressmen tell us they would work for "we the people" unless the big corporations pay them enough money so that they would go to work for them instead?

The pharmaceutical lobby is the biggest lobbying group in the country. So... Surprise! Legislation gets passed in Washington that is favorable to the pharmaceutical companies at the expense of sick people. And somehow, the reverse never happens. Legislation never gets passed that is favorable to "we the people" at the expense of the drug companies. A good example of this is the Medicare Prescription Drug Improvement and Modernization Act of 2003, which prevents the government from negotiating prices with drug companies who provide prescription drugs covered by Medicare. Wikipedia cites a piece by the Center for Public Integrity which reports that as a direct result of this legislation:

61 percent of Medicare spending on prescription drugs is direct profit for pharmaceutical companies!

In the course of researching this sector, I came across a documentary film titled *Big Bucks, Big Pharma* that I found to be extremely well done and informative. The film is narrated by Amy

Goodman, and it features a series of interviews of doctors, journalists, writers, and a former pharmaceutical representative who is now working for reform. One of the doctors who is prominently featured in the film is Dr. Marcia Angell. Here is her quote from a PBS interview about health care.

> "Our health care system is based on the premise that health care is a commodity like VCRs or computers and that it should be distributed according to the ability to pay in the same way that consumer goods are. That's not what health care should be. Health care is a need; it's not a commodity, and it should be distributed according to need. If you're very sick, you should have a lot of it. If you're not sick, you shouldn't have a lot of it. But this should be seen as a personal, individual need, not as a commodity to be distributed like other marketplace commodities. That is a fundamental mistake in the way this country, and only this country, looks at health care. And that market ideology is what has made the health care system so dreadful, so bad at what it does.'

Dr. Angell is probably the most prominent and outspoken critic of the pharmaceutical companies. She was the editor-in-chief of the prestigious *New England Journal of Medicine* from 1999 to 2000, which makes her an insider who is choosing to speak out rather than play along.

Here are some of the major points made in the documentary film, *Big Bucks, Big Pharma...*

❖ Adverse reactions to properly prescribed medications are the 5th leading cause of death in the U. S. They cause an estimated 100,000 deaths and 1,500,000 hospitalizations annually.

❖ Pharmaceutical companies spend more than twice as much on marketing as they do on research. And the vast majority of the research dollars are not spent looking for new cures. The bulk of the research money is spent figuring out how to duplicate the successful drugs of other drug companies. Then, the marketing dollars become necessary in order to compete with other drug companies trying to market the same drug under a different name. The consumers end up paying for all of this chicanery in the form of higher than necessary drug costs.

❖ The top selling drug in the world at the release date of the film was Lipotor. Lipotor is one of a number of very similar drugs called statin drugs that are prescribed to lower cholesterol. One of the biggest reasons all of these statin drugs are doing so well is that the FDA recently changed the guidelines for "normal" health in regard to cholesterol levels. Overnight, people formerly not deemed to be at risk for heart attack and stroke due to cholesterol levels became candidates for prescription medication to lower their cholesterol levels. Similar changes were made in regard to health guidelines for blood pressure, which also had an immediate and direct result on profits for pharmaceutical companies. I'm sure you will find it to be no surprise that many of the people involved in changing these guidelines had financial ties to drug manufacturers.

❖ The pharmaceutical drug, Vioxx, made by Merck & Co., is known to have caused up to 160,000 strokes and heart attacks. Studies have shown that Vioxx was no more effective in treating arthritis than older, much less expensive drugs, which do not carry the risk of stroke and heart attack as a side effect.

❖ Drug companies make huge profits marketing drugs that are protected by patents. Then, very often when the patent is about to run out, the drug company desperately finds ways to extend it. One way this is done is to change the formula ever so slightly, and then market the new, but basically the same drug as "improved". A good example of this is Prilisec, the purple pill, which became Nexium, the new purple pill, which is basically the same thing but costs three times as much, and was the most advertised drug in America when it was introduced. Another way drug companies have been able to extend their patents is to "find", or maybe more accurately, to "invent" new diseases or conditions, which they can be prescribed to treat. This was done by GlaxoSmithKline in order to extend its patent on Paxil which was originally patented to treat major depressive disorder and now treats this new, made-up condition called social anxiety disorder. The question here is "How many thousands of slightly shy people have now been needlessly subjected to the dangerous side effects of this dubious drug because GlaxoSmithKline executives wanted to create more profits and decided to do so by inventing a new disorder?" Another example is Eli Lilly and their drug called Prozac. When their patent was about to run out on their anti-depression drug, the executives there decided it could be extended by creating a new disorder called premenstrual dysophoric disorder and marketing a new drug called Sarafem which is actually identical to Prozac in every way but costs three times as much.

❖ Pharmaceutical companies spend more than $4 billion per year airing television ads marketing their drugs directly to consumers. That is a staggering number. But most of their marketing efforts are still directed at doctors. In 2004 alone, drug reps from pharmaceutical companies gave more than $16 billion worth of samples away to doctors. Today, there are approximately one of these drug reps for every 4.5 doctors practicing medicine in the U. S. In addition to giving away the free samples, these drug reps spend billions on meals, trips, tickets to events and other gifts for doctors and medical students. Much of their budget is called "education" because otherwise, the gifts and events would be illegal. All of this money is, of course, spent in order to persuade doctors to prescribe medications manufactured by the companies they represent. After all, these corporations must make a profit and grow larger... Right?

❖ In order to be approved by the FDA, a new drug only needs to demonstrate its effectiveness against a placebo, which means the new drug must be better than "nothing". There is no requirement in the approval process to compare a drug to existing drugs.

And guess what? Since the release of *Big Bucks, Big Pharma*, researchers from the University of California published an article in the October, 2010, issue of the *Annals of Internal Medicine*, reporting that of the 167 placebo-controlled trials published in peer reviewed medical journals in 2008 and 2009, 92% of those trials never even described the ingredients of their placebo pills. I think anyone would have to agree... That is not good science.

Marcia Angell makes a good point when she says, "You can't blame the drug companies. They are just making profits like they are designed to do. My greatest criticism would be for the institutions that have allowed themselves to be corrupted by the drug companies."

Then, of course she goes on to identify the Congress and the FDA as the institutions to which she is referring.

In the next section, we will take a look at the other business sector that is wreaking havoc in our health care system.

INSURANCE COMPANIES

As stated in the previous section, the United States is the only developed nation that depends upon for-profit health insurance companies as the providers of health care for its citizens. Fortunately, we do have Medicare, that covers people 65 and older, and Medicaid, that covers poor people. According to the Kaiser Family Foundation website which cites the U. S. Census Bureau for their source, in 2015, Medicare and Medicaid covered 34% of our citizens, and another 2% received military related health care coverage. According to the same source, in 2015, 9% of our population was uninsured, 49% of us had employer-based health care coverage, and the remaining 7% of us had non-group policies, mostly through the Affordable Care Act exchanges.

This means more than 150 million of our citizens receive health care through for-profit health insurance companies. Anyone who studies health care in the U. S. in an effort to understand why it is so expensive and so inefficient when compared to health care in other developed nations understands very well the role that for-profit insurance companies play. The main reason for this is pretty obvious… the "profit" reaped by the for-profit health insurance companies increases the costs of providing health care. The provider in single payer systems, being the government, does not take a profit. Hence, the cost of providing health care in other developed nations with single payer systems is roughly 2%. Here, in the United States, when you include profits, administrative costs, and marketing costs, the cost of providing health care amounts to 20%. Actually, before Obamacare, the cost of providing service through for-profit health insurance companies was even higher, but the legislation required that 80% of health insurance premiums go towards actual health care.

If there is a reason other than cronyism that our legislators passed health care coverage allowing "for-profit" insurance companies to continue to participate, I would certainly like to know it.

But there is more.

As stated previously, in all of the other industrialized nations, every citizen is guaranteed to receive health care as a basic right of citizenship. In those countries, health care is paid for by the governments in a "single-payer" system, with the government itself being the single payer. But here in the United States, when doctors, hospitals, and other providers of health care look to be paid for their services, they first have to determine whether to seek payment from Medicare, Medicaid, from one of the for-profit health insurance companies, from the individual who is receiving the care, or very often, from a combination of these alternatives.

To further complicate matters, Medicare has one set of rules regarding payments, Medicaid, another, and each of the for-profit health insurance companies has their own payment guidelines, along with a set of forms that must be properly sent to them in advance of payments. Often, payments are denied by the health insurance companies, and often, those denials are for seemingly arbitrary and contestable reasons, leading to even more administrative expenses on both ends. The result of all of these complications regarding payments for medical services arising from the inclusion of the for-profit health insurance companies is that all of these health care providers, being the doctors, hospitals, and all of the other providers of health care, must include a staff of personnel whose sole responsibility is dealing with all of the various payers.

This staff of personnel who handles billing serves to dramatically increase costs of providing health care in the United States as compared to other countries with single-payer systems. For example, according to a study by Health Affairs published in September, 2014, administrative costs for hospitals in the United States averaged 25% of all hospital spending, as compared to 12% for such costs in Canada and 16% in England. In a recent National Public Radio broadcast, Harvard economist, David Cutler cited the Duke University Hospital which employs 1,300 billing clerks in a 900-bed hospital as an example of these exorbitant administrative costs.

Here are some comparative figures regarding health care costs for various developed countries I found on Wikipedia.

Country	Per capita expenditures on health care	Healthcare costs as a percent of GDP	% of government revenue spent on health care	% of health costs paid by government
Australia	$3,137	8.7	17.7	67.7
Canada	$3,895	10.1	16.7	69.8
France	$3,601	11.0	14.2	79.0
Germany	$3,588	10.4	17.6	76.9
Japan	$2,581	8.1	16.8	81.3
Sweden	$3,323	9.1	13.6	81.7
UK	$2,992	8.4	15.8	81.7
US	$7,290	16.0	18.5	45.4

The table on Wikipedia also had columns for life expectancy, infant mortality, physicians per 1000, and nurses per 1000, which I omitted in order to emphasize numbers I thought more important in regard to our discussion. But, I will tell you that in regard to the numbers for physicians per 1000, and nurses per 1000, the US was pretty closely in line with the average numbers for the other countries. However, despite spending more than twice the average amount as the other countries in terms of per capita expenditures on health care, the US was last in life expectancy and had the highest infant mortality rate by far. Also significant is the fact that although the US spends roughly the same percentage of government revenues on health care as the other countries, yet somehow we only succeed in paying a little more than half of the total percentage of health care costs paid by the other countries on the list.

Evidently, this is what happens when health care becomes a commodity instead of a right. As Dr. Marcia Angell asserted in her PBS interview, "The US is the only country to treat health care in this manner." Furthermore, the US is the only country to allow for-profit insurance companies to deal in health care. Because we allow this, the cost of administering health care is 20% for us, versus 2% for a government administered, single-payer system. The 20% figure, of course, includes a healthy profit for the "for-profit" companies that administer our systems, as well as a lot of inefficiencies, which I assert are designed by the insurance companies to make getting payments for services harder for hospitals, doctors, patients, and other health care providers. Clearly, allowing for-profit insurance companies to be involved in our health care system is a mistake that must be rectified as soon as possible.

There are numerous other types of insurance being offered to businesses and individuals by insurance companies. Among them are auto, home, life, property, casualty, and disability insurance, to name just a few. Basically, if you as a consumer have a need, then the insurance industry will try to find a way to accommodate you in a manner that will allow them to profit. I see no problem in such an arrangement. Certainly, when you omit the health insurance companies from this discussion of insurance companies, the other sectors previously discussed provide much more to complain about than the insurance industry. Besides, it looks like the insurance industry is in for a very rough ride due to climate change and the resulting rising sea levels, severe droughts, flooding, and stronger storms.

Here, in the United States, the responsibility for oversight and regulation of the insurance industry is at the state rather than the federal level of government. Also, there is a nonprofit coalition of state insurance agencies called the National Association of Insurance Commissioners, which serves to create some consistency between the various state regulatory bodies. State agencies are responsible for making sure insurance companies operating within their borders are financially sound enough to pay claims and also are charged with protecting the public against fraudulent insurance practices. After looking into this situation, it appears the public is not being taken advantage of too badly in this area. But from what I know about big business and their ability to influence government, and laws, and governmental oversight, I must tell you I'm a little surprised to be saying that.

MEDIA AND BROADCASTING COMPANIES

Although there is no company within this sector big enough to make it onto any of the Top Global Economic Entities lists, this sector does contain some very big and influential companies. Among them are Comcast, Walt Disney, Twenty-First Century Fox, Time Warner, Time Warner Cable, Direct TV, and CBS, all of which are in the top 400 of the Forbes 2015 list of the world's largest public companies.

The main business focus for Time Warner Cable, and Direct TV is the providing of Internet, television, and telephone services through the mediums of cable and satellite dish. The other five companies are also providers of either cable and/or satellite services, plus they are the owners of multiple television stations.

Additionally, these five companies all produce television shows and movies, and they all provide news programming, some of which runs twenty-four hours a day. Other sectors in which these companies are involved include book publishing, newspaper and magazine publishing, radio broadcasting, film distribution, theme parks, and resorts.

Television viewers know Comcast through its NBC and Telemundo broadcast networks. Disney owns ABC, ESPN, and the Disney Channels. Time Warner owns CNN, HBO, Cinemax, TNT, and TBS. Twenty-First Century Fox owns Fox, Fox News, and the Fox Sports Channels. And, CBS owns CBS, Showtime, and TMC.

Not too many years ago, when most people received television broadcasts through either rooftop or set-top antennas, this television channel landscape was a lot simpler. Now, with the advent of cable and satellite providers, channel selections are much more diverse. Cable and satellite providers often operate in monopolistic situations without sufficient governmental oversight, and for this reason, prices paid by consumers are probably higher than they should be. Fortunately for me, for my cable providers, I can choose between AT&T U-Verse, and Time Warner Cable. Or, if I wanted, I would also have the option of utilizing one of the satellite providers. Usually, consumers at least have the ability to choose between cable and satellite, providing most of us with a modicum of relief from having to deal with one of these huge companies in a completely monopolistic situation. But, regardless of whether you have the ability to choose between several providers, or just one, dealing with these huge, monopolistic, or even semi-monopolistic companies can be very frustrating.

These days, many consumers are tiring of the struggle and are electing to forgo cable and satellite services altogether. Many of these people are opting instead for an HD antenna through which they can receive local broadcasts of the four major networks, plus PBS and a few other smaller stations that hold licenses to broadcast locally through the airwaves. Many of these "cord cutters" supplement the broadcast stations' "through the airwaves" content with one of the Internet streaming services like Netflix, Amazon, or Hulu, which they access through their smart TV's or through one of the video streaming devices available today. These video streaming devices include Roku, Apple TV, Amazon Fire TV, and Chromcast. Of course, for this alternative to work, these consumers need a solid and reliable high-speed Internet connection, which puts them right back in the marketplace of the cable providers.

Through their television and radio programming, plus their newspaper and magazine content, not to mention their films and their book publications, Comcast, Walt Disney, Fox, Time Warner, and CBS provide the U.S. population with a huge percentage of its media content. According to Wikipedia, "Concentration of media ownership," also known as "media consolidation", or "media convergence", is a process whereby progressively fewer individuals or organizations control increasing shares of mass media.

Of course, in the absence of media bias, this concentration of media ownership is no problem. The danger is, with such high percentages of media ownership being held in fewer and fewer hands, it becomes much easier for a few people to inflict their own bias on increasingly higher and higher percentages of the viewership, the listeners, and the readers.

Media consolidation could (and probably should) provide a reason for the reinstatement of the Fairness Doctrine, a FCC policy that has not been enforced since 1987. The Fairness Doctrine evolved out of the reality that in the early days of broadcast television and radio, there was not enough bandwidth available for the FCC to be able to grant licenses for radio and television stations to everyone who wanted them. Since only a limited number of licenses were available, the FCC developed a policy they called the Fairness Doctrine, which required holders of broadcast licenses to devote some of their airtime to discussing controversial matters of public interest, and to provide airtime to contrasting views in regard to those matters. Later, with the advent of cable and satellite providers, and the proliferation of new channels that came along with them, this bandwidth limitation became less of a problem. Initially, back in the 1970's and into the 1980's, when cable television was just getting started, all of those additional channels were much more widely held. Now, because of media consolidation, most of those numerous channels are once again owned by just a handful of companies.

It was the Reagan administration that put an end to the Fairness Doctrine. After the Reagan-led FCC stopped enforcing it, Congress passed a bill directing the FCC to reinstate it that never became law because of President Reagan's veto. Then, in 1991, another attempt by Congress to reinstate the Fairness Doctrine was thwarted when President George H. W. Bush threatened another veto. In the years since, the subject has come up many times in Congress, but somehow, it never finds the support it needs.

These days, it seems that each of us has staked out our ideological position in regard to where we fit on the liberal-to-conservative spectrum. I am old enough to remember when Walter Cronkite anchored the CBS evening news, and Chet Huntley and David Brinkley co-anchored for NBC. Today, instead of the trusted Cronkite, Huntley, and Brinkley, we have the 24-hour news cycle with talking heads on all of the major news channels, with all of them constantly looking for something they can sensationalize in order to promote themselves as an important "news person". Wherever we fit on the liberal-to-conservative spectrum, there is a news provider that caters to our particular beliefs and ideologies. When the news we receive is always slanted towards our own biases, then what could ever cause us to question those biases?

I used to get most of my television-based news from The Daily Show with Jon Stewart. But unfortunately, Jon got tired of what he called "turd mining" being his term for watching CNN and Fox News every day in order to expose their lies and absurd assertions on his comedy show. But, even after Stewart's departure, my sources for television news continues to be comedy shows. These days I rely upon Real Time with Bill Maher, and Last Week Tonight with John Oliver. If I were not so satisfied with my comedic sources, I might rely more on some of the MSNBC programs for my television news. Meanwhile, my ideological opposites, being the Tea Partiers, the Ayn Randers, the Christian Coalitioners, and the rest of the right-wing Republicans, tend to get most of their television news from Fox and CNN. Given this is our situation, I believe the reinstatement of the Fairness Doctrine would provide a lot of people with information they are currently not receiving. Certainly, the extreme polarization of our population's political viewpoints would only be helped by exposing people to alternate viewpoints, and especially by exposing Fox viewers to some of the faulty and untrue news reporting they have been gobbling up as the truth for far too long.

The reality of media consolidation leads to the possibility that the few corporations and individuals who control the vast majority of the media might utilize their powerful positions in order to impose their own biases on a naïve and unsuspecting public. Historically, the people of the United States have depended upon the checks and balances set out in the U. S. Constitution to protect us from abuses of power by any of the three branches of our government. During the past one hundred years or so, a crucial fourth check has entered the scene… Journalism.

The question is…. When five huge corporations hold the ownership of the majority of our country's media, what assurance do "We the People" have that journalists will perform their duties in regard to keeping us all informed and exposing wrongdoings by huge corporations and our government? Obviously, since the focus of these huge corporations is to continue to grow larger while continuing to increase their profits, it is very easy to see how this watchdog responsibility on the part of journalists might conflict with the goals of their corporate owners.

For instance,

How would you rate the performance of journalists in exposing the faulty logic of the Bush administration in its run-up to the Iraq War? How is it that such a large part of our population thought that Sadam Hussein had something to do with 9/11? Why was the "faulty", or should we say "fudged", intelligence regarding Hussein's weapons of mass destruction not exposed in the months before the war began?

How about the reporting during the past twenty years in regard to global warming and climate change? Certainly, it is easy to see that the only reason there has been any question as to the reality and the causes of this global crisis is because the corporate media have not done their very easy job of reporting on the facts, and on discrediting those who attempt to question the reality of the situation.

What about the financial crisis? Rather than contribute to the confusion about the causes, couldn't the journalists have helped to shine a light on the criminal acts performed by the individuals holding high positions within the major banks, insurance companies, rating companies, and others? Wouldn't our world be more secure if a couple hundred of these criminals were behind bars instead of behind their desks?

What about our health care system? Why haven't the journalists helped the people understand the simple fact that health insurance companies have no reason for existence other than to extract a profit for themselves? Why don't people understand the dire need for regulation of the pharmaceutical companies, hospitals and other health care providers? Why don't people understand that health care should not be treated as a commodity, and that it is highly immoral to allow our health care providers to squeeze every last penny out of sick people simply so huge corporations can continue to profit and grow larger?

For that matter.... Why is it even necessary for me to write this book? Especially, why is it necessary for me to write this chapter examining business sectors, or Chapter 6 about our world's biggest problems? After all, I'm not even a journalist. I'm just a guy who read Ishmael. Why is it up to me to write about these things? What is keeping the journalists from doing their jobs?

Do you think it is within the power of any of the four major broadcasting networks to shine a light on any of these issues in order to enlighten the general public about the truth? If they wanted to, do you think ABC could singlehandedly put an end to the ridiculous controversy regarding the reality of global warming, and whether or not it has been caused by human activity? Could CBS make a solid case for completely re-vamping our broken health care system into a single-payer system with adequate regulations of the providers? Could NBC make the case for arresting the criminals behind the financial crisis? Could Fox have stopped the Iraq war before it started?

To be sure, many journalists have gone before me saying basically the same things I am saying here about the war in Iraq, and about the other issues set out above. Somehow, though, the truth always seems to get buried beneath conflicting reports utilizing the very effective mechanisms of spin and fear. The reality represented by the inability of journalists to effectively perform their watchdog duties points to a serious flaw that needs to be addressed by our leaders... that is, if we have any leaders who are not already bought and paid for by the corporate interests. Somehow, though, we need to figure out a way for the people of this country to have better access to the truth about important matters. The reinstatement of the Fairness Doctrine could provide a very significant first step in this regard. The real key, though, is through the abolishment of corporate personhood.

So... as set out herein, life in this richest and most powerful nation on earth, and the world's first modern democracy, is far from ideal. The media here in the Land of the Free has its own agenda, which apparently does not include providing us with the unfettered truth, especially if that truth is considered to be contrary to the interests of its corporate owners. When looked at from the reliability of the news provided to its citizens, what is the difference between life here in the U.S., and life in communist China, or life in Russia? Without a doubt, there are obvious differences in the degrees of censorship and media bias present between the supposedly democratic U.S. media and the medias of Russia and China. But aside from the differences in the degree of censorship and bias, the main difference seems to be that here in the U.S., we are in denial about the existence of any media bias or censorship. Here, we declare that our media to be free and uncensored, when the opposite is true.

In a free and democratic society, as we hold ourselves out to the world as having here in the U.S., access by the voters to the truth is crucial. Media bias… or worse… media censorship, is a recipe for dysfunction at best, or outright oppression at worst.

Where do you think the U.S. falls on this dysfunctional to oppressed scale? Do you think the reason the media has not done their job in regard to informing the American public is because of incompetence? Or, do you think there might be powerful forces directing the deception from behind the curtains? Unfortunately, my answers to these questions can only be speculative ones. I don't have any hard evidence to back me up, but I do believe the correct answer has to be intentional deception.

Even though we don't have any hard evidence linking the answer to intentional deception, one thing I can do, is take a closer look at the likelihood of the truth being that the answer is incompetence. For incompetence to be the answer, it would have to be true that the management of NBC, CBS, ABC, Fox, CNN, and all of the other television news providers have not looked closely enough at the issues of global warming in order for them to understand the reality of the situation. I consider this possibility to be highly unlikely. The reality of global warming is really not that complicated. The only reason there is any controversy whatsoever in regard to the subject of global warming is because the media has given a voice to those who try to deny its existence by hiring pseudo scientists to put out statements casting doubts about the real scientists and their work on this matter.

Certainly, I think it is safe to assume that these media executives all have the requisite intellectual capacity needed to see through that bullshit. Next, if the correct answer was incompetence, it would mean that none of these extremely intelligent and powerful men have examined the issues affecting our broken health care system and come to the obvious conclusion that the reason our health care system is broken is because our country is the only developed nation in the world that considers health care to be a commodity that should be purchased and paid for in the same manner as any other commodity within a laissez faire capitalistic system.

It would mean that none of these rich, intelligent, educated, and powerful men in charge of these media giants understands that insurance companies are serving no beneficial purpose whatsoever within this broken health care system, and that the participation of insurance companies in the health care system only serves to raise the costs while providing the insurance companies with an opportunity to extract a profit for themselves. If the correct answer is incompetence, it would mean that none of these high-powered executives saw the flaws in the faulty or possibly fudged evidence regarding the presence of weapons of mass destruction in the run-up to the Iraq War. And, it would mean that none of these highly successful individuals understands that the real reason for the financial crisis was the criminal acts performed by hundreds of their top-executive counterparts within the financial industry.

As you can see, I consider the possibility that the answer lies in incompetence to be highly unlikely. So, if the answer is not incompetence, then the correct answer must be that we are being intentionally deceived. The question then becomes.... Who, exactly, is responsible for deceiving us?

Again... I cannot pretend to have the answer to that question. I can only point to the reality that humongous corporations benefit from each of these deceptions. And when major corporations benefit, their top executives and their major shareholders benefit as well.

Some other questions we might ask are... Is this deception the result of men being in positions of power who believe laissez faire capitalism is the best way our culture could possibly be ordered? Is this a situation where powerful people believe it is okay for them to participate in deceptions simply because they believe themselves to have the right answer, and they also believe that the end justifies the means? Or, could the answer be that this deception on behalf of the media is simply about personal gains? Are these deceptions being made for purely financial reasons? If so, how rich do these men want to be? Is there any level of wealth that will be enough for them?

Although I feel safe in answering "No" to the last question posed, I do not think it is necessary for us to know the answer to the rest of these questions. The reason I say this is, because whatever the answers to these questions are, the abolishment of corporate personhood will take care of it. And also, once we have brought this broken culture in for a soft landing, and established a new culture based upon the reality that everything is connected, problems like these will only be a memory.

Another supposedly democratic country with a dysfunctional media is Italy. According to *Forbes Magazine*, the 179th richest man in the world in 2015, with a net worth of $7.7 billion, is seventy-nine-year-old Silvio Berlusconi, three-time Italian Prime Minister, and a notorious scallywag. Without a doubt, Berlusconi's exploits are the stuff of legends. According to a recent Guardian article, Berlusconi estimated in 2009, that over the previous 20 years, he had made 2,500 court appearances in 106 trials, at a legal cost of more than 200 million Euros. Although, many of these trials have been civil actions, many have also been criminal ones. The charges filed against him have included embezzlement, tax fraud, perjury, false accounting, bribery, and soliciting prostitution with a minor. Several trials have resulted in acquittals, but he has also been convicted several times. Remarkably, Berlusconi has not only been able to avoid incarceration, but he has been able to remain in power throughout.

How did he accomplish this? Simple... Berlusconi owns three national television networks, a huge publishing firm, a major newspaper, and dozens of magazines, all of which gives him incredible influence over the public opinions in his country. Also, according to another recent *Guardian* article, "That concentration of media power in his hands means that any political fight appears like a contest between a nuclear power and a kid with a dagger. Whenever anyone dares criticize Berlusconi, the dogs of war are unleashed, and a smear campaign is mounted."

When Berlusconi came to political power back in 1993, it was illegal in Italy for any person or any company to own national television networks. Berlisconi figured out he could buy up local TV stations and have them each broadcast the same content, thereby effectively circumventing the law. The rest... as they say... is history. And remember, Italy is rated as a fully democratic country and is ranked No. 29 on the Democracy Index, a fact that definitely underscores the potential power of the media when misused.

Another big, controversial issue involving this sector is Net neutrality. Net neutrality is the term that refers to the current FCC rule that requires all Internet content, and also all Internet end users be treated equally by providers of Internet. Of course, the Internet providers don't like Net neutrality. They want to end Net neutrality so they can charge certain users like Google, Yahoo, Facebook, Netflix, Amazon, and many others, for the increased Internet traffic resulting from the millions of users of their websites. Much like the

19th Century quest for corporate personhood by the railroads, the corporate interests who are trying to bring an end to Net neutrality know they only have to win once. And, they also know there is nothing stopping them from trying again and again. So, much like Southern Pacific Railroad in the 1860's, 1870's, and 1880's, they keep trying... A campaign contribution here... A well-placed appointment of a crony there.

The latest big attempt to end Net neutrality was actually thwarted by HBO's John Oliver when he spent a 13-minute segment talking about an impending FCC decision as to whether or not to continue the policy of enforcing Net neutrality. In his show that aired on June 1, 2014, the piece included a hilarious segment comparing Obama's appointment of Tom Wheeler as Chairman of the FCC, to a family hiring a dingo as their babysitter. As Oliver pointed out, since Wheeler was the former head of the cable industry's lobbying arm, the comparison was appropriate.

At the end of the piece, Oliver posted the Internet address for the FCC website's public comments section and called for all Internet commentators to visit the site to voice their opposition to the FCC proposal. Oliver's show is widely credited with causing the FCC site to crash and in steering the FCC decision towards continuing the policy of enforcing Net neutrality. Personally, I agree with those who are saying John Oliver's show was the deciding factor that prevented the FCC from going the other way on this. Hopefully, John Oliver will be there to help thwart the corporate interests on their next attempt as well.

Just like every other business sector we have examined in this chapter, it appears that the lunatics have taken over the asylum. Once again, when you look just below the surface, it is apparent that giant corporations are running our insane culture, and "We the People" have very little say in the matter.

But it is important to remember.... There is an easy fix that is readily available for us. And it lies in the reality that

CORPORATIONS ARE NOT PEOPLE. After all, the only reason "We the People" are in this ridiculous situation in the first place is because of a Supreme Court case from 1886 that tried to tell us otherwise. This wrong can be righted. It is time to bring an end to the ludicrous concept that artificial creations called corporations should have the same rights and protections as people under the U. S. Constitution and the Bill of Rights.

Democracy depends upon an educated and enlightened voting public. We are going to have to see to it that people have access to dependable and accurate news... Something that is sorely missing at this time. And speaking of democracy... The democracy here in the U. S. in our post soft landing world, will be the successor democracy to a pretty good one established by our founding fathers. After achieving a successful soft landing as advocated herein, I would suggest that we should take care to be more vigilant in our defense of democracy this time around. Fomenting revolution is not an easy thing to do.

AGRICULTURE AND THE FOOD INDUSTRY

The business of commercially growing corn, soybeans, wheat, rice, cotton, fruit, vegetables, nuts, and beans is only one facet of this huge sector. Another is comprised of all the giant corporations involved in support roles to the growers, including the companies who provide the seeds, fertilizers, pesticides, and herbicides. Next, are the ranchers, farmers, fishermen, feedlot owners, and slaughterhouses that provide beef, chicken, eggs, pork, fish, turkey, and other meat. Another huge piece of this business sector is comprised of many of the world's biggest corporations who manufacture and market our processed and packaged food. Finally, there are the grocery and supermarket chains who sell the produce, meat and the packaged processed and ultra-processed foods to the public, and the restaurant chains, and fast food chains who sell prepared meals.

The Farmers

For the purposes of this discussion, the farming end of this sector will be divided into those farmers who grow the commodity crops of corn, soybeans, wheat, cotton, and rice, and those who grow the fruit, vegetables and other crops more often found in the produce section of our grocery stores. Some of the big corporate players involved in growing the commodity crops are Archer Daniels Midland, Cargill, Bunge, and Louis Dreyfus. The practice of plowing large fields and planting one crop in them was developed over the past one hundred fifty years, and the development of modern farming equipment along with fertilizers, herbicides, and pesticides made it possible. For a while, as crop yields increased substantially, the technique of monocropping appeared to be a beneficial innovation. Now, though, we are finally coming to understand how this practice that was once considered a good thing, has been shown to be responsible for, the loss of the land's ability to withstand both drought and excessive rain, the release of carbon that was formerly sequestered underground into the atmosphere, the depleting of the microorganisms necessary for soil health, and the pollution of our rivers, streams, and oceans due to the runoff of millions of tons of herbicides, pesticides and nitrogen fertilizer used on these crops. This practice of large-scale mono-cropping is not sustainable, and we are very close to hitting the wall represented by that fact.

The U S Department of Agriculture (USDA) reports that in 2017, farms for cropland in the U S covered approximately 339 million acres, with more than three-quarters of that area, or about 259 million acres, planted for either corn, soybeans or wheat. For comparison, the state of Texas is comprised of just under 172 million acres, so the approximately 259 million acres planted every year in corn, soybeans, and wheat represents the total area covered by about one and a half Texases. On the produce side, the USDA reported that in 2017, 1.5 million acres were planted in dry, edible beans, 4.4 million acres in vegetables, 1.1 million acres in potatoes, .2 million acres in sweet potatoes, and 5.7 million acres in orchards growing apples, oranges, almonds, pecans, and other fruits and nuts.

Commodity Crops

Of the 259 million acres planted in corn, soybeans and wheat in 2017, 91 million acres were corn. It is important to note, however, that the 91 million acres of corn were a type of corn know as field corn, sometimes called dent corn, and it is completely different from the sweet corn all know as corn on the cob. According to the USDA, 500,000 acres of farmland are planted each year in sweet corn, and typically, sweet corn is not genetically modified. Sweet corn is used primarily for human consumption, and it is highly nutritious. Typically, we consume this sweet corn either fresh as corn on the cobb, frozen, or canned. 92% of field corn is genetically modified. Forty percent of field corn is used for ethanol, and another thirty-six percent is fed to cattle, pigs, and chickens. Another eleven percent is exported. After processing and being turned into corn meal, corn flour, hominy, grits, corn oil, or high fructose corn syrup, approximately eleven percent of the field corn harvested finds its way onto our grocery shelves.

Soybeans have been an important crop in China for three thousand years. Here, in the U. S., we started growing a lot of soybeans in the 1940's. Until 2018 we had been the number one producer of soybeans in the world for many years, but Brazil has now overtaken us as the number one producer, and the two other biggest producers are Argentina and China. According to the USDA, we planted 90 million acres of soybeans in the U. S. in 2017, and 94% of the soybeans planted were genetically modified to be Roundup resistant. Less than one-half of one percent of soybeans planted are organically grown. Typically, soybeans are left in the field until the leaves fall off and the pods have dried. Then the soybeans are picked and processed by one of three methods involving either leaching or heating and pressing. After processing, the soybeans are reduced to 80% meal and 20% oil. 97% of soybean meal is fed to poultry and livestock and 3% goes into soymilk and other food products for human consumption. 68% of the soybean oil is used for processed food for people, and 25% is used for biodiesel. The last 7% of soybean oil is used for industrial purposes like paints, plastics, cleaners, and solvents.

Because of the government subsidies, which are very significant, farmers are highly motivated to plant corn, soybeans, wheat, cotton and rice, which are the only crops eligible for the subsidies. The subsidies began in 1933. In the 1930's, during the Great Depression, at a time when there were also extreme drought conditions, there was a very real threat of failure of this essential business. After a price collapse in commodity prices when a drop in demand from Europe caused a food glut, Congress passed legislation authorizing the first farm subsidies as a means to ensure our citizens had enough food. The subsidies were supposed to be temporary, but in 1949 they were made permanent. Over the years, there have been a lot of legislative changes to the basic subsidies, and today farmers of corn, soy, wheat, cotton and rice are the only ones who receive them. Of those corn, soy, and wheat farmers, the richest 10 % of them receive about 75% of the total subsidies, which makes a completely ridiculous situation even more ridiculous.

Produce Crops

California is by far the biggest producer of produce crops. In terms of the number of crops grown, the area cultivated, and the value of those crops, none of the other states even come close to California. According to the USDA, in 2017, produce farms in California represented 39.1% percent of the total area harvested for produce crops, and the produce crops harvested in California represented 56.7% of the total value of all produce crops grown in the U. S. The next three largest states in terms of area farmed were Florida,

Minnesota, and Wisconsin, and the next three states in terms of value of the crops harvested were Arizona, Florida, and Georgia. Produce crops are seasonal, and during wintertime, many produce crops are imported from Mexico and Central and South America. According to the FDA, 35% of our fresh produce is imported, with most of that being the produce imported during the wintertime here, which is the summertime in the Southern Hemisphere. I live in Texas, so the produce I buy that was grown in California might have traveled 1,500 miles to get here, and the produce I consume that was grown in Central and South America travels even further.

Recently, there has been a big movement towards farming more produce locally, which, of course, at the very least saves a lot of energy by not having to transport the food long distances from farm to table. Also significant of course, is the carbon dioxide that will not be generated from burning the fuel necessary for the transportation of your food that would otherwise have contributed to global warming. When food is grown closer to where you live, it is easier for you to monitor how it is grown and raised, and easier for you to know whether pesticides and herbicides were utilized in its cultivation. And in the event of an economic crisis or other event that would serve to interrupt your access to food grown further away, your access to food would be much more secure. Another huge benefit is that when your produce is locally grown, you have the opportunity to consume it earlier than you would if it were transported long distances, thereby accessing nutrients that are lost as time goes by after produce is harvested.

Realistically however, the most important reason for encouraging the growing of produce locally is because we are hopefully on the verge of transitioning as a culture away from our fast food and processed food diets towards a more plant based diet, and therefore our demand for fresh produce may be about to increase dramatically. When and if this increase in demand for fresh produce occurs, a part of the increased demand would be met by converting large tracts currently devoted to commodity farms growing corn and soybeans into produce crops, but this ability to meet some of the increased demand for fresh produce through the development of local sources would also be very important.

Seed, Fertilizers and Chemicals

The seed, fertilizer, pesticide and herbicide niche of the agribusiness sector has historically been dominated by Monsanto, who recently merged with Bayer. If there is a prototype of an evil corporation, I don't believe there could be a better example than Monsanto, the company that brought us the herbicide, Roundup and the genetically modified corn, soybeans, wheat and cotton designed to survive repeated applications of the poison designed to kill everything it touches except for these genetically modified crops.

But even if these crops can be genetically modified to enable them to survive being poisoned by the glyphosate, in Monsanto's Roundup, do any of us actually want to consume a crop that has been slathered in the stuff? And most especially, does anyone want to risk direct exposure to this poisonous substance that has been designed to kill everything except for the genetically modified crops? Finally, some justice is being done. In 2018, a landmark lawsuit rendered a verdict against Monsanto for a groundskeeper who developed non-Hodgkin's lymphoma after spraying Roundup for years and awarded damages of $289 million. In 2019, two more subsequent lawsuits found for the plaintiffs and awarded damages of $80 million in one, and $2 billion in the other. As of August 2019, more than 18,400 additional plaintiffs have filed actions against Monsanto alleging exposure to Roundup has caused them to suffer, and in many cases to die, from this form of cancer that has been demonstrated to result from exposure to glyphosate.

Monsanto has been around as a company for well over one hundred years. Many would say it is fitting that the two companies who brought us mustard gas in WW1, (Bayer) and Agent Orange in the Vietnam War (Monsanto) should merge into one company. By the way, Monsanto's resume, in addition to Roundup and Agent Orange, also includes DDT, the terrible pesticide that was introduced in 1944, and finally banned 30 years later after having been shown to be responsible for bringing several prominent bird and reptile species including the horny toad and the bald eagle, to the brink of extinction.

The other incredibly evil thing the seed companies have done is that they have patented their seeds and have been aggressively enforcing those patents. Neighboring farmers have been wiped out by legal costs because the wind blew some of these patented seeds onto their land. Am I wrong, or does this remind you of some sort of an evil plot in a James Bond movie?

Meat, Fish, and Poultry

The beef, chicken, eggs, fish, pork and turkey part of the agriculture and food sector is dominated by such well-known corporate giants as Tyson, Cargill, Sysco, JBS, and ConAgra. According to the association website for National Provisioner, in 2018, the top ten meat and Poultry Processors had over 399,000 employees in 384 processing plants that generated sales of more than 164 billion dollars.

Starting with the violence and cruelty represented by the manner in which these sentient living beings are killed in the slaughterhouses, there is so much wrong here. Next is the harm being done to our planet because of all the damage that is occurring in our effort to supply meat to all of the people who want to consume it. All over the world, our primeval forests with their irreplaceable, diverse, precious ecosystems that are teeming with life that is dependent upon those forests are being cut down just so they can be turned into pastureland. The waters within our rivers, streams and oceans are being fouled by the animal waste from feedlots. Our antibiotics are quickly losing their efficacy because we are using them so liberally on the poultry and livestock that are packed in together so closely on the feedlots and poultry farms that antibiotics are necessary just to keep them alive. The methane generated by livestock and dairy cattle is a significant contributor to the greenhouse gases that are causing the global warming and climate change. And then there is our own, personal health. The debate about whether or not it is healthy to consume meat has been going on for decades, but study after study shows that people who eat little or no meat have less heart disease, strokes, cancer, diabetes, and obesity than regular meat eaters. At some point, we need to ask ourselves... If it is bad for the animals, bad for the planet, bad for us, and not necessary for our health and well-being, then why are we doing it? Aside from the undeniable fact that a hamburger is delicious, can anyone point to a single benefit of consuming meat with every meal that begins to counter even one of these negatives, let alone all of them?

Ultra-Processed Food

There are numerous large, well-known companies providing the processed and packaged foods in this sector, and some of the company names we are all familiar with are Nestle, General Mills, Kellogg's, Mars, Campbell, Coca-Cola, Pepsi, Kraft Heinz, and Smucker, to name just a few. Unfortunately for all of us, another way of saying "processing and packaging" is "adding sugar, preservatives, artificial coloring, sodium, fats, and other dubious ingredients". Also, the act of processing our food often removes the vitamins and minerals that were originally present in the food's natural state, so in many cases artificial forms of these processed out vitamins and minerals are added back in. Basically, these companies profit by taking our real food that was grown in a field somewhere, and then turn it into something that can be packaged for the supermarket shelf and marketed to us as both delicious and healthy. While in some products, a case can be made the food does actually taste good, it is much more of a stretch for these companies who market this processed food to make us believe it is healthy for us, even though they may tout the fact that their product has been "fortified" with vitamins and minerals. In actuality, our consumption of all of these highly processed foods over the past sixty years, with all of their added sugar and preservatives is one of the main causes of the corresponding uptick we have seen in cases of cancer, obesity, diabetes, stroke, and heart disease.

Our culture got its start ten thousand years ago when some smart farmers in Mesopotamia and elsewhere figured out that grains could be harvested and stored for long periods without spoiling, thereby providing a level of food security that had never before been experienced. What these giant corporations are doing today with ultra-processed foods is similar, in that the processed and packaged foods will last a long time without spoilage. But while adding sugar, preservatives, and artificial flavors and coloring to these foods is convenient for these huge corporations, it is definitely not good for us, the consumers.

Grocery Stores and Supermarkets

Of course, another way our food of today and our food from ten thousand years ago is similar is that it is still locked up. According to both the number of stores and in total revenues, with 4,253 stores and $288 billion in sales, the biggest grocery store chain in the U. S. is Walmart. A top ten list of the other biggest chains includes Kroger, Albertsons, HEB, Aldi, and Whole Foods. In terms of corporate greed and malfeasance, there is a lot wrong with the business sector of food and agriculture. Walmart, of course, has a lot to answer for in terms of its substandard treatment, low pay, and lack of benefits to its employees. However, it appears to me that the other large supermarket chains do not have Walmart's problem of treating their employees poorly, and this grocery store portion is not to blame for many of the other problems of this sector either. Whole Foods got its start here in Austin in 1980, and I've been shopping there since moving here in 1990. The chain comes in at number ten on the largest grocers list and at number four on another list I found online of the best grocery stores. Whole Foods is known for stocking thousands of organic products, for banning products that contain more than 100 commonly used preservatives, flavors, colors, and other ingredients, and for providing meat and eggs from animals that have been ethically treated and have not given antibiotics and hormones. Other supermarket chains on these lists have succeeded by utilizing similar health conscious and environmentally responsible strategies in order to attract and keep customers.

Restaurant and Fast Food Chains

The restaurant and fast food portion of this sector, however, brings numerous highly significant and negative side effects to our own personal health and wellbeing, and also to the environmental health and wellbeing of our planet. According to Wikipedia, Subway and McDonald's have the most locations. Subway has the edge over McDonald's in number of locations worldwide (42,431 to 37,855), but McDonald's has more than double the annual revenue of Subway ($25 billion to $12 billion.) Some other biggies that everyone is familiar with are KFC, Burger King, Pizza Hut, Domino's, Dunkin', Baskin-Robbins, Taco Bell, Wendy's, Hardee's, Arby's, and Chick-fill-A. If you live in an urban area or even a small town in the U. S., and you have a hankering to ingest some empty calories, it is likely that you will not have to travel far to find them.

Fast food is bad for you and fast food is bad for the planet. Most fast food is full of carbohydrates and provides little or no fiber. Plus, it is loaded with sugar, fat, and sodium. Eating fast food wreaks havoc with your blood sugar, and year after year, the repeated spikes in blood sugar caused by consuming fast food has been the cause of millions of cases of type 2 diabetes. Without a doubt, many heart attacks, strokes, and cancers can also be blamed on fast food, especially in regard to the resulting tendency towards obesity and all of the problems that go along with not maintaining a healthy weight. To be sure, there are not a lot of organic ingredients in fast food, so your fast food meal is also going to include meat, dairy and eggs from animals that have been fed antibiotics and hormones, which you also get to consume along with your meal. Basically, the formerly sentient animals that you are consuming with your happy meal have been treated cruelly and inhumanely in feedlots and factory farms, and then have been slaughtered violently in huge meat packing operations. Plus, the wheat that has gone into the making of the bread, pizza crust, or other gluten product that is a part of your meal has most certainly been slathered in glyphosate, which is just one of the poisonous herbicides, pesticides, preservatives, and other chemical you ingest each time you partake of fast food. Employees of fast food companies are notoriously underpaid, and since they are not making a living wage, the rest of us supplement the profits of the fast food companies by funding the welfare programs these fast food employees require in order to achieve their basic needs. And the packaging that goes into your fast food meal wreaks havoc with the environment.

I was born in 1954, and the first McDonald's opened in 1955, so the onset of fast food pretty much coincides with my life. It took me a while, but thankfully, I finally figured out that eating fast food was not good for me. I began cutting down on fast food and eating healthier food about twenty-five years ago, but there have been plenty of ups and downs on my own personal journey to healthy eating. I think it was about 1995 when I read John Robbins classic book, Diet For a New America. Reading the book made me understand that providing meat for our worldwide diets was wreaking havoc on our planetary health, so I decided to give it up. Then, a year later, after not eating meat for a year, I realized how beneficial to my own health it was to not eat meat. These days I'll often go weeks without any meat, then eat a piece of fish or chicken. Little by little I've given up eating foods that my body tells me I should avoid. This includes bread, and all gluten, dairy, including cheese and ice cream, and beef and pork. I consider pizza to be one of our culture's great innovations, but because of my body's intolerance for wheat and dairy, I haven't had a piece of pizza in probably ten years. Michael Pollan, who famously said, "Eat food. Not too much. Mostly plants," would be proud of me. My diet is not perfect. I still consume too many sweet and salty between meal snacks. But if everyone ate like I do, the fast food businesses would die out pretty quickly.

The Wikipedia list of the world's largest fast food restaurant chains includes Applebee's, Denny's, IHOP, Chili's, and Waffle House, all of which are in the top 50, and all of which have more than 1,500 locations. Although I would differentiate these restaurants from the classic fast food chains because instead of ordering at the counter or at the drive-in window, a waitperson comes to take your order at the table, it can be easily argued that the menus of these large, corporate chain restaurants provide many more terribly unhealthy eating choices than even semi-healthy ones.

Possibilities for Reform

The possibility of achieving positive change by reforming this business sector of Agriculture and Food is huge. If everyone knew that everything was connected, then decisions about what foods we consume for our nourishment and how they are grown would be made by responsible people who are concerned about individual health and the health of the planet, and not by corporations whose sole criteria for making decisions is their own profit and growth. As with the other business sectors examined in this chapter, we need to take our government back from these huge corporations who have stolen it from us. And the way we do that is by abolishing corporate personhood.

Also, another large portion of the blame for our problems with this sector can be placed on bad choices made by each of us as individuals. And accordingly, this part of the fix is easy... We can simply choose again. For instance, instead of loading up on junk food and ultra-processed food, we can collectively choose to eat a healthy diet comprised primarily of plants. And instead of allowing ourselves to be so dependent on far away factory farms, we can choose to grow much more of our food locally and responsibly. We can choose to dramatically reduce our consumption of meat. We can choose to stop consuming sugary drinks. We can choose to cease the production of most of our highly processed foods that do not serve us. And we can choose to cease feeding so much of our corn and soy to animals, to cease converting corn and soy to ethanol, to grow fewer commodity crops and to grow the ones we do grow in a responsible manner that promotes a healthy planet.

When we are all consuming a fraction of the meat that we are consuming today, we can begin to treat the animals in a much more ethical manner, and we can stop treating them with antibiotics and hormones. Also, when we are consuming less meat, we can reduce the amount of corn and soy that is grown simply to feed to our poultry and our livestock. When we are growing less corn and soy, we can choose to do so without irrigation, pesticides, herbicides, or fertilizers.

Regenerative Agriculture

While researching all of the world's biggest problems in order to write the previous chapter, and while researching all of the business sectors in order to write this chapter, I have become intimately familiar with a lot of terrible problems that can seem pretty overwhelming. Of course, through all of this, I have been buoyed by the knowledge that our problems can be solved by collectively rejecting the notion that everything is separate and collectively embracing the truth that everything is connected. And also comforting is the knowledge that we can easily take our world back from the corporations who have stolen it from us by abolishing the insane concept of corporate personhood. But aside from those two broad comforts, maybe the most encouraging fact that my research uncovered was the existence of a movement by many farmers to embrace a manner of farming termed regenerative agriculture.

According to the Regenerative Agriculture website, regenerative agriculture practices are guided by 4 principles, which are uniquely applied to each specific climate and bioregion. These are:

1. Progressively improve whole agroecosystems (soil, water, and biodiversity).
2. Create context-specific designs and make holistic decisions that express the essence of each farm.
3. Ensure and develop just and reciprocal relationships amongst all stakeholders.
4. Continually grow and evolve individuals, farms, and communities to express their innate potential.

Like most of us, before encountering regenerative agriculture while researching this piece, I had this concept that farming crops naturally depleted the nutrients in our soil, which could only be rectified by the application of fertilizers designed to replenish the soil with those depleted nutrients. But the heroic pioneers in regenerative farming practices like Gabe Brown of South Dakota, Allan Savory of Zimbabwe, Joel Salatin of Virginia, Charles Massy of Australia, and others, have shown us that our practice of monocropping, and especially the manner in which we till the soil, has eradicated the microorganisms necessary for soil health. What we didn't understand previously is that healthy soil contains a rich and diverse biosphere of micro-organisms, most of which are too small to see with the naked eye. Thankfully, these brave and innovative and intelligent pioneers have shown us the practice of no-till or minimum till farming can regenerate the soil fertility through the application of cover crops, crop rotations, compost, and animal manures. When you begin to become familiar with this practice, you will quickly discover how surprisingly easy it is to restore soil health through these and other simple practices. With the return of the microorganisms, comes the return of the soil's ability to provide nutrients to our crops without the necessity of commercial fertilizers. The practice of regenerative agriculture has the potential to address and to solve some very serious problems in a short time, and the movement is gaining momentum... Yahoo! Regenerative agriculture is an incredibly positive development that can work wonders in terms of helping to solve some really big problems very quickly.

Proper Diet

Figuring out how to achieve a proper diet while living in this insane culture is much like swimming upstream against a strong current. It can be done, but it takes a lot of effort, a lot of self-reflection and a lot of questioning of cultural norms to be able to figure out how. Looking back on my own experience, I can see that listening to what my body tells me was a huge part of my own success.

As a young man, my body was fit because of my youth and because my athletic pursuits of high school football and other activities had made it so. During those years of relative youth, my body was able to withstand a pretty big onslaught of terrible but tasty food, alcohol, and even cigarettes. When I listened to my body during those times, it was generally in response to cravings for food or drink. Fortunately, even during my youthful years of relative debauchery, it was always important for me to be physically active, so the physical exercise was always there to help counteract the bad food, and the alcohol and the other poisons I subjected it to. Even while mired in this state of unconscious hedonistic consumption, it was obvious that cigarettes were harmful, and I gave them up repeatedly, twice for two years, and once for a year, before giving them up altogether when I was 34.

It has been 32 years since my last cigarette, and thankfully, it appears that my temporary organic vehicle has survived those patently stupid years of smoking. It took me another fifteen years to give up alcohol. I was 49 when I finally decided I had drunk enough alcohol for this lifetime. Not wanting to be the beer drinking dad to my three-year-old son provided the motivation for me to do that. With beer and cigarettes out of the way, diet related matters suddenly became more obvious to me. As I related earlier, I gave up meat for the planet but ended up embracing the personal health aspect of not eating meat through the experience of noticing how much better I felt without it. Wheat and dairy were also eliminated from my diet after I finally began paying attention to the adverse reactions my body would give me after consuming them. Ultra-processed foods like mac and cheese, breakfast cereal, candy, energy bars, and fast foods are not a part of my present diet.

These days I try to eat organic fruits and vegetables as much as possible, and often my body will complain to me pretty quickly if I eat a fresh fruit or vegetable that was not organically grown. It is a great pleasure to have been able to embrace the truth and wisdom of Michael Pollan's dictum to "Eat food. Not too much. Mostly plants." While it is true that I no longer have the pleasure of biting into a tender and juicy steak or hamburger, piece of pizza, doughnut, cinnamon roll, piece of birthday cake, or other meat, cheese or gluten infused foods, I do still enjoy the pleasure of biting into delicious salads, vegetable dishes, and soups that I get to enjoy and savor while also knowing that I am nourishing my body while consuming them. Most definitely, I can still enjoy many culinary delights while eating healthily.

Casa de Luz

During the past few years I have settled into a routine of preparing a few organically grown vegetarian dishes that I enjoy over and over again. I am not bragging when I tell you these dishes are so delicious and healthy that I never get tired of them. Even if it is only me eating them, I can cook enough at one time to last me several days, so the shopping, preparation, and cleanup involved in cooking these dishes for myself are not too cumbersome.

But even more convenient than cooking for more than one person at a time is eating out. For the past seven years I have been eating lunch regularly and dinner sometimes at an absolutely wonderful place serving organic vegetarian fare in Central Austin called Casa de Luz. (Spanish for "House of Light") Their website prominently proclaims as follows:

"See us as your FARMACY
Let thy food by thy medicine and medicine be thy food –
Hippocrates"

And above the entrance door to the dining hall in beautiful script it says,

When diet is wrong medicine is of no use.
When diet is correct medicine is of no need.
Ayurvedic Proverb   -

Casa is open every day from seven in the morning to eight-thirty at night, and they serve breakfast, lunch and dinner. All of the offerings are vegan and organic. There is no menu that you order from at Casa. Breakfast is buffet style, but every lunch and dinner meal features a soup, a salad with a homemade nut or seed dressing, and a main plate with a featured vegetarian dish, a leafy green with a homemade sauce made from nuts or seeds, a grain such as brown rice or quinoa often with a tasty seed, nut, or mushroom topping, a legume, and a fermented cabbage, beet, or other veggie. To those of us who eat there often, the food is absolutely delicious, and I believe most who eat the fare at Casa for the first time agree. Admittedly, some who try it for the first time and are not used to eating healthy, vegetarian fare, consider it bland, which it most definitely is not.

One of the great things about Casa is the dining hall features mostly large tables that are conducive to communal dining. Because of this, everyone who eats there regularly eventually gets to know each other, which is one of the features of Casa dining that many people enjoy very much. When you are seated with several individuals who are conscious enough and conscientious enough to understand the importance of healthy eating, the conversations usually transcend the trivial, and can often be pretty enjoyable. Many of the topics discussed in Soft Landing have come up on more than one occasion with fellow Casa de Luz diners I have only just met.

The dining hall sits on the back of a beautiful property adjacent to Lady Bird Lake near downtown. When the founders of Casa acquired it in 1989, the grounds were the site of a rundown former meat packing plant. Today, the whole place radiates beauty and good vibes. I could go on and on about how great of a place Casa de Luz is. I have never heard of another place like it, and I believe it is unique in all the world. When your travel brings you to Austin, please don't miss an opportunity to check it out.

But the main reason I bring up my experience of eating regularly at Casa is that I believe Casa de Luz offers a blueprint for us to use as a means of providing meals to all people everywhere in our post soft landing world. As you know, I am advocating that we provide basic needs including food to all people everywhere with no questions asked. Keeping this in mind, the Casa de Luz way of feeding people could be used as a model for a certification process for meal providers in our post soft landing world. Once certified, any dining establishment could provide meals for anyone who enters at no cost to the customer. Every citizen would be entitled to two free meals per day at any Casa certified provider. Certified providers would then be compensated by the government at a rate that would provide a reasonable profit, say fifteen to twenty dollars per meal. These days, Casa probably averages about 300 meals per day. I foresee these certified post-soft-landing Casa de Luz style dining establishments might serve anywhere from 50 to 500 meals per day. In a city the size of Austin, there might eventually be as many as two thousand such Casa certified providers. I also imagine that many of them might be located within former fast food establishments.

Of course, a big downside to this idea is the negative impact it would have on the non-certified restaurants who will have a hard time competing with the delicious and nutritious free meals provided by the certified Casa de Luz providers. Perhaps this could be solved by some sort of a grading curve, whereby non-certified restaurants could be partially certified and thereby receive up to fifty percent of the compensation given to Casa certified restaurants with the balance of the dinner tab being paid out of pocket by the customers. I would imagine that each of us would also be given some grocery store credit as well, so meat eaters and other citizens who have not yet fully grasped the concept of healthy eating, or even upscale diners who prefer five star accommodations, would have options and would not be forced into eating Casa-style all at once.

Conclusions on the Food and Agriculture Sector

Just like all of the other business sectors we have examined, the inmates have taken over the asylum. All of the biggest, most important decisions about how our food is grown, what food is grown, and how it is processed, produced, and marketed are being made by huge corporations whose sole criteria for making any decisions is profit and growth. If we, the people were more involved in these decisions, then without a doubt, we would be looking at many other important decision-making criteria including sustainability, environmental health, pollution, effect on climate change, and most definitely, we would be looking at how healthy each of the foods is for our consumption.

I find it extremely ironic that ten thousand years ago, our new culture took a terrible wrong turn when somebody locked up the wheat and barley, and now, the manner in which we are farming these same grains is causing so many problems for us today. Ten thousand years ago, farming innovations involving wheat, barley and rice led directly to food surpluses that enabled specialization of labor and hierarchal society enabling the first civilizations to develop. But aside from that positive development, when somebody put a lock on that stored grain, this new development in the manner in which we fed ourselves turned out to be problematic for all of us. Today, the food is still locked up, and the farming of wheat and barley, corn, soybeans, rice, and cotton, is the root of some of our biggest societal problems.

But as set out herein, the corporations are not the only problem. Also key to fixing this situation is each of us as individuals needs to arrive at a place where we can choose to eat a much healthier diet that contains a lot more fresh produce than our current collective diet does. As long as there is a demand for empty carbs, for meat with every meal, and for sugary drinks several times per day, the corporations are going to provide them for us. Consciousness has to be raised so that people are capable of understanding the choices they are making. When we choose to eat a healthier diet for ourselves, we are also choosing to live on a much healthier, as well as a much saner planet.

BANKING AND THE FINANCIAL INDUSTRY

Citigroup, the company our government bailed out from insolvency with a $45 billion cash infusion because they were insolvent and "too big to fail", comes in at No. 57 on the Institute for Policy Studies list of the world's largest economic entities from the year 2000. Bank of America was a little further down at No. 84. Of course, there has been a big shake-up in the banking world since the list was made. J. P. Morgan & Chase & Co. is now way up there on current lists. But, seriously... what benefit to society is there for these banks to be so large? Keep in mind that this list includes both companies and countries. All three of these banks bring in more revenue than more than half of the world's countries!

Of course, the biggest reason these banks have become so large is because they are not just banks anymore. Thanks to the repeal of the Glass-Steagall Act of 1933 by passage of the Gramm-Leach-Bliley Act of 1999, these bank holding companies also control insurance companies and investment banks. In 1933, the Glass-Steagall Act made it illegal for one company to operate as both an investment bank and a commercial bank, or an insurance company, or in any other combination of the three separate, financial areas. Then, the Graham-Leach-Bliley Act made it okay again. And the reason the Financial Services Modernization Act, as the Gramm-Leach-Bliley bill came to be known, was passed, was to enable a merger between Citibank and Travelers Group, Inc. During the two years leading up to the passage of the bill, which was after the merger had been finalized, but prior to the governmental approval... which could not have been given without the repeal of the Glass-Steagall Act... over $300 million was spent on lobbying by the banking, insurance, and brokerage industries. This total included $58 million in campaign contributions, $87 million in soft money contributions made directly to the Republican and Democratic parties... or, as I prefer to call them... the Republican and the "Republican Lite" parties... and $163 million on just plain old lobbying expenses. Once again, with the passage of this bill, the corporate interests prove it is not votes, but money, that controls who our elected officials are working for. At the time of the bill's passage, the New York Times quoted the chief lobbyist for the American Bankers Association, as saying, "If I had to guess, I would say it's probably the most heavily lobbied, most expensive issue in a generation."

As a result of the passage of the Glass-Steagall Act back in 1933, JP Morgan was forced to split into three entities. After the break-up, JP Morgan continued to operate as a commercial bank, and Morgan Stanley was formed to operate as an investment bank. And a third entity was spun off as a British merchant bank. Now, as a result of the repeal of the act, Morgan Stanley, and also Goldman Sachs, the last two major investment-banking companies left in the United States, have both converted to bank holding companies. Since that conversion was made in September of 2008, Morgan Stanley has purchased another former major investment bank, Smith Barney, from Citigroup, and is now operating as Morgan Stanley Smith Barney.

Everyone needs a bank. Even the poorest among us needs the services of a bank. For most of us, it is just not practical to conduct our daily lives on a cash basis. Our employers need to be able to pay us by check and we need a place to deposit our paychecks. Then we need a way to spend that money after we put it into our bank accounts. That means we need checking accounts and debit cards for sure. It appears we are on the verge of transitioning to mobile apps on our smart phones that can accomplish these tasks. Google, Facebook, PayPal, and Apple are all working on various versions. I would imagine the banks are huddling with their lobbyists at this moment to work on their game plan to legislate their way out of this potential loss of business.

Also handy for the more affluent among us, are credit cards and savings accounts, along with the ability to borrow money when we need to. Of course, the problem that many of us have with borrowing money is that the only time banks will consider lending it to us are those times when we don't need it.

In this modern world, there are services that many of the more affluent people elect to purchase like limousine service, or cosmetic surgery, or pet grooming, or lawn mowing service, or personal trainers. Then there are the more essential services that everyone needs like electricity, natural gas service, garbage removal, telephone, Internet, and cable TV service, water, sewer processing, car insurance, home insurance, health insurance, or banking. When a service falls into this category of essentialness, then it is the obvious responsibility of our government to protect "we the people" from abuses by the companies providing that essential service. In turn, those companies who are allowed by society to profit by providing those essential services, must either play by the rules, or be penalized for taking advantage of their situation. And in the case of banks, those services are not only essential in that everybody needs them, but these banking services are crucial to the stability of our economy. In recent times, it is in this responsibility to protect its citizens from abuses by companies providing essential services... like banks... that our government has failed us most dramatically. In the specific case of the banking and financial industry, this failure is very evident.

The Financial Crisis

I am, of course, referring to the financial crisis that began here in 2007, causing economic chaos throughout the world. But what is not evident about the failure of our government in its duty to protect "we the people" from abuses by the banking and financial industry is how the government failed us. Or maybe I should say that it is not evident to enough of us. If it was, then we just might have a revolution on our hands. Certainly, there are a large number of congressmen who took the bankers' and the Wall Streeter's money and then went to work for the banks and for the Wall Street investment firms instead of for the people who elected them.

If more people understood how things work in Washington, these congressmen, and probably the president as well, would certainly not be re-elected. At the very least we would see a mini revolution when almost every member of our United States Congress was voted out of office as they came up for re-election.

Like every other sector we have already looked at and every other sector we will examine after this one, our government is not performing its duty in regard to regulating these giant corporations and protecting "we the people" from their abuses of power. The problem is that the companies have gotten so large, so powerful, and so rich, that they are able to direct the legislation that affects them and also able to dictate the amount of regulation that will be enforced upon them.

After the financial crisis, Congress created the Financial Crisis Inquiry Commission as a part of the Federal Enforcement and Recovery Act of 2009, which was signed by Obama on May 20, 2009. The 10 commissioners delivered their reports in January of 2011. After more than a year of inquiry, only six of the commissioners joined in the signing of the final report. One dissenting statement was signed by three of the remaining commissioners, and another dissenting statement was prepared and signed by the last commissioner.

The following are the major causes of the financial crisis that were listed in the majority report:

- We conclude widespread failures in financial regulations and supervision proved devastating to the stability of the nation's financial markets.
- We conclude dramatic failures of corporate governance and risk management at many systemically important financial institutions were a key cause of this crisis.
- We conclude a combination of excessive borrowing, risky investments, and lack of transparency put the financial system on a collision course with crisis.
- We conclude the government was ill prepared for the crisis, and its inconsistent response added to the uncertainty and panic in the financial markets.

- We conclude there was a systemic breakdown in accountability and ethics.
- We conclude collapsing mortgage-lending standards and the mortgage securitization pipeline lit and spread the flame of contagion and crisis.
- We conclude over-the-counter derivatives contributed significantly to this crisis.
- We conclude the failures of credit rating agencies were essential cogs in the wheel of financial destruction.

The dissenting statement signed by three commissioners stated that the majority explanation was too broad, and asserted that "when everything is important, nothing is." This dissenting statement went on to state that there were ten essential causes of the financial and economic crisis, namely:

Credit bubble They assert that the initial credit bubble was caused by capital surpluses in China and other large, developing countries who loaned these savings to the United States and to European countries.

Housing bubble They assert that many factors contributed to the housing bubble.

Non-traditional mortgages They say, "Tightening credit spreads, overly optimistic assumptions about U. S. housing prices, and flaws in primary and secondary mortgage markets led to poor origination practices and combined to increase the flow of credit to U. S. housing finance."

Credit ratings and securitization They say, "Failures in credit rating and securitization transformed bad mortgages into toxic financial assets."

Financial institutions concentrated correlated risk They say, "Managers of many large and midsize financial institutions in the United States amassed enormous concentrations of highly correlated housing risk. Some did this knowingly by betting on rising housing prices, while others paid insufficient attention to the potential risk of carrying large amounts of housing risk on their balance sheets."

Leverage and liquidity risk They say, "Managers of these financial firms amplified this concentrated housing risk by holding too little capital relative to the risks they were carrying on their balance sheets."

Risk of contagion Here is the "too big to fail" problem, which also recognizes the interconnectedness of these financial institutions. When one behemoth goes belly up owing zillions to others, then the disaster quickly spreads.

Common shock This one recognizes that the burst of the housing bubble affected many financial firms at the same time.

Financial shock and panic This one recognizes that ten firms either failed, almost failed, or re-structured in September of 2008, causing financial shock and panic.

Financial crisis causes economic crisis They say, "The financial shock and panic caused a severe contraction in the real economy. The shock and panic ended in early 2009. Harm to the real economy continues through today.

And the second dissenting opinion, which was signed by only one of the commissioners, asserted that there was only one real cause of the financial crisis, the Community Reinvestment Act of 1977, which led to a U. S. government housing policy aimed at increasing home ownership through an "intensive effort to reduce mortgage underwriting standards." According to this commissioner, it was the existence of 27 million subprime loans and other risky loans that was the direct cause of the crisis. According to this commissioner, the 27 million subprime loans' only reason for existence was bad U. S. housing policy on behalf of the U. S. government.

If ten commissioners who studied the problem for eighteen months couldn't come to an agreement as to what caused the financial crisis, then what hope do we have of figuring it out ourselves?

In conducting my own, personal research for this sector, I, of course, did not delve as deeply into the subject as did these ten commissioners and their staffs. I did, however, look at a lot of material. And, like the lone commissioner on the Financial Crisis Inquiry Commission who wrote his own, dissenting opinion, my conclusion regarding the cause of the financial crisis is somewhat simplistic. I assert, however, that more Americans would agree with my conclusion than would agree with his. It seems very evident to me that the financial crisis was caused by the greed of the executives running the largest commercial banks, investment banks, financial insurance companies, and ratings companies.

Their greed, combined with a lack of governmental regulation and oversight led to widespread fraud and criminal negligence on behalf of these financial executives. It was the invention of CDO's, (collateralized debt obligations), MBS's (mortgage-backed securities), and CDF's (credit default swaps), that enabled these executives to book fictional short-term profits from which they extracted huge bonuses and other financial compensations. Then, when the housing bubble burst, and these investments failed, their companies became insolvent, causing our entire economy to come to a sudden halt. Afterwards, these criminals walked away from the wreckage with their own, personal fortunes intact, having already extracted their billions in bonuses. It is blatantly obvious to anyone who looks closely, that these executives had deliberately placed the companies they were entrusted with managing, into extremely dangerous positions, only because of their desire for personal financial gains.

It happened like this.... After the invention of the CDO's and the MBS's, a securitization chain was developed from which every entity on the chain extracted a profit... that is everyone except for the poor schmucks who ended up owning the toxic financial inventions when the bubble burst. These "profit extractors" included the mortgage broker, the mortgage underwriter, the ratings company, and the investment bank that packaged loans into the MBS's or CDO's, and then sold them as a big package of safe and secure loans, backed by either real estate or other tangible property such as cars or boats. The Wall Streeters loved the new way of doing business because once their part was done, they were no longer liable and were free to spend their huge profits. The incredible success of this securitization chain was like a drug for these Wall Street types. They couldn't get enough. So, after the initial success, the demand became enormous for more housing loans that could be stuffed through the pipeline. This enormous demand led quickly to lax lending policies, and predatory lending was one consequence of that.

Then, after the pipeline had been in operation for a while, some genius at AIG (just kidding about the genius part) invented CDF's (credit default swaps). By this time, many owners of the CDO's and MBS's could see the need to insure their investments, which, despite their AAA rating, were looking riskier and riskier. So... AIG sold billions of dollars worth of them. And, since the derivatives market was unregulated, there was no requirement on the part of AIG to set aside funds to meet potential claims made against these securities. Instead, huge bonuses were paid to AIG executives that were based upon this fictional profit.

By mid-2008, the housing bubble was rapidly deflating. On September 7, the federal government took over Fannie Mae and Freddie Mac. Then, in mid-September of 2008, in one 48-hour period, Merrill Lynch ran out of cash and was acquired by Bank of America for $2 per share, Lehman Brothers declared bankruptcy, and the AIG bailout began with an initial credit line from the Federal Reserve Bank of $85 billion.

The day after being bailed out, AIG paid out $61 billion in claims against its credit default swaps, representing 100 cents on the dollar, effectively transferring the settlement of these dubious obligations of AIG's unregulated derivative sales from the investment banks to the U. S. taxpayers. The bailout of AIG eventually cost the taxpayers more than $150 billion.

According to Wikipedia, one week following the bailout in mid-September of 2008, AIG employees and distributors participated in a California retreat that cost $444,000 and featured spa treatments, banquets, and golf outings. Then, the Associated Press reported on October 17 that AIG executives spent $86,000 on an English hunting trip. And on November 10, ABC News reported that AIG spent $343,000 for yet another outing at a lavish resort in Phoenix.

Then, in March of 2009, AIG announced they were paying $165 million in executive bonuses. The total bonuses for the financial unit were estimated at $450 million, and for the entire company, at $1.2 billion. The fact that these trips were made and these bonuses were paid represents a huge failure on behalf of the U. S. government in its obligation to oversee this bailed-out company.

I found it really hard to find good sources in print media that described the events of the financial crisis and also explained what caused it. Considering that the Financial Crisis Inquiry Commission couldn't even agree on the causes, I guess this is somewhat understandable. There is no doubt that what happened is complicated. And there is no doubt that there are many causes and contributing factors. But the best source I found for explaining what happened and how and why, was a movie called *Inside Job* that was produced, written, and directed by Charles Ferguson, who also won awards for his previous film about the Iraq War called *No End in Sight*. Matt Damon was the narrator for *Inside Job*, and deservedly, it won the Academy Award for the best Documentary Film for 2010.

The movie begins with a segment on Iceland, whose financial system and economy crashed roughly the same time as our own did. Significantly, though, Iceland has appointed a special prosecutor and people are already facing jail time for their criminal acts that caused the financial crisis in that country. Unfortunately, that is not happening here.

Then, turning to our own situation here in the U. S., Damon explained how investment banks used to be small, and investor owned and operated. For instance, Morgan Stanley had only 110 employees in 1972. Then, the investment banks went public and raised billions in stock issues, transforming them into the behemoths we see today.

Inside Job showed us how we had enjoyed more than 40 years of uninterrupted prosperity in the United States until financial deregulation began here in the early 1980's. In 1982, the S & L's were deregulated, and by 1990, hundreds had failed, costing U. S. taxpayers $124 billion. Significantly, several thousand Savings & Loan executives went to jail for looting their companies.

The movie points out an extremely interesting and very significant historical fact in that one of the most famous and high-profile S & L executives to be prosecuted hired a financial consultant named Alan Greenspan to represent him. Charles Keating went to jail, and, after collecting his $35,000 fee from Charles Keating, Alan Greenspan was appointed by Ronald Reagan in June of 1987, as Chairman of the Board of Governors of the Federal Reserve.

The movie had a segment about the bursting of the Dot Com bubble in 2001. And the point was made that Elliot Spitzer investigated wrongdoing by the investment banks and found that all of the big firms had knowingly promoted tech stocks they knew would fail. In December of 2002, the following ten banks settled with the state of New York for $1.4 billion.

Bear Stearns	$80 million
Credit Suisse	$200 million
Deutshe Bank	$80 million

J. P. Morgan Chase	$80 million
Lehman Brothers	$80 million
Merril Lynch	$200 million
Morgan Stanley	$125 million
UBS	$80 million
Goldman Sachs	$110 million
Citigroup	$400 million

Damon then points out that this agreed settlement by these banks was not an isolated instance of wrongdoing. Since deregulation began, the world's largest financial firms have been caught laundering money, defrauding customers, and cooking their books… again and again and again. Many examples were given, and the information is easily accessible to anyone who is interested. It is interesting to consider that if Elliot Spitzer had not been caught using an escort service and had instead been allowed to continue his oversight of the financial industry, we might be living in a totally different world today.

Inside Job shows us that in the year 2000, the financial industry was dominated by the following five investment banking firms:

Goldman Sachs
Morgan Stanley
Lehman Brothers
Merrill Lynch
Bear Stearns

Two financial conglomerates:

Citigroup
J. P. Morgan Chase

Three securities insurance companies:

AIG

MBIA

AMBAC

And three ratings agencies:

Moody's

Standard & Poor's

Fitch

And the last hour of the movie tells the story of how the executives at many of these companies basically ran our financial system into the ground for their own, personal gains. It's really an incredible story, and one of the most incredible things about it is that the people responsible have apparently escaped culpability. Not only that, but many of them are still in charge of our financial system today.

Here is a great quote from an interview with Martin Wolf, the Chief Economic commentator for the Financial Times.

> "It wasn't real profits. It wasn't real income. It was just money that was being created by the system and booked as income. Two or three years down the road, there's a default. It's all wiped out. I think it was. In fact, in retrospect, a great big, national… and not just national, but global… ponzi scheme."

And the points the movie makes about the participation of academia also need to be mentioned. I'm quite sure there are two professors from Columbia University, as well as another from Harvard, who were especially sorry they agreed to be interviewed for the film.

After walking us through all the intricate details of what transpired and who benefited, the movie ends with a segment about how Obama has appointed many of the same people to positions in Treasury, the Federal Reserve and the SEC. For instance, in 2010, at the time the movie came out, Timothy Geithner, was our Secretary of the Treasury. Ben Bernanke was still the Chairman of the Federal Reserve System. And Larry Summers was Obama's Chief Economic Advisor. All of these guys were major players before and during the crisis. The point is well made in the movie that it is hard to bring about reform and to prosecute the criminal wrongdoings that occurred, when all of the same people are still running things.

The movie ends with Damon telling us,

> "For decades, the American financial system was stable and safe. But then, something changed. The financial industry turned its back on society, corrupted our political system, and plunged the world economy into crisis. At enormous cost, we have avoided disaster, and are recovering. But the men and institutions that caused the crisis are still in power. And that needs to change… They will tell us that we need them. And that what they do is too complicated for us to understand. They will tell us it won't happen again. They will spend billions fighting reform… It won't be easy… But some things are worth fighting for."

The *Inside Job* DVD has some great special features. Here is a quote by Charles Ferguson from the "Making of Inside Job" section, which provides an apt ending for this section on the financial crisis…

> "It is really not that complicated. The details are complicated because it's a complicated industry. But the underlying principles are really very simple. And, in fact, one point that has really not been made sufficiently,

frequently about the crisis, and, I think about the issues in general, is... Even if you didn't do a single thing about increasingly stringent regulation of financial practices... If you were to put 75 senior financial executives in jail for the rest of their lives... I have a funny feeling that financial crisis in the future would become less frequent."

<u>Monetary Reform</u>

As stated in the beginning of this Banking and Financial Industry section, there are several banks in the Top 100 of the annual lists setting out the world's largest economic entities; a list that includes both corporations and countries. That fact, in itself, is significant. But even more significant than that is the fact that there are four U. S. banks in the top ten of *Fortune Magazine's* list of the most profitable U. S. corporations. So, how is it that these four banks are way down on the Fortune 500 list in terms of annual revenue, yet all rank in the top ten of U. S. corporations in terms of profit? Simple... These banks all have the ability to create money out of thin air! It's pretty easy to make a profit when, much like waving a magic wand, you can simply wish money into existence.

This is what it means to have a fractional reserve monetary system. I bet most of us think when we go to a bank to apply for a car loan, a home improvement loan, or a mortgage loan, that, much like when we borrow money from a friend, and that friend has to reach into his or her pocket to extract the money they will loan to us, a bank likewise must have somehow earned the money it will loan to us. We assume the money we are being loaned must exist as an asset somewhere on the bank's balance sheet. But that is not how it works. Because of our fractional reserve banking system, banks have the power to create the money they loan to us.

This is a very important point that is not widely understood. So, please allow me to say it again...

WHEN THE BANK LOANS US MONEY, THEY ARE ACTUALLY CREATING MONEY THAT DIDN'T EXIST BEFORE THEY LOANED IT TO US. ALMOST EVERYONE THINKS THE BANKS MAKE THEIR MONEY ON THE INTEREST PAID TO THEM ON THESE LOANS. IN ACTUALITY, IT IS THE PAYMENT OF THE PRINCIPAL ITSELF THAT PROVIDES THE MOST PROFIT TO THE BANKS.

Our present, fractional reserve banking system has its roots in medieval times. In medieval times, gold and silver coins were commonly used as money. Then, in part because of the variance in the quality and amount of gold or silver in the coins being used, goldsmiths, who were experts in evaluating the value of individual coins, began taking coins for safekeeping and issuing certificates representing the fair value of each coin. These certificates were then used as mediums of exchange in place of the coins.

Although the certificates were intended to represent the right of the holder to exchange the certificate for the gold and silver that had been deposited, many of the goldsmiths eventually realized their customers rarely came to actually redeem the certificates. This provided an opportunity for some of the less trustworthy goldsmiths to fraudulently issue multiple certificates for the same gold and silver. In this manner the precursor to our modern fractional reserve banking system was born. Of course, when the medieval public became suspicious there might be a problem with their ability to redeem those certificates, all the holders would show up at once to collect on them, thereby exposing the fraud. And, similarly, since the inception of fractional reserve banking, which is based upon this model, there have been many, many runs on banks when depositors became nervous that the money they had deposited for safekeeping might not be there for them. The desperate depositors would line up to get their money, the bank would be forced to admit they didn't have it, and the bank would fail.

This deceptive practice of fractional reserve banking has somehow been going on for almost a thousand years. Except that our present system is backed by our government and administered by the Federal Reserve, our current fractional reserve banking system is really not very different from the fraudulent one first started by those dishonest goldsmiths a thousand years ago, Although the participation by the government and a central bank provides more stability, this fractional reserve system of today is very similar to the old goldsmith ruse because the public in medieval times, like our public in these modern times, did not realize their deposits are not actually there for withdrawal. As a result, our supposedly honest bankers like JP Morgan Chase, Wells Fargo, Bank of America, and Citibank, are really performing very similar deceptions on us that those first dishonest goldsmiths attempted.

Currently banks are required to keep only ten percent of their deposits on hand for demand from their depositors, meaning the fractional reserve requirement is ten percent. In accordance with the fractional reserve requirement that is administered by each country's central bank, the other ninety percent of their depositor's funds may be loaned out. Incredibly, we live in a world where for-profit banks are allowed to create money out of thin air in order to loan it to us. This means that for every net increase in deposits, there is a direct link to that bank's net revenue. This is the main reason there are four banks included in the top ten of Fortune's list of our nation's most profitable corporations. It is also the main reason the CEO's of those four banks brought in $77.3 million between them in salaries, bonuses, and other compensations in the year 2016 alone.

And the exorbitant compensation rates do not stop with the CEO's. According to an article by CNN, the top executives from the nine banks that received the first batch of government aid through the Troubled Asset Relief Program, better known as TARP, paid their top executives in the previous year (2007) more than $930.6 million. This included $76.7 million to seven executives of Bank of America, $70.6 to seven executives from Citigroup, $94.9 million to five executives from JP Morgan Chase, $82.9 million to seven executives from Merrill Lynch, $70.6 million to six executives from Morgan Stanley, $94.2 million to six executives from New York Mellon Bank, $61.2 million to five executives from State Street Corp., $57.4 million to six executives from Wells Fargo, and a whopping $321.9 million to just five executives from Goldman Sachs. To re-cap, that is more than nine-tenths of a BILLION DOLLARS that was paid to fifty-four bank executives IN ONLY ONE YEAR!

How would you react if you woke up tomorrow morning and you suddenly realized that every time somebody asked you for a loan you could simply snap your fingers and the money would magically appear in your hand? Would you tell them, "Here is your fifty dollars. If you don't return the full amount to me plus interest in one week, I am going to send my associate, Guido, over to your home, and he is going to bring me that big flat screen TV I have seen hanging on your living room wall"?

Hopefully, if you were suddenly given the power to create money out of thin air, you would act a little more responsibly. But seriously, why are we allowing for-profit banks to have this magical power to create money for their own benefit? If banks were somehow providing a benefit to our culture that warranted such a reward, then I could understand why we might allow this. But banks are notorious for acting exactly the opposite of beneficially towards our culture. As Matt Damon noted in Inside Job, banks have been caught laundering money, defrauding customers, and cooking their books, over and over again. Anyone who expects any sort of altruistic actions from a bank is clearly not thinking correctly.

Once again, I assert this ridiculous situation where for-profit corporations have such immense power over us, exists only because we the people do not understand it. If enough of us were better informed about this little piece of our reality, then the public outrage that would result from that understanding would force our legislators to either rectify the matter, or risk losing their next election to a candidate who promised action. But, unfortunately, the issue is somewhat shrouded in complexity. And, so far at least, that complexity has been enough for the people and the banks who are profiting unjustly to continue the charade.

Let's take a moment to try to unravel this complexity.

The first of the other two main components of our insane culture's worldwide monetary system is central banking. Every nation on the planet except for North Korea, Iran, and Cuba, now issues its own fiat-based currency and operates under a fractional reserve banking system administered by a central bank. The only other countries who don't have their own central bank are the nineteen members of the Eurozone who have all adopted the Euro as their currency under a system administered by one central bank called the European Central Bank. Central banks are charged with overseeing and regulating the banks within their country, or, in the case of the Eurozone countries, and with monitoring and adjusting the money supply.

Here, in the U. S., our central bank is the Federal Reserve, and the current Chairperson of the Fed is Jerome Powell. There is no getting around the fact that our Federal Reserve System is complicated in its makeup, and also in its function, duties and responsibilities. The Federal Reserve was established by Congress and signed into law by Woodrow Wilson on December 23, 1913. In order to appease those who were concerned with bankers potentially having too much power on one side, as well as those who were concerned about the government having too much power on the other side, the Federal Reserve was designed as a quasi-governmental institution that contains both public and private components. Although the composition and the workings are so complicated, that I do not feel qualified to pass judgment on whether it serves us or not, I have looked deeply enough to see that on the surface, at least, it seems to work fairly well towards achieving its mandates, which are "to promote sustainable growth, high levels of employment, stability of prices, and moderate long term interest rates". To me, the most glaring problem with the Fed is its obvious complicity in the continuation of the insane practice of allowing our for-profit banks to profit from fractional reserve banking.

The last of the three main components of our worldwide monetary system is fiat money. "Fiat" means "trust", so fiat money stands for trust-based money. Fiat money is money backed by nothing but trust or confidence in the issuer, and that trust is propped up the laws within each country that require their nation's currency to be accepted as legal tender for any business or commerce conducted within their borders. Our U. S. dollars used to be a hard currency that was convertible to gold, but after a period of inflation caused by Federal Reserve policy and practices that made conversion of dollars to gold impossible, Richard Nixon ended that practice in 1971.

Because all money that exists has been created through borrowing, our monetary system is often referred to as a debt-based system. Here in the U. S., a small portion of our money is created by the issuance of government bonds, (otherwise known as deficit spending) but, by far the biggest portion of our money supply comes into existence as a result of our fractional reserve system through loans made to businesses and individuals by for-profit banks.

As with some of the other issues I have researched and written about in this chapter and in the preceding chapter, researching this issue has provided me with the most astonishing revelation about how "we, the people" have been bamboozled. In this case, the bamboozlers are the bankers who are enabled in their deception by the Federal Reserve. These present bamboozlers and their predecessors have been putting a big one over us for a thousand years. In fact, when I think about it, I am reminded of organized religion, because much like Christianity and Islam, the bankers are still here in our modern world, working their deceptions on the general public, largely because they have been doing it for so long, most people don't even think to question it.

But if one takes the time to look a little closer, a little deeper, it becomes apparent there is something terribly wrong with our monetary system. And most certainly, the main reason we need monetary reform is to rectify this insane situation whereby for-profit banks are profiting from the creation of money. In a sane culture, do you think we would tell all the businesses except for banks that the way to succeed in business is to provide a good or a service that people are willing to pay for, and to figure out a way to profit by doing so, but we would tell banks not to worry because they can simply waive a magic wand and money would magically appear for them to profit from?

The only way any changes are ever going to be made is if enough people understand how crazy our current system actually is. So, let me say that again. If we are ever going to fix this, then this point MUST be understood. WE ARE ALLOWING FOR-PROFIT BANKS TO PROFIT FROM CREATING OUR MONEY! Every dollar that is loaned to us for every house, car, boat, motorcycle, or whatever, represents new money created by the bank who loaned it to us. That bank gets to profit from the creation of the money they loan to us, and they get to use it to pay exorbitant compensation packages to their top executives, donate to political campaigns and political parties, and among other things, pay lobbyists to keep the wheels greased with the politicians they elected with their campaign donations, so that they may keep the deception going.

Again, the only reason I can see for this ridiculous situation to continue is because not enough people understand it. My assertion is that of the small percentage of the population who actually do have a good understanding of our monetary system, the only ones who actually like things the way they are, are the bankers and their associates, including many of our politicians, who profit along with them. Unfortunately, there is a lot of disagreement among the balance of the people who understand our monetary system about what should be done to fix it. In fact, a big part of the problem in achieving reform is this disagreement among the reformers about which method of reform to pursue.

According to what my research has shown me, those who advocate for reform all choose a path that reflects their political ideology and their worldview. For instance, Libertarians advocate either a return to the gold standard or a return to free banking whereby each bank would be free to issue its own currency and to loan as much or as little of its deposits as it wanted. With free banking, these banks would all either succeed or fail with no help or interference from government or from a central bank. There would be very little regulation or oversight, and no Federal Deposit Insurance to guarantee depositor's funds when their bank fails. Of course, with a gold standard, the money supply would be fixed because of the finite gold supply. This would discourage inflation and also make deficit spending by the government very problematic.

Of the more progressive minded reformers, many advocate a fiat-based system where money is actually spent into existence by the government without debt, and where either there is no fractional reserve banking allowed or the fractional reserve requirement is much higher. Another popular choice for progressives is public banking, which refers to a system whereby our for-profit banks would either be nationalized or required to convert to full reserve banks, and public banks would take over the fractional reserve duties so the profits from creating money out of thin air could be utilized to fund the government.

As you would expect, having become familiar with my political bent and worldviews over the preceding pages, my own recommended reform more closely resembles a progressive one than a conservative or libertarian one. As set out above, I am asserting in the strongest possible terms that the main problem with our current monetary system is the fact that for-profit banks are profiting by the creation of money through our fractional reserve system. This is truly insane, and absolutely must be stopped as soon as possible. To me, the next most pressing problem in this area appears to be debt in general, especially third world debt. And, of course, any new monetary system will need to devise a manner in which to peg each country's own currency to every other country's in some sort of fair and balanced way.

With the caveat that I have only spent a few weeks studying this extremely complex subject, I offer the following:

First: We must end the insane practice of allowing for-profit banks to profit from the creation of money through the fractional reserve system. This is by far the biggest problem arising from our current monetary system. Admittedly, the fix to this may be painful, but hopefully, knowledgeable and fair-minded people will contribute to solving this in the best manner possible. A conversion to full reserve banking by for-profit banks, along with the creation of public banks that could take up the role of lending to individuals and businesses, and send their profits to fund the government, would seem to me to be a viable alternative. I also would advocate for governments having the power to create money in order to fund government activities without the need for issuing bonds. Hence, my solution would include a part of our money creation being debt based, (being that part created by loans from public banks to individuals and businesses), and a part being directly spent into existence by governments without the need for the issuing of bonds.

Second: We need to effect a debt jubilee that at the very least extends to all Third World debt, and student loans. Especially considering the genesis of all presently existing debt as it pertains to for-profit banks, we need to strongly consider what should be done about all other debts, including both secured and unsecured ones. To me, the need to forgive Third World debt and student loans is obvious, while the rest is more complicated and nuanced. I recommend this matter be studied by the present-day equivalent of a tribal council whose members are all grounded in their sense of connection to all things.

Third: Given that our world's central banks have all been created in order to prop up a corrupt and insane fractional reserve banking system, somebody is going to have to take a very hard look at the makeup, responsibilities, duties, and authority of our central banks, and make appropriate adjustments. Personally, I see no problem with a fiat-based currency administered by a central bank for every country. We simply need to weed out and clean up the corruption.

I contend that for-profit banks are being allowed by our culture to unfairly profit in this manner, emboldening those working in that field to constantly push the boundaries in an effort to ascertain what else they can get away with. And, very obviously, they have been able to get away with a lot. There does not appear to be a lot of altruistic people with a social conscience working in high executive positions in the banking and financial industry. Clearly, there is no place for such people there.

In this crazy country, we will devote resources to rooting out and punishing the desperate poor among us for welfare fraud amounting to a few hundred dollars, yet nobody in the banking and financial world ever gets indicted for crimes their companies admit to having done, and for which their companies (and not them, personally) have paid billions of dollars in fines. Clearly, there are individuals behind these admitted crimes who are personally responsible. Yet, nobody ever goes to jail, or even gets indicted. What kind of a world are we living in when our law enforcement personnel consistently look the other way when individuals within giant corporations like our banks are obviously responsible for the criminal taking of millions of dollars, yet work so hard to put less-advantaged people behind bars for crimes involving tiny fractions of the money stolen by banking and financial executives?

As stated previously, the obvious fix involves the removal of the ability of for-profit banks to profit from fractional reserve banking. For the sake of everyone except those few individuals who are profiting, and for the sake of the environment, the natural world, and the rest of the Community of Life on this planet, this insane practice MUST be dealt with as soon as possible.

Closing Thoughts on Our Corporate Rulers

And, as we have seen, our world is not being served by the fact that the giant corporations in the other business sectors are also making most of the important decisions affecting their businesses either. Poll after poll shows how the American people support change regarding issues that would improve our daily lives but adversely affect the bottom lines of huge corporations. But because of the power wielded by the corporations, and especially because of the money the corporations spend on lobbying and on political contributions, nothing ever gets done.

In this chapter, we have looked at pharmaceutical companies and questioned whether it serves us to allow them to make zillions of dollars selling us dubious drugs that mostly mask symptoms of illness rather than treat the underlying disease, and at the same time saddle us with their terrible side effects. We looked at oil companies whose main product is one of the main causes of global warming, and who are also directly responsible for much of our pollution and deforestation. We looked at car companies and questioned whether we should live in a world that is so dependent upon the personal automobile. We looked at defense contractors who profit from war and therefore have a vested interest in keeping our world mired in strife and conflict, and we have questioned whether we should allow them to have so much influence over these matters. We looked at health insurance companies and questioned whether for-profit corporations should have a place in our health care system, especially when their sole purpose in being there is to extract a profit for themselves. We looked at agricultural companies and questioned almost everything they do, including whether our food production should be so centralized and so dependent upon shipping and distribution. And, we have questioned whether our present governmental-backed system of subsidies representing billions of dollars that mostly goes to big corporations to grow corn, wheat, and soy, which are used either to feed our livestock or to make processed foods that are not beneficial to our health, is serving us. And we have looked at banks and the financial industry and among many issues, we especially questioned whether banks should profit from the creation of money. In all of these cases, the answers to the question of "Should we?" is "No!" But in every case, the corporations have grown so large and so powerful, they have taken the decision-making process away from the citizens of this country, and made decisions about how things will be that benefit the corporations and their profit-making capabilities to the detriment of the citizens, the environment, and the natural world.

It is a travesty that we have allowed our world to be organized in a manner that facilitates profit and growth for a bunch of stupendously large corporations. Instead, we should choose to organize our world in a manner that benefits all of the natural world, including all people everywhere, and protects our beautiful planet from pollution and deforestation.

We must abolish the insane legal concept of corporate personhood and return our world to one where people and not giant corporations decide how things will be ordered. The abolishment of corporate personhood will not be easily accomplished. There are just too many politicians who are beholden to their corporate masters and want to continue being paid off by them. The insane concept of granting legal protections as persons to artificial entities that can live forever, don't need breathable air or drinkable water, and can't be incarcerated, will most definitely come to an end when we have successfully achieved a Critical Mass of people who understand how things came to be this way and stand ready to transform our culture to a sane culture that is based upon the reality that everything is connected. However, in order to fix this issue of corporate rule, we don't have to wait for the entire culture to be transformed. I contend that the abolition of corporate personhood and the return of our government to "We, the People" could be considered a logical first step for a culture that is attempting to return itself to sanity.

This brings us to the end of Part Two, wherein we have examined our world of today. My intention in the first two sections of this book has been to describe the history and the present state of our culture. At the same time I've been endeavoring to illuminate the undeniable connection between our problems, and the fact that our basic beliefs dictated by our fairy tale cultural myth fosters a false sense of separation. Finally, I have spent a lot of time describing how things would be much better if we returned to a culture based upon our knowing that everything is connected and we are a part of the world and a part of the Community of Life.

What follows is that in order to make meaningful and positive changes we are going to have to put an end to our insane and destructive culture and replace it with a new culture based upon the reality that everything is connected. The only way that is ever going to happen without a lot of struggle and strife is voluntarily through the achievement of that all-important Critical Mass of people who understand our situation and stand ready to make changes.

When enough of us understand how things came to be this way…. When enough of us understand how our culture was born when the people of one tribe out of a world full of tribal people decided to reject their positions as Responsible Members of the Community of Life and begin acting as if the world was made for man only…. When enough of us understand there actually is a law governing evolution and our insane culture is operating in violation of that law…. When enough of us understand the reality of our situation as one species out of millions of species of life that has evolved on this planet, and that our particular species of life is no more or no less special than any of the other species of life…. When enough of us…

Part Three

Soft Landing

8

We Are Not Humanity

◊

In the previous two chapters, we took a look at a list of serious problems. Our world has been in big trouble for a long time and apparently, much like in Quinn's boiling frog analogy, things are just getting worse. Recently, the gulf between the rich and poor has grown tremendously. People all around the world are starving, just as they have for millennia, except now that our world population has increased so dramatically, we have millions more hungry people than ever before. Billions of our impoverished people struggle to provide basic needs for themselves and their families. People are dying from HIV/AIDS, cholera, malaria and many other easily preventable diseases. Women continue to die every day from easily treatable complications from childbirth.

Our polar ice caps and our glaciers are melting and our sea levels are rising. Our storms are getting stronger. The last of our ancient forests are on the verge of being destroyed. And along with them, the last of the world's remaining tribal people are on the verge of being killed or assimilated into our culture, just as all of the other tribal people around the world have been killed or assimilated before them. As their habitats disappear, entire species are becoming extinct at a rate not seen since the cataclysmic event 65 million years ago when a huge asteroid struck the Yucatan Peninsula and wiped out the dinosaurs.

More chemicals and other dangerous contaminates continue to be dumped into our already polluted atmosphere, rivers, streams, lakes, aquifers, and oceans. The very air we breathe is actually dangerous to the health of many of our city dwellers, especially to our children. Commercial fishing in our oceans is decimating fish populations around the world. North Korea recently tested another nuclear weapon. The possibility that either a country or a terrorist group would use these terrible weapons is indeed a very real and a very scary one.

As has been the case for thousands of years, everywhere we go on this planet, we must be conscious of the fact that there are people around who will steal our stuff if we do not take care to secure it. And worse, many others would forcibly take our cash and other possessions away from us if they thought they could do so and get away with it. Many of these bandits would have no concern whatsoever if their victims end up wounded or even killed in the process. Rapists of women, and sexual and physical and psychological tormenters of children wreak havoc every day all around the globe, causing trauma that is very often carried by their victims for their entire lives.

The United States continues to be mired in wars in Iraq and Afghanistan. Other armed conflicts, where one side is doing its best to kill and terrorize as many members of the other side as possible, are ongoing in more than twenty-five other locations around the world. And all over the world, people continue turning to drugs and alcohol to provide themselves with some escape and mental relief from the constant underlying anxiety caused by living with all of these problems. Others drink or take drugs in an attempt to cover up their own mental problems resulting from their personal childhood traumas. Many are addicted, and many more are on the verge of being addicted as well.

Will things ever be better? Can poverty be alleviated? Can we ever stop killing each other in senseless wars? Will we ever stop destroying our planet's ecosystems and polluting our environment? Can we ever stop worrying about the need to protect ourselves from criminals, rapists, and abusers?

If we press the powers in charge of running this insane culture for an answer to these questions, they will first try to tell us.... "We live in a complicated world and each of these problems has its own set of causes, and therefore, its own set of complicated and very expensive solutions. Benevolent governments and charitable organizations and philanthropists are donating funds, and many of our smartest people are working very hard on these problems, but the solutions are complicated and require a lot of time and money. We are trying our best, and we ask that you be patient while we work towards solutions."

Then, if we continue to try to look for a deeper solution, our culture, when pressed, will tell us the problems are there because of basic flaws in humanity itself.

"People are greedy," our culture will tell us. "And lazy. Additionally, people are weak, immoral, violent, and dishonest. It is because of these basic flaws in human nature that we have these problems. If people would only behave better, then everything would be okay."

But unfortunately, when we complain about all of these problems, this second answer our culture gives us is sufficient to satisfy many of us. And that is because superficially, at least, there certainly appears to be some truth to it. It is easy to look at the terrible results of human greed, and sloth, and immorality, and violence, and dishonesty. Yes... these are definitely human traits. There is no denying that.

But there are some of us who can no longer be put off when our culture tries to tell us, "We are trying our best". And that is because we have been given the great gift of understanding that our culture itself is the cause of these problems.

These negative human tendencies that our culture tries to blame our problems on are all magnified because we all live in an insane culture that believes incorrectly that **the world was made for man to conquer and rule**. They simply wouldn't be a problem if we were living in a sane culture. Belief in this fairy tale myth fosters a false sense of separation. And it this false sense of separation that tells the person with tendencies towards greed that it is only natural and right for him to gather all the money and possessions and wealth he can. After all, our culture believes in the survival of the fittest, doesn't it? Doesn't that make it okay for the smartest, or strongest, or most cunning of us to succeed and thrive, and even to amass immense wealth?

And what about those who don't have enough to eat? Or a place to sleep? Or, a place to go where they can protect themselves from the elements and keep their possessions secure? Or, what about those of us who live in squalid, unsanitary environments with no access to health care? Do we answer this one by listening to that same cultural myth that tells the greedy people it is okay to be greedy? That the disadvantaged among us are poor because they are lazy, or weak, or simply mentally challenged? Do we chalk all of these problems up to that other secondary cultural myth that tries to mollify us by telling us there are not enough resources available for us to be able to provide these things?

How about the violent, immoral, and dishonest people among us? Would they still be violent, immoral and dishonest if they lived in a culture that was based upon the truth that we are a part of the world and the Community of Life? If these people woke up every morning into a world where everyone understood that everything was connected, and nobody had to worry about any of their basic needs, such as food or shelter or health care being met, would these negative human traits still manifest?

Most of the problems discussed in the previous two chapters are problems experienced all over the world by the people of our culture. But here is the good news.... Ours is not the only culture on this planet! The Bushmen of the Kalahari represent another culture that is completely separate from ours. Are they polluting their environment? Are the Australian Aborigines suffering from overpopulation? Are the Tahumari of Mexico allowing their poor people to starve? Are the Baniwa in Brazil cutting down their rainforest? Are those tribes all comprised of enlightened people with extremely high levels of consciousness who have learned to overcome their basic human flaws? Of course not! Those people are simply all a part of cultures that do not foster insane behavior like ours does.

Although it is true that we members of this insane culture represent the largest part of the human population on this planet, it is certainly not true that we represent humanity itself. It is not because of some flaw in human nature that the people of our culture behave so badly. The reason so many of us behave so badly is because these negative tendencies are brought out and magnified by our insane culture that fosters separation when the reality is connectedness.

As we have established, our culture is based upon a fairy tale myth that tells us the world was made for man to conquer and rule. Adherence to that fairy tale myth results in a false sense of separation. All of our harmful secondary cultural myths arise out of that false sense of separation.

The true nature of reality is that we are a part of the world and a part of the Community of Life. If we could only transform our culture into one that embraces that truth, then most of these problems would simply melt away. Those "other cultures", like the Bushmen, the Aborigines, the Tahumari, the Baniwa, and a few lucky others that still exist, know this to be true and live their lives accordingly. Growing up in communities who adhere to this great truth fosters and confirms a sense of connection. Connection with our environment., connection with the other members of the Community of Life... and connection with each other as well.

Patchwork programs simply cannot fix our culture. Enough of us need to wake up and realize that the only way to stop this destruction is to remake our culture into a new one that is based upon the true reality of our world.... **We are a part of the world and a part of the Community of Life.** The great news is that you and I both understand this very significant fact. Instead of letting this insane culture crash on its own, you and I stand ready to help bring it down for a soft landing.

But unfortunately, the bad news is that the truth about this situation eludes most of the rest of us. And since you and I cannot save the world by ourselves, it is this lack of understanding by the majority of our population that is our main hurdle to saving the world. But there is hope. As many of us found out by watching Avatar.... Jake Sully's insanity could, indeed be cured! For each of us then, our task becomes to cure the insanity of a hundred... who will each cure the insanity of a hundred.... And so on, until eventually we will succeed creating a Critical Mass of people who are capable of saving the world from the insane culture (ours) that is destroying it.

9

Outlaws No More

Resuming Our Role as Responsible Members of the Community of Life

◊

In the same manner that Jesse James, Butch Cassidy, and Billy the Kid were outlaws in regard to our culture, our culture has been acting as if we were all outlaws in regard to the larger culture that includes the rest of the Community of Life. Appropriately, the sheriff and his deputy have come to arrest us. They are standing on our porch with an arrest warrant that says we have been violating the peacekeeping law for the past ten thousand years. As the sheriff hands us the warrant, we take a look at the name badge on his starched shirt and see that his name is Global Warming. We glance at the deputy's name badge and see that her name is Overpopulation.

Our outlaw culture is finally on the verge of being held accountable for our crimes against the planet and our fellow members of the Community of Life. For ten thousand years, we have enjoyed the life of an outlaw... robbing, and raping, and pillaging our way to conquering the world, just as we were instructed by our culture's founding myth. But we have hit a wall.

Sheriff Global Warming and Deputy Overpopulation are telling us that our crime spree is over. Our culture can either resume our role as Responsible Members of the Community of Life, or these officers of the law are standing ready to administer our punishment.

Sheriff Global Warming is not going to fuck around with us. And neither is Deputy Overpopulation. They have both come to tell us we need to get our shit together. And they are dead serious.

Although the warrant says we have been committing this crime of violating the peacekeeping law for ten thousand years, it is only very recently, relative to the ten-thousand-year period, that overpopulation and global warming have reached the point where the threat they pose is real. It wasn't until 1804, that our worldwide population reached 1 billion. Considering it took us ten thousand years to reach the 1 billion mark, it is remarkable that the second billion of population was achieved in only a little more than 100 years after the first. I think any of us who have put any thought into the topic of population and overpopulation would feel comfortable with the ability of this planet to carry 1 to maybe 2 billion of us. But in the 93 years since reaching that milestone of 2 billion, we have added another 5.8 billion people! That is way more people than should reasonably be here. What is worse, our worldwide population is still exploding.

And like overpopulation, global warming has only become a problem in recent times. Fifty years ago, we didn't even know global warming was taking place. Certainly, if we could roll back our greenhouse gas emissions to the output levels from fifty years ago, we would all be immensely safer from this very real threat than we are with today's levels.

But, the additional 4 billion people added to our worldwide population during the past fifty years has changed things considerably. In 1927, when our worldwide population hit the 2 billion mark, there were a little more than 20 million cars in the United States. Today there are more than 253 million. Needless to say, the addition of all of those people, and all those automobiles, and all those factories, and all those refineries, and all those power plants, have had a tremendous impact on the health of our environment, as well as on the well-being of the rest of the Community of Life.

It has been more than twenty-five years since I first read *Ishmael* and got so excited about finally having the proper, basic information about how things in our world became so screwed up... and how it could all be fixed. The disappointment I experienced when many of my friends read the book at my urging and then hated it, provided a difficult but a very valuable lesson for me.... This soft landing is not going to be as easy to achieve as I naively thought it would.

But today, twenty-five years later, our problems are also much bigger. The world economy is teetering on the edge of collapse. Our storms are getting stronger. Our glaciers are melting, and our sea levels are rising. In those twenty-five years, our worldwide population has increased by another 31%, from 5.4 billion, to 7.8 billion. Corporate greed is much more apparent. The chasm between rich and poor is widening. The middle class is disappearing. And consequently, more people are desperately looking for answers.

Unfortunately, the vast majority of the people looking for answers are still tricked by our fairy tale cultural myths into blaming our problems on superfluous stuff like bad economic times, or wars, or incompetent governments run by the party of their political opponents, or unfortunate weather patterns. Others blame our problems on the lies our culture tells us like "There is Not Enough". And way too many others see the problems resulting from human greed, and dishonesty, and jealousy, and violence, and hate, and prejudice, and incorrectly place the blame for our problems on basic flaws in humanity.

Still others welcome the end of the world, because their religion has not only predicted it, but tells them the end of the world is a good thing, because the cataclysmic end of the world will be the time when their faith in Jesus and their faith in God in Heaven will be rewarded by the salvation of their eternal soul. I suppose if these fools get impatient waiting for the apocalypse, they could consider converting to Islam and blow themselves up on a crowded bus.

But there is good news. Some of the people who are seeking answers now, who weren't asking questions before the problems got worse, are actually looking for solutions where they need to be looking... at the very foundation of our culture. When these people find their answers, then there is a very high likelihood they will be able to influence others to find the same answers. Some, like me, will write a book. Others may write blogs that become widely read and very influential. Others might start "Save the World" organizations and raise a lot of money for education. Others might contribute their time and money to such organizations. Still others might make movies, or TV shows, or YouTube videos, or write, record, and perform songs that help people to see the truth of our situation.

But even the ones who don't do any of these things will end up having a big influence on their friends and families just by being around them and speaking their truth. And that is because there will be others who will recognize the truth when they hear it from them. Who knows when one of us might reach an individual who will end up having a huge impact? Achieving the Critical Mass of people who "get it" and understand we must bring this culture in for a soft landing before it crashes on its own is a monumental task, but one made more doable with every soul who connects the dots from "How things came to be this way," to "We must return our culture to one based upon the reality that everything is connected."

Of course, the building of the Critical Mass has been going on for a long time already. Daniel Quinn made huge contributions to the effort with the publication of Ishmael in 1992. As you know, I give Quinn and his telepathic gorilla credit for waking me up to our situation. He may not have been the first person to point out the failings of our modern culture, but he was the first to put the Great Forgetting and the peacekeeping law into the explanation of how things came to be this way. Through reading Ishmael, I learned that our ten thousand-year-old culture is flawed at its very foundational level. And, if your goal is to help save the world, there is nothing more valuable than having this very basic knowledge at your disposal.

Another author who deserves a lot of credit for shining a light on our flawed culture with the goal of helping us to resume our roles as Responsible Members of the Community of Life, is David Korten, who wrote the classic non-fiction work, *When Corporations Rule the World*. The book was first published in 1995 and was revised and updated in a second edition published in 2001. I contend that *When Corporations Rule the World* is David Korten's *Soft Landing*, although I should probably have said that the other way around. I can only dream that *Soft Landing* might someday approach the impact that Korten's book has had on contributing to the Critical Mass. I do think, however, that anyone who reads both of these books will see the similarity as I do. The differences are a result of our differing backgrounds and experience, and on the sources of our inspiration, with mine being Ishmael and his being his background in economics combined with his business experience.

I recently read *When Corporations Rule the World* again and noticed a reference to another book that sounded interesting. It came out in the year 2000, and because I was in Costa Rica at the time, that must be the reason I missed it. The book is *The Cultural Creatives, How 50 Million People Are Changing the World*, by Paul H. Ray and Sherry Ruth Anderson. The authors are married to each other, and both have PhD's. Paul is a macro sociologist, and Sherry is a psychologist. In terms of relevance to *Soft Landing*, I consider *Cultural Creatives* to be a very important work. The book is based on analysis from more than nine years of surveys conducted by Paul Ray's company containing questions used by the authors to classify people according to their cultural beliefs. The survey material was supplemented by additional interviews and focus groups.

I want to report that I took a lot of comfort from my recent reading of *The Cultural Creatives*. Ray and Anderson make the point that a lot of us feel as I do (did?) that we are out there all alone with our radical worldviews. But it turns out we are not so alone as it seems. We just have a problem recognizing each other and connecting with each other. It is indeed very comforting for me to know there are another 50 million Americans and 200 million people worldwide out there who share at least enough of my anti-cultural sentiments so that Ray and Anderson deem it appropriate to lump us together into the *Cultural Creatives* category.

Yes…. It is comforting to know there are more kindred spirits already out there than I imagined there were. But without a doubt, there are still not enough of us. What are we supposed to do? Sheriff Global Warming and his deputy, Overpopulation, have already handed us our arrest warrant. Do we make a run for it? What would that even mean?

The way I see it, we have no choice but to keep our heads down and focus on adding to that budding group of cultural revolutionaries I call the Critical Mass. And hope that Sheriff Global Warming and Deputy Overpopulation give us a little more time to get our shit together.

10

A New Human Consciousness

An Unforeseen Dividend of Living in a Sane Culture

Until we bring this flawed and doomed culture in for a soft landing, all of us will continue living in a culture that is insane. It is insane because it is based upon a fairy tale myth that tells us all that God created the world for man to conquer and rule. Belief in this fairy tale myth fosters a false sense of separation. In reality, everything is connected and we are all a part of the world and a part of the Community of Life.

And guess what? Living in an insane culture takes a toll on us. Very few of us are able to exist in this insane culture without being adversely affected by it. Who among us is able to live every moment in the present, totally open and accepting to everything that comes our way? How many of us even realize this to be a goal that we should strive for? Only very few of us do not experience periodic bouts of depression or anger or fear or pride. Many of us even live our lives almost totally within the grip of one or more of these terrible afflictions. The miniscule minority of us who are able to live in this culture and not go in and out of these types of temporary insanities are the ones who are the most developed spiritually. And what do those spiritually advanced people tell us about their experiences of higher consciousness? Without exception, they tell us there are no words to describe their experiences. In other words, their experiences go beyond the ability of our symbols to depict them.

But what if another form of consciousness was available to us... A form of consciousness that is not based upon symbols and abstract reasoning... A form of consciousness where living every moment in the present, totally open and accepting to everything that occurs, comes naturally to everybody.

I recently read a scientific publication by an anthropologist named E. Richard Sorenson that describes just such a consciousness. The piece is called *Preconquest Consciousness*, and it relates his studies of the tribal people Sorenson lived among and studied in New Guinea, the Andaman Sea, the Philippines, India, Nepal, Polynesia, Mexico, South America, and elsewhere. Sorenson says in the article that it actually took him decades to comprehend the extent of the differences in their way of perceiving and thinking from ours. Initially, and for many years thereafter, he mistakenly thought of these people as naïve and primitive and ignorant and unsophisticated, just as most everyone else from our culture has for millennia. But, as he came to understand them, he realized that these people lived an entirely different reality than the one we are a part of in our modern world. He referred to them as being liminally conscious, meaning their perceptions and their consciousness was much more focused "in the moment" than ours. Here is Sorenson describing liminal awareness:

Most of us know about subliminal awareness – the type of awareness lurking below actual consciousness that powerfully influences behavior. Freud brought it into the mainstream of Western thought through exhaustively detailed revelations of its effects on behavior. But few, including Freud, have spoken of liminal consciousness, which is therefore rarely recognized in modern scholarship as a separate type of awareness. Nonetheless, liminal awareness was the principal focus of mentality in the preconquest cultures contacted, whereas a supraliminal type that focuses logic on symbolic entities is the dominant form in postconquest societies.

Sorenson says that finally, after many years of anthropological study, he came to understand that these tribal people who he had the privilege to live amongst, had a completely different way of cognition than we do. Prior to being conquered or assimilated, or just corrupted by our very presence, these people existed without a need for abstract reasoning. According to Sorenson:

> In the real life of these preconquest people, feeling and awareness are focused on at-the-moment, point-blank sensory experience – as if the nub of life lay within that complex flux of collective sentient immediacy. Into that flux individuals thrust their inner thoughts and aspirations for all to see, appreciate, and relate to. This unabashed open honesty is the foundation on which their highly honed integrative empathy and rapport becomes possible.

> Where consciousness is focused within a flux of ongoing sentient awareness, experience cannot be clearly subdivided into separable components. With no clear elements to which logic can be applied, experience remains immune to syntax and formal logic within a kaleidoscopic sanctuary of non-discreteness. Nonetheless, preconquest life was reckoned sensibly – though seemingly intuitively.

Later in the article, Sorenson says:

As fascinating as we may find the impact of conquering cultures on preconquest groups, it pales before the challenge of epistemology posed by the existence of a system of cognition not based on symbolic logic. We of Western training may find it virtually impossible to see how truth can be demonstrated without recourse to symbols that are logically controlled. When I first came face-to-face with these experientially-based modes of cognition wherein logic was irrelevant, they slid right past me. I did not even see them. Even when I did begin to catch on, I tended to doubt such perceptions once I was again within the confines of Western culture. It took years of repeated, even dramatic exposure before these initially fragmentary mental graspings were able to survive re-immersion in Western culture. Experiences repeated, however, eventually make their mark and I began to question whether symbolic logic was actually the only means to get at truth. Now I rather think that alternative routes to truth may exist within the immediacy of a type of experiential awareness that perhaps moves in extra-sentient directions not yet brought into the realm of our modern sense-of-truth. My slowness in this matter leads me to believe it may take modern humankind some time to identify and make use of these perhaps more rarefied mental capabilities.

According to Sorenson, these tribal people employed a "system of cognition not based upon symbolic logic." Alternatively, he calls it "preconquest consciousness," "liminal awareness," and "intuitive rapport".

Here are more of Sorenson's comments describing these tribal people's form of cognition:

It took a long time for me to realize that they had evolved their own sophisticated type of cognition that was simply different from what I (or anyone I knew) was used to. And I came to realize that such mentality could not be considered primitively ignorant if only because it was so sensitively intelligent and beneficially responsive. It moved more facilely, more harmoniously, and more constructively than do the mentalities associated with today's postconquest world. Furthermore, it provided for an astonishingly rewarding and zestful life.

Sorenson ends his piece with the following comment:

Finally, in the ultimate analysis, we do not yet have a way to know if the postconquest type of consciousness that dominates the world today represents a positive or negative shift in the evolution of mentality. This question of fundamental values bears on all of humankind and on the future of humanity. Thus, of all the questions raised, it is the one that most demands an answer.

Okay then... Dr. E. Richard Sorenson... Let's try to answer your question!

First, thank you very much for posing it. After all, without your studies and your article, we wouldn't even know to ask it!

To me, the initial analysis is obvious. The manner of cognition of the tribal people is based upon the reality of connectedness. Their consciousness results in an intuitive rapport with their fellow tribal members and it keeps them connected to the present moment where everything that comes their way is greeted with openness and acceptance. Sorenson doesn't say much about whether the tribal people experience an intuitive rapport with the other members of the Community of Life, but it is easy to see the potential. And remember, Robert Wolf wrote about similar experiences in Original Wisdom, which included an account of Wolf being escorted back to camp by a tiger. Wolf also described the typical morning at the Sng 'Oi camp as beginning with a discussion of the group's shared dreams from the previous night. (They always dreamt about the same thing as a group.)

In contrast, our manner of cognition is based upon abstract symbols (words), on which we build our reality through logic and reasoning. Our minds are rarely focused on the present moment, but rather are usually pre-occupied in either the past or the future. And even if our minds are focused on the present, there exists a cognitive gap due to the fact that our minds must translate whatever is happening into the abstract symbols that allow us to comprehend it. The "real world" cannot help but be separate from the reality our words are attempting to represent.

But is it really the destiny of humanity to return to our preconquest way of cognition? Do we really need to discard all the seemingly progressive achievements that have been made possible by our logical analysis and our abstract reasoning? Or, alternatively, as Dr. Sorenson poses the question... now that we know about this alternate earlier form of consciousness, can we take the opportunity to examine it closely looking for ways in which we might improve on our present form?

Thinking about these questions logically.... (What other option do I have?) It would seem a shame to have to discard one system of consciousness for another. Now that we know there are two systems out there, why don't we investigate whether we can conceive of a new, improved form of consciousness that is perhaps a hybrid of the two? Is that, in fact, what Dr. Robert Wolf and possibly Dr. E. Richard Sorenson have already done for themselves?

While ruminating on this question, I thought back to the time when I was a nineteen-year-old college student at the University of Oklahoma. One beautiful Spring afternoon, I decided to "take the plunge" and experience windowpane acid for myself. Like many before me and many since, my experience of "tripping" was an incredibly powerful one. At one point, I experienced the very real feeling of leaving my body and actually journeying to an astral plane where I encountered other "people" who appeared to me as puffs of smoke, but who I could actually speak with. Later, I had a tough time finding my way back into my body. But in the end, that difficulty only made the experience all the more powerful. Being young, and inexperienced in such matters, as well as quite clueless about the possibility of such things as out-of-body experiences, I was much like a fish out of water. But when I woke up the next day, I had an extremely tangible and very powerful personal experience under my belt that told me without question that there is more to this reality than just normal day-to-day experience.

Thankfully, I was smart enough to know intuitively that taking more acid was not the answer. What I needed was explanations. But where I would get them, I wasn't sure. It was a couple of weeks later when I told a musician friend what had happened that I received the suggestion to read. He suggested that I start with *Stranger in a Strange Land*, the classic science fiction work by Robert Heinlein. And now that I have read Sorenson's piece on *Preconquest Consciousness*, I think *Stranger in a Strange Land* may contain the answer to this question of whether we can develop a hybrid form of consciousness.

The main character in Heinlein's novel is Valentine Michael Smith, a young man who was actually conceived and born during the voyage on the first manned trip to Mars. He was still only an infant when the ship crash-landed on Mars, and he was the only member of the voyage to survive the crash. For the next twenty-one years, Michael Smith was raised and cared for by Martians. Then, when the next manned mission made it to Mars, Michael Smith was brought back to Earth when they returned. As the story unfolds, we found that Michael Smith could leave his body at will, and he also had other abilities like the ability to communicate telepathically, and to move objects by telekinesis, and the power to make "wrong" things like Federal agents and their guns and helicopters disappear.

Later, as Smith grew in his understanding of life on this planet (in our insane culture), and developed relationships with friends, we were introduced to terms like "grok" and "water brother" and sayings like "Thou art God" and "I am only an egg." But the reason I bring this classic story up is because, after visiting the churches of his time and finding them very lacking, Michael ended up forming his own church which he called the Church of All Worlds. And the path to enlightenment in the Church of All Worlds was a simple one.... All you had to do was learn the Martian language.

Of course, this is only a fifty-year-old work of fiction. But could it possibly contain the answer to our question of a hybrid form of consciousness? Could our symbols be somehow tweaked so that our abstract reasoning is thereby brought back into alignment with the reality of connectedness? Or could the answer be even simpler? Could it be that we only need to modify our basic beliefs? If we all begin our lives in this world knowing that everything is connected and that we are a part of the world and Responsible Members of the Community of Life, then could our new consciousness be built upon that basis? Now that we know there is an alternate form of consciousness that provides people with what Dr. Sorenson calls "an astonishingly rewarding and zestful life", I think it just might be possible.

11

Changing Minds

◊

Creating a Critical Mass of people who understand our present worldwide culture is flawed at its very foundational level is the key to saving the world. Right now, as you read these words, there are millions of people who already understand the truth of what I am saying and stand ready to help make the necessary changes. But those of us who already "get it" also understand there are not yet enough brothers and sisters standing with us. The best thing we can do right now is to help other people understand our situation. There must be enough people who understand the need for change, and stand ready to make it happen, so that the changes can be made even as those opposed to changes attempt to prevent the cultural shift from happening. In order to achieve this, we are going to have to change a few million more minds.

A few months ago, Trump was acquitted of two Articles of Impeachment in the Senate. Sadly, the U. S. Senate has no problem with turning our 231-year-old democracy over to an authoritarian leader. As has been the consistent situation ever since Trump was sworn in, our fragile democracy continues to lurch towards authoritarianism. The vote in the Senate to acquit was 52-48 and 53-47, with Mitt Romney casting the only vote to convict by a Republican Senator.

Let's take a look at the polls for the Presidential approval rating and see if they can give us any clues as to the status of the Critical Mass. Using the numbers from the FiveThirty-Eight website, which utilizes a weighted composite of all scientifically viable polls, Trump currently has a 51.9% Disapproval rating and a 43.9% Approval rating. Looking at the accompanying charts, I can see these current numbers are slightly more in Trump's favor than the average from the first three years of his presidency, and presumably, this is due to a bump in polling because of his recent acquittal in the impeachment trial. According to FiveThirty-Eight, Trump's lowest approval rating has been 37.1% which occurred at the end of his first year in office, and his highest was 44.7% which occurred just after being sworn in. The average over the three years appears to be just under 42%. The disapproval rating has been above 50% ever since March of 2017 and appears to average about 53%.

Now, let's take a look at the numbers for the Presidential candidates during the Democratic primary election. If you followed the contest for the Democratic Presidential candidate, then you are aware of the two "lanes" that comprise this party. The first is the Progressive lane of Bernie Sanders, Elizabeth Warren, and Tom Steyer; and the other is the Moderate lane of Joe Biden, Michael Bloomberg, Pete Buttigieg, and Amy Klobuchar. The contest began with over 20 declared candidates, and at time I am writing this, the field has been reduced to only eight. According to the FiveThirty-Eight composite polling, Bernie Sanders is leading in the Progressive lane as well as overall, and is currently polling at 24.2% nationally. Elizabeth Warren is at 11.7% and Tom Steyer has 2.2%. This indicates that the Progressive lane has about 38.1% of the Democratic voters. Michael Bloomberg is leading the Moderate lane with 16.5%. He is followed by Joe Biden at 16.4%, Pete Buttigieg at 10.1%, Amy Klobuchar at 5.3%, and Tulsi Gabbard at 1.7%, indicating the Moderate lane includes approximately 50% of Democratic voters.

If you look at the positions of these candidates on the issues, you will see the Progressive lane Democrats agree with many of the assertions I have made in this book. Clearly, Bernie, Elizabeth, and Tom all want to take our government back from the corporations who have stolen it from the people of this country. They don't say so, but based upon their positions on the issues, I am guessing they would be just as impressed as I am with Ishmael and of his explanations of how things came to be this way.

On the other hand, the Democratic candidates in the Moderate lane seem to be a lot happier with the status quo. Key to understanding the difference between the Progressive and the Moderate lane Democrats is that the Progressives want to reform health care by converting to a Medicare-for-All system. The Moderates want a public option that would keep the totally useless insurance companies in business, extracting a profit just for screwing things up. I am guessing these Moderate lane Democratic candidates all understand real reform would require the removal of for-profit insurance companies from the system. Hopefully, their reluctance to do so is due to calculations as to how their position on this particular issue affects their electability, more so than pressure from the companies or the potential of loss of contributions. Either way, it sucks that they would take this position. I would pick any of them as a "lesser of two evils" choice over Trump, but I'm not a fan of Moderate lane Democrats. This country is in need of real and meaningful reform. Moderate lane candidates would take us in the right direction, but only in baby steps.

To me, these polls are very illuminative in regard to the status of the Critical Mass. According to the Presidential approval rating polls, somewhere in the neighborhood of 43% of our voters are staunch Trump supporters. Although some of these people are reachable, my assessment is it is going to be really tough to extract significant numbers of ardent Trump supporters and add them to our Critical Mass. But that leaves 57% that are either already a part of the Critical Mass or are in a much better position than the ardent

Trump supporters to be convinced to join us. Arguably, most of the 38% of this 57% that are supporting the Progressive candidates for President are either already with us or could potentially be brought on board fairly easily. The other 62% of the 57% of us who are not ardent Trump supporters may take a little more convincing, but if we truly want to save the world, then a big part of our task is to do just that.

To recap:

- Approximately 43% of us are ardent Trump supporters. My assessment is that most of the people in this category will probably die while still holding their racist beliefs. We can and should try to reach as many of the people from this group as possible, but realistically, our task is to enlighten their children regarding the reality of connectedness.

- Approximately 22% of us are Progressive lane Democrats. Many of the people in this category are already a member of the Critical Mass we are advocating for in this book, and the balance are ripe to be recruited.

- Approximately 35% of us are Moderate lane Democrats. It is the people in this group who are key to saving the world. Somehow, we need to make enough of these "Moderate lane Democrats" understand that everything is connected, and that we need to resume our roles as **Responsible Members of the Community of Life.**

Are you interested in saving the world? I know I am. And guess what? We can do it! All we have to do is to convince enough people of the veracity of the truths set out in this book so that we can achieve the Critical Mass. I remember very well going through a huge personal transformation when I read Ishmael. I hope some of you who read Soft Landing, will experience that same tremendous sense of relief I did when I read Ishmael and learned there is a way out of this mess. And the way out of this mess is that when enough of us finally "get it", then we can transform this culture into one that actually works... not only for us humans... but also for this beautiful planet and the rest of the Community of Life.

During the process of writing this book, I have tried my best to identify and understand the various categories of people who resist the truths contained herein. Without a doubt, if we want to save the world, we are going to have to find a way to reach a lot of them. Through my analysis of our situation, I see four main categories of people who are resistant to understanding and acknowledging the reality of connectedness. These are:

- Religious people.
- Ultra-conservatives, Tea Partiers, and right-leaning people who believe in trickle-down Reaganomics, who I sometimes refer to as "Ayn Randers".
- Racists.
- People who are simply afraid to consider there is something terribly wrong with our culture because it would mean that their whole lives have been based upon a lie.

Simply because their egos have not developed sufficiently to transcend their own personal needs and desires, many of the people who fit into one or more of these categories could read this book cover to cover and still resist the truth and logic of the explanation of how things came to be this way. Many people are so wrapped up in their own dysfunctional emotions, they could never conceive of a worldview that encompasses our entire culture, or one that requires us all to act responsibly as a member of the Community of Life on this planet. These people are simply not ready for the truths contained herein. In order to bring them along, the first step is to help with their ego development. The egos of millions of our children are stunted by unresolved childhood traumas resulting from physical and sexual abuse, neglect, bullying, or exposure to other violent acts.

In many cases, these children could be helped in school, but unfortunately, many of our schools of today are not up to this task. A universal curriculum of emotional intelligence taught by qualified teachers would not only serve to help many children in their ego development but could identify students who need specialized help and care because of traumas they have experienced. In fact, all of our teachers should be screened for emotional intelligence, and those falling below a certain level should be disqualified from a teaching position on any subject. We could also take another huge step forward by transforming our educational system into one that provides free, high-quality schooling for all of our children everywhere. Currently, our teachers in our public education systems are not well compensated. That should change. Currently, our children from higher income neighborhoods receive a higher quality education than children from lower income neighborhoods. That should change. Currently, our children must mortgage their futures by taking out student loans to pay for their college educations. That should change.

Even among those of us who do not suffer from stunted ego development, very few of us understand the reality of our situation. Our government here in the United States has been stolen by huge corporations and the 1%. Most of us don't even understand how a good government would function in order to benefit us all. Our present government is set up to benefit big corporations and the wealthy. It was not designed to be that way. As evidenced by the

Preamble to the U. S. Constitution, the founder's hearts were in the right place:

> We the People of the United States, in Order to form a more perfect Union, establish Justice, insure domestic Tranquility, provide for the common defence, promote the general Welfare, and secure the Blessings of Liberty to ourselves and our posterity, do ordain and establish this Constitution of the United States of America

It was mostly during my lifetime that our government was stolen from us. It happened little by little, and hardly anyone noticed. Now, at this point, there is hardly anyone left who has a good understanding of what functions and duties our government should be doing on behalf of all of us. And that makes it really hard to fix. Most of us see the way our government is working for the benefit of the corporations and the wealthy and we assume the dysfunction is the result of our government being flawed in some basic way. They don't see that it is working just as the corporations and the wealthy who stole it from us are intending for it to work.

The only fix available is for us to somehow achieve a general awareness among our voting population of how our government has been stolen. After that, we still have a functioning democracy and the fix is easy. First, it happens in the voting booth. Then, we abolish corporate personhood.

One hundred percent of the Republican Party is comprised of people from one or more of the categories outlined above. This means the Republican Party, which is one of the two dominant political parties in this country, is totally comprised of people whose basic beliefs align with a world where everything is separate. Clearly, in order to achieve the all-important Critical Mass, we are going to have to somehow reach a significant number of Christians, Ayn Randers, racists, and fearful people. That is why I have been working so hard to debunk Christianity and to demonstrate the insanity of consuming our last remaining natural resources for the sole purpose of maintaining the wealth of our already privileged upper class.

Religious People

Certainly, many of the members of the organized religions are a difficult bunch to convince. They think they already have the answers, and they are not the answers we are providing here. Without a doubt, many religious people are guilty of intellectual laziness. They look at the big questions like, "What happens when we die?" And, "Who, or what is responsible for creating this fantastic universe we live in?" And, "Who am I and why am I here?" And they decide the questions are too hard for them to answer for themselves. So, they simply defer to the "experts" of organized religion. The fix for these people, therefore, is for them to take the time to examine these beliefs, so their belief in a fairy-tale God who is separate from us, and who created this world just for us to conquer and rule, and who will judge us when we die, and many of their other unfounded beliefs, including especially their belief in "salvation by faith," can be debunked and rejected one changed mind at a time.

Ayn Randers

The libertarians and the conservatives, on the other hand, are guilty of greed and irresponsibility. They use the flawed philosophy of Ayn Rand that tells them the world will work best if everyone acts in their own self-interest. What then, is the fix for greed, irresponsibility, and selfishness? Maturity, of course. Basically, these people need to grow up. Ron Paul, who ran for President as a Republican and a Libertarian in the 1988, 2008, and 2012 elections, may have given the appearance of a very mature person, but I assure you, inside that craggy old noggin is the immature mind of a self-centered teenager. Admittedly, a pretty smart teenager. Even one with some pretty good ideas. But, a teenager, nonetheless. And, as these libertarians, Ayn Randers, conservatives, and Reaganites mature, they need to dig a little deeper with their thinking, and hopefully... eventually... they will be able to identify the flaws in Ayn Rand's philosophy, and embrace the truths contained in this book that tells us everything is connected.

Racists

Another very significant and very problematic group are the racists. Ever since the 2016 election, I have been saying that Donald Trump has accomplished one very good thing for our country. And that is by winning the election, and by governing with his 41 to 44 percent approval rating, and by leading those almost weekly rallies attended by the thousands of ardent and enthusiastic followers, Trump has served us all very well by shining a flashlight down into the deepest, darkest recesses of our collective basement. For the first time in a very long time, we have all seen the surprisingly large population of rats scurrying around down there in the darkness.

Until Donald Trump got elected, we did not know they were there. Now we do. And that is a good thing. It is a good thing because that is the type of information we need if we are going to be able to find a way forward. These are the same people that Hillary called "Trump's basket of deplorables". Calling them that may have cost her the election. But it is important to understand that she was not wrong. There is no question that racism is deplorable. But saying it out loud probably cost Hillary the election because calling them deplorable energized them and brought them to the polls in order to defeat her. Certainly, calling them Trump's basket of deplorables was one of the half-a-dozen things that occurred just before the 2016 election and combined to contribute to her surprising loss.

But I'm not running for President. I'm just trying my hardest to help create a Critical Mass of people who see that our flawed and doomed culture must be replaced with a culture that recognizes the truth that everything is connected before it crashes. There are a lot of labels I could put onto these ardent Trump supporters. I could even call them racists, though I will try not do that too often. I want to try to be a little bit careful about what I call them, because some of them can still be reached, and I do not want to alienate them like Hillary did.

Although these ardent Trump supporters represent the group whose minds will be the hardest of all to change, some of them can and will join us. If we can somehow help some of them to see that their racist thoughts and feelings are flawed, and that holding those flawed thoughts and feelings are detrimental to not only to the people of color who are the objects of those flawed thoughts and feelings, but especially they are detrimental to the racists themselves, then some of them can become former racists, which is a very powerful thing. We need them here with us, so in an effort to make nice, I will sometimes substitute the phrase "ardent Trump supporters" when I really mean to say "racists".

But saying that begs the question; "Are all ardent Trump supporters racists?" Considering that Trump burst onto the scene in 2015, riding the escalator down to the basement of Trump Tower (How appropriately symbolic was that!) to make his announcement speech, in which he asserted that Mexico was sending people who have lots of problems, I think it is pretty hard to deny that anyone who is an ardent Trump supporter, at the very least, has to not mind having a leader who is racist. In that speech he said those immigrants that Mexico was sending to the U. S. are "bringing drugs. They're bringing crimes. They're rapists. And some, I assume are good people." And later on, in the same speech he also said, "I will build a great wall on our southern border and I'll have Mexico pay for that wall."

Like I said, we all owe a debt of gratitude to Trump for shining his flashlight down into our collective basement. Largely because this surprisingly large segment of our population welcomed such statements from a Presidential candidate, Trump's campaign easily won the Republican nomination for President. As far as Trump's appeal to the racist segment of our voting population, it also didn't hurt that before running for President, Trump had famously been the person driving the blatantly racist "birther" controversy about Barack Obama.

And going back to 1989, his racist fans could also take comfort in Trump's participation in the rush to judgment of the five Black and Latino boys called the Central Park Five, who were convicted of assaulting and raping a white woman as she was jogging through Central Park. Three weeks after the incident, and before the trial began, Trump took out full page ads in all four New York papers advocating a return of the death penalty so these kids could be properly punished. All five were convicted and sent to prison, then exonerated by DNA evidence seven years later. According to several accounts of recent interviews, Trump will still assert the guilt of these kids when asked about it today.

Then, since taking office, there is Trump's family separation strategy at the southern border wherein thousands of children have been separated from their parents and placed in cages. Another example of Trump's blatant racism is the fact that he tried unsuccessfully to ban all Muslims from entering the United States. Continuing down the list of examples of Trump's racist behavior, there is the tragedy in Charlottesville, after which Trump announced there were good people on both sides, including the side that was comprised of white supremacists, neo-Nazis, neo-confederates, KKK members, and white nationalists.

Just recently, during the State of The Union Address, Donald Trump awarded the Presidential Medal of Freedom to Rush Limbaugh, an avowed racist. Do you think it is possible that even a small portion of the ardent Trump supporters are completely oblivious to all of these racist positions and views held by the President? On the contrary, these racist positions and views of

Donald Trump are quite obviously one of the big keys to his popularity.

In the intervening time since the 2016 election, it has become obvious that our country is being ruled by Trump's basket of deplorables. Significantly, a 41 to 44 percent approval rating translates to an 80% majority in the Republican Party. This means that any Republican Senator or Congressman who crosses Trump will most certainly lose his seat in the next election... not to a Democratic rival, but to another Republican, chosen, approved, and inserted by Trump into the Republican Primary. Three years into the Trump Presidency, our fragile democracy is teetering on the edge of authoritarianism. It remains to be seen.... Will this be a good thing because it exposes flaws and defects in our present manner of government? Or, will it signal the end of democratic government for the United States? Apparently, the answer will come in November (2020) at election time.

Fearful People

One of the biggest categories of people I gave copies of Ishmael to who didn't appreciate it, were people who just weren't willing to question whether or not their whole lives might have been based upon a lie. When you think about it, the significance of this realization is immense. This one, I can certainly understand and even sympathize with. I think it takes a lot of courage for people to be willing to question whether or not our culture might be flawed at its foundational level as is ours. It is fear, plain and simple, that holds a huge percentage of people back from even considering whether or not our culture is insane and most certainly is destined for a crash landing in the very near future. (That is, of course, unless we can bring it in for a Soft Landing!)

How then, can we reach these fearful people? For, in order to successfully achieve that all-important Critical Mass of people who "get it", a lot of people who fall into this category are going to have to be won over.

Maybe we can help these fearful people deal with their fears. First, they need to understand it is their fears that are holding them back. Then they need to understand there is never any reason to allow fear to have control over them. Here is an excerpt from one of my all-time favorite books, *Das Energi*, by the songwriter and musician, Paul Williams:

Fear is the greatest enemy of awareness.
It leaves shame and guilt far behind.
Fear is the force that holds us back.
And we need not be held back any longer!
Listen.
There is a way to deal with fear.

First: Accept that fear is not needed, that there is never a reason to let it live. Carry this knowledge with you always. It is your first line of defense.

Second: Learn to recognize your fears, in all their forms, in the earliest stages possible.

Third: Learn reflex. Any fear-killing mantra will do. Say I shall not fear. I need not fear. Write your own mantra. Learn it. Use it. Killing fear is like stamping out a fire. Reflex Fear: Stamp it out.

Fourth: Never, under any circumstances, think first. That will destroy reflex. Shoot first. Stamp it out. Then think. If you must.

A less fearful person is more conscious, more present, and more aware than a more fearful person. It's all about raising consciousness. Fear inhibits the free flow of energy. In this case, it prohibits people from considering whether or not they adequately understand the true nature of our reality. For the reality is…. If they have not yet examined the evidence and come to the conclusion that our culture is insane, they do not, in fact, understand our reality. The more you can clear yourself from your fears, the higher the level of consciousness you will be able to achieve. And the higher the level of consciousness you are able to achieve, the more likely you are to desire to replace our present, insane culture with a sane one.

But, as I related to you in the beginning of this book, in my own case, my learning of the truth provided me with a huge sense of relief. Looking back, I can see that I had somehow been aware on a mostly subconscious level, throughout my entire life, that something was seriously wrong. Finding out what that something was, for me, provided a grand, celebratory moment. It was a celebratory moment… not because I learned how screwed up the world was… but because I learned that there was a potential fix for our severely screwed up world! I'm sure there are many more people out there, just like me, who will experience a similar sense of joy and relief, when the reality of our situation, which includes the fact that we can fix this, is finally explained to them.

Join the Cultural Revolution

I doubt whether there will be many people who will read this far into this book and still not be convinced that our present culture is insane and must be replaced before it crashes. I imagine that most of the people who reject what I am saying in this book will have stopped reading long before reaching this chapter. However, for those few skeptics who do read this far, please allow me one more opportunity to persuade you to join us in our cultural revolution.

As to those of you who remain skeptics because of your religious beliefs… To you, I say… You are obviously an intelligent person. If you were not such an intelligent person, you never would have picked up this controversial book and read it. Considering that you are an intelligent person, how, then, have you not found it within yourself to question these unfounded beliefs in a fairy-tale God who created this world, and everything in it, just for us humans, as a test to see whether or not we are worthy of joining Him in Heaven? Just because your church has been around for a couple of thousand years does not mean that your church's belief system is founded in reality. In fact, the very fact that your religion has been around for two thousand years means that it began long before we understood many of the most basic facts about our cosmos and our place within it. The last two thousand years, and especially the last two hundred years have brought us a lot of new information that really should be considered before anyone makes any assertions about the true nature of reality, especially anyone like our religious leaders.

And I would also like to reiterate.... Giving up on your version of organized religion does not mean you need to walk away from all things spiritual. As I have been asserting herein.... The unseen world of the Shaman is real. There are many options for people on a spiritual path that do not involve turning their thinking brains over to big organizations with selfish motives. As you know from reading about my experiences with Santa Claus, Richard Hogue, LSD, out-of-body experiences, haunted houses, meditation, telepathy, lucid dreaming, etc., I have been moving down my own spiritual path for my entire life. I can't say I have all the answers, but I can tell you the fuzzy picture I started with does not seem as fuzzy as it used to. And I can tell you for sure, it has been a very interesting, and a very satisfying, rewarding journey. For me, direct experience has played a huge role, but reading has been a big part of my own journey as well. If you are interested, I have included a list of books I have read and recommend. You will find it after the Afterward.

So, please consider leaving your organized religion with its judgmental God. Your unfounded beliefs in a fairytale are holding you back from embracing the truths set out in this book. We need **YOU** to help us save the world.

Now... To you Ayn Randers out there... and to all of you Tea Partiers... and all of you ultra-conservative, right-wing Republicans.... Thank you very much for reading this far. In my experience from talking (arguing?) with many of you over the years, you probably have a hard time swallowing the fact I am advocating that we provide basic needs for everyone, with no requirements from them whatsoever. You don't think it is fair that you are so smart, and you work so hard, while so many of the people who will receive these benefits might lack your intelligence, and they might also be lazy, ignorant, uneducated, and unambitious. And, especially you don't like it that a portion of your income may be taxed in order to pay for these benefits for people you don't believe deserve them.

I am guessing that my problem convincing you of these truths must be because of your unshakeable faith in the cultural myth that tells us the strongest, and richest, and smartest, and the hardest working among us should reap all of the rewards, as well as your belief in the cultural myth that tells us there is not enough. In your opinion, the food is locked up for good reason. You believe that anyone who is not willing to work hard enough to provide food and other basic necessities for his or herself and their family deserves what they get.

Here is what I have to say to you.... Those are cultural myths because they are myths. They are myths because they are not true! They are based upon and derived from our basic cultural myth that tells us the world was made for man to conquer and rule. This cultural myth fosters a false sense of separation. And it is this false sense of separation on which Ayn Rand based her flawed philosophy of objectivism, that tells us everyone should always act in their own self-interest.

If you have any desire to help us to save the world, then please stop worrying about how hard the underprivileged among us are working and start thinking about the truth of what I have been telling you here! Everything is connected! We are all in this together! All of life is precious. Greed, on behalf of the wealthiest among us, and ignorance, on behalf of the aspirants to wealth who adhere to Ayn Rand's message, are the only reasons any person on this planet ever has to worry about basic needs.

We are all members of the Community of Life!

And we all need to resume our roles as **Responsible Members** of the Community of Life! Everything is falling apart, and it is entirely our fault! There is very little time left for us to bring this ship carrying our collective culture in for a soft landing before it is all comes crashing down!

And to all of my fellow inhabitants of this tiny little speck of dust we call Planet Earth, who believe there is a difference between white, black, yellow, or brown people, there are so many things I could say to you about why you should rethink your racist tendencies. In fact, beginning with "Everything is connected," and "We are all Africans," I've already said them all in these pages. Only you can change your own mind. Self-reflection is an incredibly virtuous undertaking. If you try, I believe you will find that you really don't have to think very deeply in order to debunk your racist thoughts and feelings. Find someone who has already overcome their racist tendencies and listen to what they have to say. I promise you, you will never ever regret overcoming this very serious flaw in your makeup.

Finally, to those of you who are simply freaked out by the immense implications of the fact that our worldwide culture is based upon a lie…. Have courage! You don't have to think very deeply in order to understand that it is preferable to have the correct information when you are attempting to ascertain the true nature of reality. Don't let fear hold you back.

And getting back to those Moderate Democrats who are supporting Joe Biden, et al instead of Bernie Sanders and Elizabeth Warren in the Progressive wing, you obviously are a lot closer to joining our Critical Mass than are the Ayn Randers, the religious faithful, or the racists. Probably, it is fear of change that is holding you back from joining us. Most of you are probably in denial about the fact that our government has been stolen from us by huge corporations and the 1%. Maybe after you read the next and final chapter that describes what our post Soft Landing world might look like, you will be a little less fearful. You are our best hope for saving the world. Please consider carefully what I have been saying here. A Moderate Democrat does not qualify as a Responsible Member of the Community of Life!

Thank you all, from the bottom of my heart, for considering my arguments. The successful achievement of our cultural revolution necessarily depends upon the creation of a Critical Mass of people who understand that connectedness is the reality and stand ready to take responsibility as caretakers of the Community of Life. Since nobody can think for another person, this Critical Mass may only be added to one person at a time, as each person is able to incorporate these truths into their own consciousness. Who knows? A last-minute conversion of such a reader might prove to be pivotal in the establishment of our Critical Mass.

At this point, I cannot think of anything else to say regarding the effort I have been making herein to add to the all-important Critical Mass. The next and final chapter is dedicated to people who are already there.

12

Soft Landing

◊

For ten thousand years, our culture has been ruled by rich and powerful individuals, with many of them acting behind the scenes through the daisy chain of their rich and powerful organizations. At any point during that ten-thousand-year period, these individuals could have come to the same conclusions set out in this book and decided to bring us all down for a nice, soft, three-point landing. But that has never happened. That leaves the rest of us with only one option. We are going to have to go into the cockpit, rip the controls out of their hands, and bring this flawed and doomed culture down by ourselves. There is a very real possibility that this struggle for the controls may turn into quite a battle. One thing is for sure, though.... We will need to see it through. We owe it to this beautiful planet, and to the underprivileged among, us, and to the rest of the Community of Life that have been exploited and neglected for so long.

I foresee this Cultural Revolution taking place as a series of mini revolutions via the voting booths that will occur country by country. The United States of America is the richest and most powerful nation on earth. Because of our size and our economic influence, not to mention our military might, it would be ideal if the Cultural Revolution could begin here. If we could make it happen here, then I imagine it would be relatively easy to export our successful transition to the other developed nations around the globe. After transitioning to the developed nations, I imagine that the developing nations would fall in line rather easily. All we would have to do is explain to them that we have decided to stop exploiting them for their cheap labor, their natural resources, and their lack of regulations, and start actually helping them to protect their forests and their natural resources, and to provide basic needs for all of their citizens.

It's easy to imagine how the Cultural Revolution could begin here in the United States. After we have achieved that all-important Critical Mass of people who understand our present culture is flawed and doomed, and cannot be fixed, and must be replaced, we simply take over the government via the voting booth. Then, with a President and a Congress comprised of people who "get it", we can go to work on making our world match our new-found collective understanding that everything is connected.

Let's take another look at the preamble to our Constitution.

We the People of the United States, in Order to form a more perfect Union, establish Justice, insure domestic Tranquility, provide for the common defence, promote the general Welfare, and secure the Blessings of Liberty to ourselves and our posterity, do ordain and establish this Constitution of the United States of America.

Like I said when we looked at the preamble the first two times... not bad. This preamble to the Constitution will even work for a government in our new, post-soft-landing culture! And likewise, I see nothing in our Constitution or its twenty-seven amendments that is a problem either. Constitution wise, I think we are already in pretty good shape in regard to the framework of our post-soft-landing government. The abolition of the concept of corporate personhood is imperative. But that is a matter of case law, not constitutional law. The only fix I see we need to make to the Constitution is the flaw that has manifested due to the development of our two-party system of government, which was not addressed in the Constitution because the founders did not foresee it happening. As we have discussed, there is an easy fix for this one…. It's called instant runoff voting, and it simply makes it possible for a third, or fourth, or even a fifth, sixth, or seventh party to participate without taking votes away from whichever of the major parties they are most closely aligned with. Perhaps this could be rectified as well with new legislation instead of a Constitutional amendment.

But I imagine that politics will become pretty simple in our post-soft-landing world. I don't see this "instant runoff" fix as being so important in our new world, as it would be if we had the fix in place today. Once enough of us are on board with the reality that everything is connected, and we want to resume our roles as Responsible Members of the Community of Life, then, unlike today, the purpose of our government should become pretty widely agreed upon. I also foresee that not only our politics, but our entire world will become much, much simpler, when our main job as a culture is no longer to exploit desperate poor people and to consume our precious natural resources just so a tiny minority of our species can remain wealthy and privileged. From the very beginning, the main focus of our government will be to aid and facilitate our citizens in implementing and maintaining our collective vision as Responsible Members of the Community of Life on this planet.

Without a doubt, our post-soft-landing world will be a profoundly different world than our world of today. When we have provided basic needs for all people, stopped cutting down our precious forests, and begun the process to cease polluting, then we will be living in a different world indeed. Just imagine all the changes we would have to make in order to accomplish these three simple things. For one thing, our economy will be completely transformed. Instead of our present economy that must grow year after year, our post-soft-landing economy will actually shrink considerably. Once the focus of our economy is no longer on growing the wealth of our upper class, we will embrace an economy that has no need for growth in order to serve us. Instead of growth, the measuring stick for our post-soft-landing economy will be whether or not it serves our new cultural ideals of connectedness and responsibility.

Since a big part of this shift to connectedness and responsibility will involve an awareness of our roles as Responsible Members of the Community of Life, our new economy will be focused on providing everyone with their basic needs while doing nothing that harms the environment or our fellow members of the Community of Life. The only way an economy could possibly accomplish this would be by shrinking. Public spending, in our post-soft-landing world, will be made on selective areas that foster these goals. All public expenditures that hinder them, like most, if not all of our defense and military spending, will be withdrawn.

It is my contention that when you consider how much it will cost to provide all people everywhere with their basic needs, and compare it to how much will be saved in other areas, that ultimately, the decision to provide basic needs to all people everywhere will prove to be a net gain financially. Even if I am wrong about this, there is no question that there will be financial trade-offs that will serve to offset the costs of providing these basic needs. The question is…. Will they offset them completely, or only partially? When you consider the cost savings coming from reduced crime rates, reduced prison populations, savings in healthcare, and mental healthcare, reduced alcoholism and drug addiction, plus the financial savings from not needing to continue to fund most of the present welfare programs, not to mention the cost benefits of no longer having to fund wars or fight terrorism, it is easy to see the possibility that the costs of funding basic needs for everyone could very likely be offset in their entirety. No more spending for corporate welfare is another huge area for savings. Then, on the revenue side, converting to public banks will provide a huge boost in revenue. I can't say how all of this will shake out financially, but I can certainly see the potential for a net gain.

One of the big questions our post-soft-landing leaders will need to address is how quickly we should make the transition. Clearly, the shorter the transition, the more likely are the chances that things will get messy. Whether the transition is short or long, a lot of very tangible assets in corporate stocks will surely diminish in value, and many will disappear entirely. The great bulk of these "at risk" corporate stock holdings are owned by the wealthy, but unfortunately, a lot of IRA's and 401K's owned by middle income individuals and families will also be affected. This particular piece of messiness will need to be dealt with in some manner.

I am advocating that we evolve our government, just as we have evolved, and as our consciousness is evolving, into an enlightened form of social democracy. After all, if the afore-mentioned evolution had not taken place, then we would never have been in this position where it is possible for us to achieve the Critical Mass that will allow us to make these changes to our government in the first place. Once again, I want to interject my contention that the preamble to our U. S. Constitution fits perfectly with this ideal. This contention that such a cultural transition is permitted under our present Constitution is extremely key, because if that were not the case, the Cultural Revolution could not happen in the voting booth.

Once we have elected a President and a majority of Congressmen in both Houses, then we can set to work to transform our culture. One of the very first steps will be to abolish corporate personhood via the legislative process. Once we have abolished the insane concept that corporations are entitled to the same protections provided to individuals under the Constitution and the Bill of Rights, then we can set about to transform our world from one that thinks and acts like everything is separate, to one that operates from the knowing that everything is connected.

There is no rational reason why we, as a society, cannot provide basic needs to all of our citizens, while asking nothing of them in return. Once we have accomplished that, then, much like today, commerce will provide each of us with an opportunity to benefit financially through our participation. Like today, possible ways we might profit include participating as an employee, a consultant, a business owner, an entrepreneur, or an investor. But unlike today, all money-making activities that harm the environment will be expressly prohibited. And unlike today, the poorest among us will no longer be exploited by their desperate need to provide their families with basic needs. Since we will all be living in a world where the food is no longer locked up, and all of our other basic needs have been provided for all people everywhere, then if a potential employment opportunity does not provide a fair wage, a safe working environment, reasonable hours, and other benefits, such as vacation, sick leave, and family leave, then we can simply choose not to work.

Once this transformation has taken place, many of the goods and services that are presently available in our economy will either disappear or become much more expensive than they are today. Eventually, the well-known market forces of supply and demand, in conjunction with any governmental subsidies or regulations deemed appropriate by our new, post-soft-landing leaders, will run their course, and all of these factors will dictate the prices and the availability of goods and services. And that is as it should be.

Much like today, I see a place in our post soft landing world for individuals and for companies to profit from entertainment and professional sports. As stated above, supply and demand will ultimately dictate the prices for these things, so the top professional athletes, actors, musicians, writers, directors, and others involved in sports and entertainment will probably not be bringing in the zillions they are bringing in today. Or, maybe they will make zillions, but if they do then the progressive income tax in our post-soft-landing world would even things out. I imagine that even though the financial rewards may be somewhat diminished, the personal ones, such as the self-satisfaction gained from participating in the creative process, or the thrill of striving to achieve your absolute best as an athlete, will remain as potent in our post-soft landing world as they are today.

One important area I have not yet mentioned is whether there will be a need to re-distribute the vast wealth currently held by individuals. My feeling on this is that as long as we have taken the control of the government away from the corporations, and as long as our government remains a government "of, by, and for the people", then I don't believe it will be necessary to re-distribute the wealth of individuals, at least not all at once. Certainly, a lot of the wealth currently held by individuals is ill-gotten, and much of it was acquired in a manner very similar to that first criminal act from ten thousand years ago, when somebody first locked up the food. But the way I see it, individuals within our post-soft-landing world are going to have a hard time maintaining this wealth when they no longer have the large corporations and the government aiding them.

It may take some time, but I believe this problem will eventually take care of itself. Certainly, many wealthy individuals will be a part of the Critical Mass that will transform our culture initially. And, many more will join us willingly after the transition. Those who don't may find the amount of pleasure they derive from enjoying their luxurious and consumptive lifestyle in our post-soft-landing world to be somewhat diminished.

Let's take another look at all of those never-ending problems that we examined in Chapter 6 and see how well my contention that transforming our culture would solve them holds up in our post-soft-landing world.

Hunger, famine, starvation, poverty, homeless people, the lack of affordable health care, pollution of our air, land, and water, the loss of our rainforests and other precious timberlands, overpopulation, ozone depletion, global warming and climate change, war, terrorism, the threat of nuclear war, rampant crime, overcrowded prisons, police brutality, governmental corruption, alcoholism and drug addiction, racism, sexism, physical, emotional, and sexual abuse, suicide, depression, gun violence, and mass shootings.

I asserted in Chapter 6 that these problems were a direct result of us living in an insane culture that is based upon the illusion of separation. And I further asserted that we were going to be stuck with all of these problems until we transform our culture into one that is based upon the reality that everything is connected. So, what would happen to all of these terrible problems if we achieved the three measuring sticks for ascertaining whether or not we have successfully transformed our culture? Once again, these are (1) the providing of basic needs for all people everywhere with no questions asked, (2) the ceasing of the cutting down of our precious forests, and (3) the cessation of pollution. And for the purposes of this discussion, add to that list the abolition of corporate personhood signifying that large corporations would no longer be calling the shots in Washington D. C. and in our state capitols.

When we provide basic needs, stop polluting, and cease cutting down our precious forests, almost half of these terrible problems will disappear immediately simply because those problems are the direct result of these things. Therefore, immediately after achieving our successful cultural revolution, our list would be reduced to this:

Overpopulation, global warming and climate change war, terrorism, the threat of nuclear war, rampant crime, overcrowded prisons, police brutality, governmental corruption, alcoholism and drug addiction, racism, sexism, physical, emotional, and sexual abuse, suicide, depression, gun violence, and mass shootings.

Let's take a quick look at each of these remaining problems that I contend are just one step away from being solved directly.

Overpopulation

The only fix I see for overpopulation is the result of an educated populous who understand the seriousness of this problem and understand that the fix lies in each of us willingly agreeing to limit our reproduction to only one child. When we have transformed out culture, then a big benefit of that transformation will result in an improved educational system which will lead to this solution for overpopulation. We will address overpopulation. It may take a little time to get started, but once we do, the fix can be achieved fairly quickly.

Global Warming and Climate Change

Corporate profits, and a desire on behalf of the wealthy elite to continue with the status quo, have been the main impediments to action on this issue. Once we have taken our government back from the corporations who stole it from us, we will finally be able to implement meaningful reforms. This will help, but unfortunately, meaningful action in regard to global warming and climate change should have begun more than thirty years ago. We have waited too long to address global warming and climate change, and because of that, we are in for some bad times. The rising sea levels are going to cause devastation of coastal cities and the displacement of billions from their homes. And the increased amount of moisture in our air is going to wreak havoc on us in the form of stronger, more damaging storms. We should have taken better care of our polar ice caps when we had the chance.

The best news in regard to global warming and climate change is that once we all live in a world we all know to be connected, and once we all know ourselves to be Responsible Members of the Community of Life on this planet, then we will be much better equipped to deal with the devastation and destruction that is coming. Everything is connected, and together, we will get through this.

War, Terrorism, and the Threat of Nuclear War

Although I wrote about these three issues separately in Chapter 6, the comments I want to make here in this post-soft-landing second look are appropriate to all three. The obvious main point here is that by providing basic needs to all people everywhere, the tension between the privileged few who have way too much and the desperate poor who struggle to provide their basic needs will be greatly diminished. And gone with it will be the historic reasons for so many of our armed conflicts. Also, once we have abolished corporate personhood, we can take away the power of the defense contractors and the arms manufacturers to influence whether we are at war or at peace, thereby greatly reducing the possibility of armed conflict.

Yes, I do believe that war and terrorism will quickly become problems of the past in our post-soft-landing world. As to the threat of nuclear war, I cannot foresee any scenario in a post-soft-landing world where we have not all agreed to give up our nuclear arsenals. Keeping any of these terrible weapons would be insane, and since our culture would at long last be sane, that would make no sense.

Rampant Crime, Alcoholism, Drug Addiction, Physical, Emotional, and Sexual Abuse, Suicide, Depression, Police Brutality, Gun Violence and Mass Shootings

These issues were all examined separately in Chapter 6, but the comments I want to make here are appropriate to all of them collectively. Once again, the main point is that by providing basic needs to all people everywhere, the tension between the privileged few who have way too much and the desperate poor who struggle to provide their basic needs will be greatly diminished because there will be no more people who are desperately poor. Add to that, when each of us wakes up every morning to a world we all know to be connected, and where each of us know ourselves, the other members of our family, and all of our neighbors to be Responsible Members of the Community of Life, then our reasons for participating in any of the activities outlined above will largely disappear.

I must say though, that some of us are so badly damaged from living in this insane world, that a cultural transition to a sane world may not be sufficient to heal us. For those of us in this position, there will be lots of help which will serve to greatly decrease the numbers of us who continue to participate in these aberrant behaviors. I contend that each succeeding generation born into our post-soft-landing world will enjoy better and better living conditions which are freer and freer from these problems.

Overcrowded Prisons

With a reduced crime rate comes an obvious reduction in the need for incarceration. But along with that, comes an obvious change in strategy away from our present "lock 'em up" mentality. I foresee our prisons in our post-soft-landing world will serve a greatly diminished population of inmates who will benefit greatly from the educational and rehabilitative programs that will be a part of these systems.

Governmental Corruption

In our post-soft-landing world, when our government has been returned to the people from the corporations and the 1% who stole it from us, the purpose of government will be much more widely agreed upon. Therefore I foresee there will be a lot more people interested in seeing our governmental duties performed as they are intended and designed to do. This increased interest and scrutiny, along with the fact that unlike today, people will actually believe in and support the functions of our government, will quickly reduce the occurrence of governmental corruption. Also pertinent is the fact that when each of us wakes up every morning to a world in which we all know that everything is connected, and where we all understand our roles as Responsible Members of the Community of Life, everyone will experience a greatly diminished motivation for wrongdoing.

Racism and Sexism

As I discussed in the previous chapter, most of us did not understand how pervasive racism was in our world of today until Trump ran for President. We all knew there were still racists among us. But most of us thought the problem of racism was largely a thing of the past, and that there really weren't that many people around today who still thought like that. You can add me to that group. I was flabbergasted to see the surprisingly high numbers who jumped on board with the Trump's racist agenda.

And writing that piece on sexism for Chapter 6 was also very illuminative for me. Before researching the issue to write that piece, I perceived sexism and misogyny to be problems that we had largely transcended. I was wrong!

Unfortunately, the reality is that we are going to achieve our Critical Mass, save the world, and transform our culture, not along with, but in spite of most of the racist and misogynistic people among us. Certainly, the members of the Critical Mass who speak our truth to the misogynists and the racists will serve to reform some of them. But many if not most of them will probably die still holding their prejudiced and misguided thoughts, feelings, and beliefs. Transcending racism and misogyny requires a level of self-reflection that unfortunately, is beyond the capabilities of most of the people who are mired in these flawed beliefs. This lack of a capacity for self-reflection is the main reason they are racists and misogynists in the first place.

Their children, however, are another story. Their children will be born into a world where everyone knows that everything is connected, and nobody has to worry about their basic needs being met. And significantly, their children will attend high-quality schools that will not only provide them with better educations than their parents but will aid them in their emotional well-being and their ego development. Large numbers of the children of racists and misogynists will transcend the flaws of their parents and join with us in celebrating our newfound place as Responsible Members of the Community of Life. It may take another generation or possibly two to reach them all, but eventually we will get there.

And that, my friends, is the end of the list of terrible problems that have been plaguing our world for so long. I don't know about you, but I think I have made a pretty good case that these problems are never going to go away until our culture has been transformed into one that is based upon the reality that everything is connected. And furthermore, once we have accomplished that, then the problems will pretty much magically disappear. But even though these terrible problems will largely be resolved, we will still have work to do in regard to reordering our economy and deciding how businesses will function within it. Remember all of those sectors of the economy we explored in Chapter 7 with an eye towards abuses of power by the corporations? Well, this will be the time when those abuses will be rectified!

When we abolish corporate personhood, the decision-making power regarding how our world is ordered will be stripped from the corporations and returned to the people. Thereafter, important decisions about issues like "How will our food be produced and distributed?" will be made by considering such important criteria as efficiency and sustainability and environmental responsibility... Not to mention whether or not the food is healthy for us to consume. Lobbying will either be banned altogether, or subject to very strict regulations. Any corporate profits will be made within the framework devised by "We the People" and not by backroom deals. Our current government is set up to serve large corporations. Our new government will serve the people and the natural world.

Considering all of this, let's take another look at all of those business sectors we examined in Chapter 7 and speculate as to how they will be transformed in our post-soft-landing world.

Car Companies

In the United States of today, we live in a culture where most people feel that they need their own automobile so they can get to and from their home to their place of employment, their school, the grocery store, and anyplace else they need to be. In our post-soft-landing world, there are a lot of factors that are going to come together to suppress this need for each of us to own and operate our own, personal automobiles. Perhaps the most prominent of these factors is the threat of global warming and climate change, which will serve to motivate all of us to drive less, and to drive more fuel efficient or all electric cars when we do drive. This, of course, is already happening. But as the effects of global warming and climate change continue to intensify, this motivation to drive fuel efficient or electric cars will only increase along with it.

And going forward, the development and sale of driverless cars will certainly lead to the sharing of automobiles which will also serve to diminish the demand for new cars. Of course, the development of mass transit options for travel will have a big impact on this sector as well. And for sure, many if not most of our future housing developments and planned communities will include plans for walking and riding bicycles or utilizing a form of mass transit instead of driving.

One thing that might help to slightly increase the demand for new cars will happen if new, stricter regulations regarding fuel efficiency and emissions are enacted, these would serve to remove older cars from the road and cause a need for them to be replaced with newer autos. I'm not exactly sure how all of this will shake out, but I would advise the car manufacturers to get ready for some big changes, with most of them being not favorable to the sale of a lot of new autos, especially after the new, fuel efficient driverless cars are in place.

Oil Companies

Because each of these sectors has so blatantly operated in its own interest as opposed to the interest of the general public, while pretending to be operating in the public interest, I consider the oil companies, the defense industry, and the pharmaceutical companies to be the triumvirate of the evil corporations. The oil companies, along with the other two sectors representing this evil triumvirate, are definitely going to see some big post-soft-landing changes. The oil business, as we have known it for the past 75 to 100 years, is about to end. Surprisingly, the end of the oil business is not coming because we are running out of oil, but because the demand is diminishing. The bulk of the demand for oil comes from transportation, and because of our awareness that carbon emissions from gasoline powered vehicles are one of the biggest contributors to the global warming and climate change crisis, transportation is undergoing a huge transformation to more fuel efficient, or all electric vehicles. With a reduced demand, comes an imbalance in the dynamics of supply and demand, resulting in a perpetually low oil price, and the loss of an incentive to explore for new reserves.

Without a doubt, the abolishment of corporate personhood will provide a meaningful blow to these powerful corporations, but I have to say, it is nice when a problem this big basically solves itself like this one did.

Defense Contractors and Arms Manufacturers

Our post soft-landing world will definitely be the cause of some large bankruptcies for companies in this sector. And that is as it should be. When we are living in a connected, post-soft-landing world, where all of us understand ourselves and our various nations to be Responsible Members of the Community of Life, we will have no need for the terrible weapons being manufactured and marketed by this sector, or for the huge armies standing by to use them. The immense amount of money we will save by not funding and equipping all of these armies will serve us much better when we spend it on more important things like education, health care, parental leave, safety nets for unemployment and illness, infrastructure, childcare, and care for the aged. The peace dividend resulting from the achievement of our soft landing will be a wonderful thing for everyone except for the defense contractors and the arms manufacturers.

Pharmaceutical Companies

The recent scandal about opioids has pretty much exposed this sector for what it is, the corporate equivalent of a sociopathic criminal. In our post-soft-landing world, the health care industry in general will enjoy a return to focusing on health and wellness through proper diet, exercise, and a positive frame of mind, and away from a reliance upon dubious drugs with their dangerous side effects that treat mostly symptoms of illness, rather than the illness itself. I concede there will still be a place for pharmaceutical drugs in our post-soft-landing world, but when our fellow human beings take back the personal responsibility for their own health and well-being, the demand for these drugs will greatly diminish. Also, after we have abolished corporate personhood, these sociopathic corporations will no longer enjoy the power and control over our legislatures and the governmental regulatory agencies. Going forward, important decisions regarding pharmaceutical drugs will be made by considering the health and well-being of each of us as individuals, and not the profits and the growth of huge corporations.

Insurance Companies

If it hasn't happened already, then very soon after the achievement of our soft landing, the health insurance companies are going to receive the death penalty. There just is no reason for us to allow these companies to continue to extract a profit while making the delivery of our health care more complicated and expensive. A Medicare-for-all universal health care system is the only thing that makes sense for us. The only reason it has not happened already is because of the power these huge companies have with our Congress to keep us from doing the obviously smart thing. In our post-soft-landing world, these huge companies will no longer be able to use their money and their influence to affect our Congress in this manner.

Media and Broadcasting Companies

Democracy depends upon an educated and enlightened voting public. I'm not sure of the dynamics about how this will happen, but somehow, in conjunction with the abolishment of corporate personhood and the realization by a Critical Mass of us that everything is connected, we will find a way to provide solid reliable information to the general public via our media and our broadcasting companies. Currently, these companies are using spin and fear to keep many of us confused and scared. Possibly, in our post-soft-landing world, we will institute reforms that will severely penalize media broadcasting companies for lies and misrepresentations.

For instance, what if there was an agency of the government tasked with oversight of the various news organizations? All news broadcasts, as well as all Internet and print news sources, would be monitored by this agency in real time. And if a broadcast or a written news piece was found to be knowingly false or misleading, the company at fault would immediately be assessed an appropriate fine (large!) and be required to broadcast or write a retraction and a correction exactly 24 hours after the false or misleading broadcast occurred or the written news piece was released. Failure to comply would result in the suspension of the broadcaster's license to broadcast, or the publisher's right to print. When you think about it, this is not too different from what Jon Stewart used to do. He called it turd mining, but we might have to come up with another term. Just a thought.

Agriculture and the Food Industry

The fact that all of the important decisions as to how our food has been grown, processed, and distributed have, up to this point, been made by giant corporations, whose basis for making decisions are profit and growth, has not served the planet, and it has not served us as individuals either. The reforms that will occur in this sector will be incredibly beneficial to our ecological systems, our own personal health, and to the rest of the Community of Life on this planet.

Today, a full forty percent of our population here in the United States is obese! Once the giant corporations are no longer calling the shots for this sector, the bulk of our population will quickly transition to a mostly plant based diet largely provided by local growers utilizing practices such as regenerative agriculture and other farming and growing techniques beneficial to us, the consumers, and are not harmful to the environment. The end is near for Sugar Frosted Flakes and other highly processed foods! And, although I can't foresee the meat industry disappearing entirely, at least not initially, I am confident that in our post-soft-landing world it will be greatly diminished.

Banking and the Financial Industry

Today, and for the past one thousand years, private banks have been bamboozling us into letting them create money out of thin air, and then loan it to us while reserving the right to utilize the full force of the legal system to require us to pay them back, plus interest. Basically, these for-profit banks have been making us jump through hoops to get some of this magical money that never belonged to them to begin with. Welcome to our fractional reserve banking system! I don't think there is a better example of how we are all living in an insane world than this practice of allowing private, for-profit banks to profit from the creation of our money.

Naturally, when we have achieved our successful soft landing, this will no longer be the practice. Our current fiat-based monetary system regulated by a Central Bank in each country, could be successfully transformed into a system that is completely beneficial for our culture by simply taking this privilege of creating money out of thin air away from giant, for-profit banks, and giving it to newly-formed public banks. Thereafter, all profits from the creation of money through this new, improved, fractional reserve system would go to funding the government. I would hope that this common-sense reform that should have happened centuries ago would happen very quickly in our post-soft-landing world.

THE NORDIC WAY

Of course, what happens after we achieve the Critical Mass of people who understand we must transform our culture from a flawed and doomed one to a viable, functioning one, will not be up to me. This is all pure speculation on my part. My role is to help create the Critical Mass. After transitioning to a new culture, these important decisions will be made by our new leaders utilizing all of their available resources, including consultations with all of the available experts in the various fields of study that need to be included in these plans and decisions. I contend that if we have provided basic needs to all people everywhere, stopped cutting down our precious forests, and begun the process to cease polluting, then we will have successfully transformed our culture from one that is flawed and doomed, to a viable, functioning, new culture that can endure and prosper. Certainly, there is more than one way our world could be ordered and still accomplish those three things.

Here is some really good news.... A strong case can be made that the Cultural Revolution has already begun! The social democracies of Norway, Sweden, Denmark, Finland, and Iceland have already implemented many if not most of the reforms advocated for herein, and they have been operating successfully for close to one hundred years already. Certainly, those countries are way ahead of the rest of us in terms of providing basic needs including universal health care, good schools and day care, parental leave, a strong social safety net for the sick or unemployed, care for the aged, social and ecological awareness, and of happiness in general. Just as the U. S. Constitution was a model and a starting point for all the modern democracies that came after us, the form of government of these successful countries, and their programs and practices, can serve as a model and a starting point for countries that want to emulate their success.

For instance, high quality, universal, free education is often touted as being one of the big keys to the success of these nations. In the Nordic countries, learning is not limited to academics; emotional and moral development, as well as social responsibility are also important. In the Nordic countries, children proudly learn of the functions of their government and how it facilitates the health, well-being, and the happiness of their citizens.

Here, in the United States, our government has to hide the fact that it has been stolen from the people by huge corporations and the 1%, so it is very difficult to make our students proud of it.

Just imagine for a minute, what a fantastic improvement an educated population would represent here in the United States! How beneficial would it be if we could agree on the actual facts, and not have to argue about them? What would be the effect here in the United States if every child could receive the same, high quality education, no matter if they lived in a city or a rural area, and no matter whether their parents were wealthy or poor, religious or secular, Republican or Democrat?

The Nordic social democracies can provide us with a blueprint for improvement. The path I have outlined in this chapter is not quite the same as the path taken by these countries, but to be sure, I would be happy to see our culture in this country and around the world transformed by either of these scenarios. But whether we go forward by proceeding down either of these roads, or by another road entirely, we must begin by achieving that all-important Critical Mass of people who understand that our present culture is flawed and doomed and must be replaced.

THE THIRD INDUSTRIAL REVOLUTION

In addition to the cultural revolution I have been advocating herein, it appears we are also on the verge of a technological revolution as well. As outlined and described in several books by Jeremy Rifkin, including *The Third Industrial Revolution, The Zero Marginal Cost Society*, and *The Green New Deal*, our world is on the verge of being transformed by technological advances for the third time in the past two hundred years. Each of these revolutions has involved significant advances in energy, communication, and transportation that have completely transformed the way we do things.

According to Rifkin, the first Industrial Revolution took place in Great Britain, and then spread to the U. S. and elsewhere. The energy driving the first Industrial Revolution was the coal that powered newly invented steam engines that were first used to automate the textile industry. The leap-forward in communication was the steam-powered printing press. And the new mode of transportation was the steam-powered locomotive. The second

Industrial Revolution was fueled by oil and electricity. The new communication systems were the telegraph, the telephone and radio and television broadcasts. And the new modes of transportation were trucks, automobiles, ships and airplanes powered by gasoline and diesel-driven internal combustion engines.

Two hundred years ago, there were only one billion human beings on this planet, and we were still in the beginning stages of the First Industrial Revolution. One hundred years ago, there were two billion of us, and we were in the early stages of the Second Industrial Revolution. Fifty years ago, we walked on the moon. Once technology got started, everything happened pretty quickly. The discovery of penicillin in 1928 has had a huge impact on our worldwide population. Today, there are almost eight billion of us, and we are in the beginning stages of the Third Industrial Revolution.

According to Rifkin, the new energy sources will be mostly solar and wind, along with all of the other renewable energy sources. Communication-wise, we will all be connected via the Internet, and the new modes of transportation will include driverless cars and trucks, as well as new mass transit systems. Technologically, we will all be connected, as will all of our homes, vehicles, factories, buildings, and all of the appliances and the heating and cooling systems within them. In his books, Rifkin describes the changes we will experience due to these new technological advances which includes a lot more sharing. Everything necessary for this Third Industrial Revolution, except the required infrastructure, is already in place. Putting the infrastructure in place will require about thirty years of effort and a lot of capital and human labor, but after that, the need for workers will be greatly diminished.

Germany in particular and the European Union in general are way ahead of the United States in terms of this build-out of the infrastructure. Rifkin has provided consulting services in regard to this infrastructure build-out for both Germany and the EU, as well as

China. Here, in the United States, we are living with a government that has been stolen from us by the huge corporations. In this case, the theft of our government means the oil companies and the car companies have been able to slow and delay the inevitable transition to renewable energy and technological connectedness. We all should have been driving electric cars powered by energy collected from our rooftops for a decade already.

Once the infrastructure is in place, we will be living in a technologically connected world. And hopefully also, one where we all know the reality of connectedness as I have been advocating herein. Imagine a world where these two realities have both manifested at the same time!

Once we resume our roles as Responsible Members of the Community of Life, our seemingly never-ending problems of today will magically disappear. Unlike today, corporations will no longer be making the decisions about how our world is ordered and organized. In fact, the oil companies that have not already disappeared through bankruptcy will be producing and distributing a small fraction of the oil they are producing today. And unlike today, they will be doing so in a much more responsible manner because our government will be performing its regulatory and oversight duties.

There will be fewer companies making cars because, unlike today, not everyone will need to own one. Because we will no longer be fighting any wars, and will no longer be worried about defending ourselves, the defense contractors and the arms manufacturers will be out of business thereby freeing up huge resources for much better purposes. The pharmaceutical companies will be a fraction of the size they are today, and they will be sharing information and technology with each other and making a reasonable profit for manufacturing only the drugs that are deemed beneficial to our health and well-being.

Having been replaced by a single-payer healthcare system, the health insurance companies will only be a memory. Likewise, the for-profit banks will be long gone, replaced by public banks who profit from the creation of our money in a new and improved fractional reserve system, then remit those profits to our government. Our media and our broadcasting companies will be thriving. However, they will no longer be permitted to utilize spin and fear as a means of controlling us. Instead, they will be providing us and our fellow citizens with all of the information necessary for us to make informed decisions as voters in a valid, healthy, and a properly functioning democracy.

Our agriculture and our food processing and distributing industry will be thriving. However, because our informed population will have transitioned to a mostly plant-based diet, this sector will be unrecognizable in terms of the differences between then and today.

Can you imagine how differently you are going to feel when you wake up every morning to a world where you know yourself and your other family members, as well as your neighbors and the rest of the people in your city, your state, your country, and your entire planet, are all **RESPONSIBLE MEMBERS OF THE COMMUNITY OF LIFE?**

<u>IN CLOSING</u>

Twenty-five years ago, I read the novel that won the $500,000 first prize in the Turner Tomorrow competition for the work of fiction judged to be the most influential towards the goal of helping to save our planet from destruction. And I was transformed by it. In the pages of Ishmael were answers to questions I was so grateful to know yet hadn't even realized I wanted to ask. Thanks to a fictional, well-educated, and extremely intelligent gorilla, I not only understand why our world is in such bad shape, but also… more importantly… what has to be done in order to save it.

Ishmael provided me with the truth that our insane culture is the root cause of all of the world's problems. Our problems can be fixed. But in order to fix them, we must take action at the most basic level…

at the foundational level of our worldwide culture. Our culture cannot be changed until a Critical Mass of people understands the need to do so, and then collectively takes the necessary action. If we are going to get out of this mess, then somehow, we need to find a way to help more people understand the truth about our culture. That, of course, has been the entire purpose of my writing *Soft Landing*.

As we discussed in the Introduction, I see three ways for people to access the truth of the connectedness of all things. These are the spiritual path, the scientific path, and the rational, logical path. Ultimately, it doesn't matter which path a person takes, as long as they arrive at the truth. However, in my estimation, the easiest path, and therefore the path that is most likely to be traveled by the most people is the logical and rational one. For me.... My own journey down the rational, logical path was accomplished in the few hours of time it took for me to read *Ishmael*. It is my hope that *Soft Landing* will provide a smooth path down the logical and rational alternative for many others.

When we achieve that Critical Mass of people who understand the need for transforming our culture, we will be standing at the precipice for the next major leap in our own evolution. When our new culture finally resubmits itself to the peacekeeping law, our species will be poised for greatness.

As I have stated a time or two previously.... The key to saving the world, avoiding a crash, and bringing us all in for a soft landing, is the creation of a Critical Mass of people who understand that our worldwide culture is flawed at its most basic level.... It cannot be fixed, and it must be replaced with a culture based upon the truth.

Everything is connected.

It is time for us to resume our roles as Responsible Members of the Community of Life.

We can save the world.

Let's get to work!

Afterword

Twelve years ago, during one of the industry downturns I have endured as an oil and gas explorationist, I wrote a chapter-by-chapter outline for *Soft Landing*. What you see today is very close to that original outline. But, as any writer knows, writing is an organic process, meaning the process of writing often leads the writer in unexpected directions. In this case, one big difference between the original outline and the finished product is the amount of words I spent criticizing religion and advocating for spirituality.

I can see now that this occurred because as I delved deeper and deeper into the main subject of the book, which is to advocate for a cultural shift in order to save the world, I found Christianity to be a huge impediment, especially here in the United States, where fundamentalist and evangelical Christianity is so prevalent. Christianity stands in the way of a person recognizing that our present worldwide culture is based upon a false premise of separation, precisely because Christianity and our culture are both based upon the same false premise that a God who is separate from us created the world just for humans. On the other hand, spirituality recognizes the reality of the connectedness of all things. And, as I continued to criticize Christianity, I felt the need to make it clear that giving up on organized religion does not require one to give up on pursuing spiritual knowledge and understanding.

As one pursues spiritual knowledge and understanding, there is no greater question a person can ask than, "What is the true nature of reality?" When you think about it, there are only two groups who have a reasonable shot at answering this biggest of all questions. The first of these groups, the quantum physicists, are definitely inching closer to accomplishing this task. But I think it is safe to say, even the smartest, best educated, and most advanced scientist living today still has some work left to do in their effort to describe the ultimate nature of reality from a scientific perspective. On the other hand, many spiritual masters may have already answered this for themselves. Or should I say they have been provided the answers through their connection with a higher power. Unfortunately, the only way any of the rest of us will know whether or not these spiritual masters have accomplished this task, is to become spiritual masters ourselves.

But, for those of us who want to spend some of our time and energy attempting to understand the true nature of our reality, but do not feel called to dedicate our lives to the achievement of actual spiritual mastery, there is something else we can do... and that is to read. This has been my path. Personally, I have no doubt that the true nature of reality includes a physical world that we are experiencing here and now, and also a non-physical world with which these spiritual masters are very familiar. I have experienced enough of the "unseen world" to know that for me, there is no question whatsoever in regard to whether or not this "world of things hidden" actually exists.

For people on the rational and logical path, it is very important to recognize the difference between knowledge and belief, and to constantly be willing to challenge our beliefs as new information becomes available. For instance, in my own case, I had no clue that it was even possible for a person to leave his or her body until I took some windowpane acid and visited an astral plane. Afterward, on the suggestion of a friend who was trying to help me to understand what I had experienced, I supplemented that knowledge by reading the science fiction classic, *Stranger In a Strange Land*. In this manner, my own spiritual quest for knowledge and understanding began in earnest. A little more than ten years later, another very intense personal experience involving ghosts provided another wake-up call. This one caused me to delve into books about ghosts, out-of-body experiences, near-death experiences and similar studies, including books about reincarnation and past lives.

Since reading *Stranger In a Strange Land*, I have read a lot of really great books focused on spirituality. Recently, I read one that resonated very deeply with me. It is *Adventures Beyond the Body*, by William Buhlman. In addition to providing "how to" instructions for out-of-body exploration, Buhlman provides his own description of the true nature of reality, which he has assembled through his explorations in the non-physical world. From everything I have experienced, and everything I have read, it appears to me that Buhlman has nailed it. (Of course, I do recognize this to be a belief, and not a knowing on my part.) He says only a small percentage of our universe is composed of the physical world, with the vast majority being non-physical. According to Buhlman, the non-physical world is very thought responsive, meaning in the non-physical realm, our thoughts, including even our subconscious, uncontrolled thoughts, have an immediate effect on our reality.

On the other hand, here, in the physical realm, although thoughts do affect our reality, the process is much slower, and therefore the disruptive effect of our subconscious uncontrolled thoughts is greatly diminished. This provides a safe environment for developing consciousnesses, such as yours, mine, and 7.8 billion other fellow human inhabitants of this little planet, not to mention the developing consciousnesses of all of the rest of the Community of Life here.

In addition to providing an in-depth description of the non-physical world, Buhlman also answers another big question.... What is the purpose of life? According to Buhlman, the purpose of life is to provide a temporary organic vehicle for a developing consciousness. I like that answer very much.

That leads me into a discussion I have had with myself many times while struggling to write this "Save the World" book. From everything I have read, and everything I have experienced, I do think that Buhlman has correctly identified the purpose of life. So, if the purpose of life is to provide a temporary organic vehicle for a developing consciousness, and that consciousness existed before joining up with the temporary organic vehicle (sometime prior to physical birth), and that consciousness will survive the physical death of that temporary organic vehicle, then wouldn't a world with a lot of problems (like ours) provide more adversity, more hurdles to overcome, and therefore provide a superior learning environment for a developing consciousness than a more perfect world as I am advocating for in Soft Landing?

On the other hand, precisely because there would be fewer problems to overcome, a more perfect, *Soft Landing* type world might churn out a lot more graduates of this "earth school", and therefore be preferable, not only in terms of "Which is more responsible?" and "What is right?", but also in terms of "Which model provides the best results in terms of helping a developing consciousness?"

This is a question that is certainly worthy of consideration. But when I think about it, the answer I always come up with is that in addition to being beyond my capabilities to answer, the question is not for me to decide. My role is to do what feels right to me. And what feels right to me is doing everything I can to save this world from being destroyed by our insane culture.

So, that is what I will do.

Recommended Reading List

Other Save the World Books

1. *Ishmael, an Adventure of the Mind and Spirit*, by Daniel Quinn

For me, there is a pre-Ishmael Don Shepherd, and a post-Ishmael Don Shepherd. The post-Ishmael Don Shepherd is definitely happier. Thanks, again, Daniel!

2. *When Corporations Rule the World*, by David Korten

I recently re-read this book and was struck by how similar it is to Soft Landing. Clearly, David Korten and I agree that it is insane for us to allow corporations to make all the important decisions as to how our world will be ordered.

3. *This Changes Everything*, by Naomi Klein

Another important, recent work focused on the insanity of allowing corporations to rule the world. The title refers to the fact that global warming is orchestrating a battle to the death between the corporate interests and the progressive forces. The only way global warming will ever be addressed in a meaningful way is if the profit of corporations is taken off the table. This will require a cultural shift as advocated in Soft Landing, and also in When Corporations Rule the World.

4. *The Last Hours of Ancient Sunlight*, by Thom Hartmann

Thom Hartmann is definitely one of my heroes. Without question, Last Hours is reaching a lot of people and having a huge impact on adding to the Critical Mass. Of course, another work of Thom's, Unequal Protection, provided the basis for the Corporate Rulers chapter in Soft Landing. I couldn't have done it without you, Thom. Please check out Thom Hartmann. He has written a lot of other important books and has a radio show that is broadcast on the Sirius satellite network.

5. *Endgame*, by Derek Jensen

Endgame is a huge, two-volume work. Derek is definitely a kindred spirit who has correctly identified our insane culture as the culprit. I prefer the voting booth method of change, which I advocate for in Soft Landing, to Derek's more militant and radical approach.

6. *The Cultural Creatives*, by Paul Ray and Sherry Anderson

Technically, this is not a "Save the World" book. It does, however, study the status of our worldwide cultural situation. The Cultural Creatives are the ones who already see the need for transforming our worldwide culture a la Ishmael, Soft Landing, Last Hours, and Endgame. According to Ray and Anderson, there are 50 million Cultural Creatives here in the U. S., and 200 million worldwide.

7. *Guns, Germs, and Steel*, by Jared Diamond

Also, not technically a "Save the World" book, I include it on this list because of its significance in describing how things came to be this way, as Quinn did in Ishmael. Interestingly, the book was the result of a question asked of Diamond by a New Guinea native named Yali, who was a friend of Diamond's. When Diamond arrived in New Guinea thirty years ago for a birding expedition, Yali asked him, "Why does the white man have so much cargo and the black man so little?" Diamond's book, in addition to providing an answer of how things came to be this way, also resulted in a refutation of racism. The book won the Pulitzer Prize, and deservedly so. National Geographic made a wonderful documentary out of the book.

8. *The Food Revolution*, by John Robbins

This hugely important book is the sequel to Diet For a New America, Robbins' first revolutionary book that came out in 1986. I have no doubt that our post Soft Landing world will be one as advocated for by Robbins. The food we eat has profound effects on our own health as well as the health of the planet. Without a doubt, this book should be included on any list of "Save The World" books.

Science Meets Spirituality Books

9. *The Tao of Physics*, by Fritjof Capra

10. *The Dancing Wu Li Masters*, by Gary Zukov

11. *The Way of the Explorer*, by Edgar Mitchell

These three books are all worthwhile reads, and the subject matter, being the similarities between science and spirituality, serves to give credence to spirituality, which is inherently un-provable. Science, especially quantum physics, has already discovered the non-physical world and is on the edge of exploring it deeper, with dark energy and dark matter being just two examples. The famous astronaut,

Edgar Mitchell died four years ago, and his passing inspired me to read his work. I'm so glad I did. The Way of the Explorer is fantastic. You will want to read it more than once.

Other Favorites

12. *Autobiography of a Yogi*, by Pramahansa Yogananda

An autobiography written by an adept spiritual master. This is undoubtedly, one of the most important books ever written. Millions have read it, and millions more should also read it.

13. *Das Energi*, by Paul Williams

This is a little book, but it has meant a lot to me. I've probably read it more than fifty times. You can read it in an hour or less. I only know two other people who have read this book who did not learn of it from me. Not surprisingly, they are two of my very best friends.

14. *Stranger In A Strange Land*, by Robert Heinlein

A classic science fiction work that introduced me to the possibilities of out-of-body travels and other psychic abilities. The book features an expose of the hypocrisy of organized religion, and the corruptness of government, as well as the possibilities for higher consciousness in a group setting.

15. *Conversations With God, Books 1, 2, and 3*, by Neale Donald Walsh

I highly recommend these three classics. They are full of timeless wisdom including wisdom about the necessity for cultural shifts. Book 3 could have been included in the Save The World section of this reading list.

16. *The Untethered Soul*, by Michael Singer

I consider this to be a masterwork because of its simplicity. It boils a description of our human consciousness down to its very essence, and it takes an extremely wise person to be able to do that. Singer wrote an autobiographical sequel called The Surrender Experiment, which is great as well. I highly recommend Singer's books to spiritual seekers.

17. *Adventures Beyond the Body*, by William Buhlman

One of my absolute favorite books. Buhlman also wrote three others that I have enjoyed, The Secret of the Soul, Adventures in the Afterlife, and Higher Self Now.

18. *Journeys Out of the Body*, by Robert Monroe

This is the first in a trilogy of classics by the famous out-of-body journeyer who founded the Monroe Institute. The first one is not very well written, but even so, it is still worthwhile. The other two, Far Journeys, and Ultimate Journey are written more skillfully. I really could have used Journeys Out of the Body in 1974, when I was trying to understand that acid trip. Monroe tells in his books of his own spontaneous out of body experiences, and how he learned and progressed as he went along. Being an engineer by trade, he examined all that happened from a scientific viewpoint, which served him well. A successful businessman, Monroe founded the Monroe Institute in Faber, Virginia to further the experience and exploration of consciousness. He died in 1995, at age 79. William Buhlman teaches at the Monroe Institute today.

19. *Voyages Into the Unknown*, by Bruce Moen

Bruce was a student of Robert Monroe, and he taught at the Monroe Institute as well. Voyages into the Unknown was Bruce's first book, and several others followed, which I also read with interest and enjoyment. Bruce died in 2017, but I wouldn't be too concerned for him. I think he already had the afterlife territory mapped out pretty well.

20. *Awakening to the Spirit World*, by Sandra Ingerman and Hank Wesselman

As I have been asserting herein, the world of the Shaman is real. This book will take you there. I included some excerpts in the Tribal Living chapter.

21. *Thieves of State*, by Sarah Chayes

I believe in government, and this book shows how government fails us through corruption. If everyone read it, we would be living in a much better world.

22. *Original Wisdom*, by Robert Wolfe

A truly incredible little book, and an important work in the area of consciousness. I included some excerpts in the Tribal Living chapter.

23. *The Third Industrial Revolution*, by Jeremy Rifkin

Just in time for the cultural revolution advocated herein, Jeremy Rifkin announces the arrival of the sharing economy, brought on by the Third Industrial Revolution. We are on the verge of implementing the infrastructure that will harness our renewable energies and automate our workforce and connect us all through the Internet of Things. This is truly an important work and has a lot of relevance for Soft Landing. See also Rifkin's other great books, The Zero Marginal Cost Society, and The Green New Deal.

As a part of my self-education process into the spiritual realm, I also read just about everything by Carlos Castaneda, Shirley MacLaine, Wayne Dyer, Jane Roberts, Marianne Williamson, David Hawkins, Dan Milmann, Raymond Moody, Eckhardt Tolle, and Byron Katie, whose works are all recommended as well. I am a huge fan of Michael Moore, whose books and movies I highly recommend. I could have added works from each of these authors to the main list, but twenty-three books are probably sufficient for a reading list like this one.

For those who are interested, here are five really great books on Buddhist meditation.

1. *The Heart of Buddhist Meditation*, by Nyanaponika Thera
2. *Mindfulness, in Plain English,* by Bhante Helepola Gunaratana
3. *In This Very Life,* by Sayadaw U. Pandita
4. *Vipassana Meditation*, as Taught by S. N. Goenka, by William Hart
5. *Practicing the Jhanas,* by Stephen Snyder and Tina Rasmussen

Save The World, Inc.

Yes! There is a way out of this mess! All we have to do is bring enough people into the growing group who understand our present culture is flawed at its very foundational level, and must be replaced with a functioning, sane culture that recognizes the reality of connectedness. When enough of us understand that things came to be this way as the result of a cultural shift that began ten thousand years ago when the original asshole locked up the food, then we will be able to transform our culture, bring it in for a soft landing, and save the world!

I wrote *Soft Landing* for the sole (soul?) purpose of helping to contribute to the already growing group of people who stand ready to resume our roles as Responsible Members of the Community of Life that will eventually reach Critical Mass and thereby save the world. Hopefully, by convincing readers of *Soft Landing* of the truths set out herein, I will exceed by many multiples the mandate given to the narrator at the end of *Ishmael*, when Ishmael instructed him to "teach a hundred people what I have taught to you."

It has now been more than twenty-five years since I first read Ishmael and became so excited about being provided with an answer as to why our world has so many problems. It took a while, but I have survived the disappointment of realizing that creating the Critical Mass is not going to be as easy as I naively thought it would when I first read Daniel Quinn's famous novel. But even though it is going to take more work and effort than I originally thought, I believe with all my heart that creating that Critical Mass is doable. Besides, no matter how difficult it is, we have to try. We owe it to ourselves, to this beautiful planet, and to the rest of the Community of Life.

I cannot think of a better way to spend the time I have left inhabiting this particular temporary organic vehicle than continuing my work on helping to create the Critical Mass. It would be wonderful if I could live to see it happen. Towards that end, I have formed a company called Save the World, Inc. and I have put up a website at:

www.savetheworldinc.com

Right now, this is a one-man operation, but my hope is that it can eventually expand to two or even more people working full-time. Please check it out. And, if you have the means and the inclination, all contributions are welcome.

Acknowledgements

First and foremost, thanks to Daniel Quinn who gave me the great gift of understanding there is a way out of this mess. I'm extremely grateful for that. *Ishmael* changed my life. I give many props to Daniel in the pages of *Soft Landing* but let me just say here one more time, "Thank you, Daniel. Even though you are no longer with us, your positive influence on this earthly plane will continue for generations to come."

Thank you, Thom Hartmann, Jared Diamond, Naomi Klein, David Korten, Derek Jensen, Neale Donald Walsh, Michael Moore, Sarah Chaves, and Timothy S. Bennett for being Responsible Members of the Community of Life and for accomplishing so much in regard to adding to the Critical Mass that will ultimately bring us all in for a soft landing and save the world. Thank you as well for sharing your wisdom with me through your books and movies. I am a better person because of your work.

My dear friend, Cathy Lee gets the prize as the most influential of my many in-person helpers. It must have been destiny that brought us together. How else do you explain the fact that just as I was starting *Soft Landing* I became good friends with an initiated kahuna, honorary Native American grandmother, and accomplished meditator as an Ashram participant who was also a professional editor, and who was interested in helping me?

My inspiration for *Soft Landing* goes back twenty-five years to when I first read Ishmael and became so enthusiastically convinced that all we had to do to save the world was to get enough people to read *Ishmael*. Back then, if it weren't for a few dear friends who understood what I was so excited about, I don't know how I could have possibly dealt with the disappointment I experienced when I discovered that most of my other friends were not interested. Thank you, Frank and Amy Ennis, Mark McNair, Janice Forney, and Stella Shapiro. You saved me, and you made *Soft Landing* possible!

These days my circle of friends has grown to include a lot more Ishmael-loving people, many of whom have generously provided their time and effort to read earlier versions of Soft Landing and give their feedback and encouragement. Thank you, Casandra Hutson, Alex Palomo, James Vance, John O'Connor, Randy Brooks, Michael Shattah, Raad Monsour, Nick Kostler, William Scoular, Rosh D'Souza, Butch Patton, Andrew Lee, and Carlos Kugler.

Special thanks to Sarah Sullivan, Jeni Lowry, Jeff Mallon, Dan Owen, Steve Lavendusky, Whitley Smith, and John Richter for always being interested in how my project was going and for providing help and insights when I needed them most. Thanks to my new friend, Will Alkin for his work on the book cover and on the website.

Thanks to Wayo Longoria for the many times he introduced me to people at Casa de Luz saying, "This is my friend, Don. He is writing a save-the-world book." What a pleasure it is going to be to hear him say, "This is my friend, Don. He **has written** a save-the-world book. If you are interested, you can buy it right over there."

Finally, special thanks to my very good pals, John Breeding, Dennis Paddie and Mikal Masters, authors and activists all. I rely on you to be there when I need you. Your friendship means the world to me.

Everything is connected!

About the Author

Photo by The Perfect Headshot

Don's says his life has been transformed by the process of writing this labor of love called *Soft Landing*. Now, after 44 years in the oil and gas exploration business, Don is attempting to transition over to being a writer, a speaker, and an advocate for the Community of Life. Hopefully, the publication of *Soft Landing* will enable him to do that.

Except for five years he spent in Costa Rica, Don has been in Austin for the past thirty years. His favorite diversions are billiards, ping pong, and jogging on Town Lake. As you would expect from someone whose sun, moon, and risings signs are all earth signs, Don is a lover of dogs, horses, and the natural world.